Crisis and Control

D0556669

Crisis and Control

The Militarization of Protest Policing

Lesley J. Wood

PlutoPress
www.plutobooks.com

Between the Lines
TORONTO

First published 2014 by Pluto Press
345 Archway Road, London N6 5AA
www.plutobooks.com

Distributed in the United States of America exclusively by
Palgrave Macmillan, a division of St. Martin's Press LLC,
175 Fifth Avenue, New York, NY 10010

First published in Canada in 2014 by Between the Lines
401 Richmond Street West, Studio 277, Toronto, Ontario M5V 3A8 Canada
1-800-718-7201
www.btlbooks.com

British Library Cataloguing in Publication Data
A catalogue record for this book is available from the British Library

ISBN   978 0 7453 3389 2   Hardback
ISBN   978 0 7453 3388 5   Pluto Press Paperback
ISBN   978 1 77113 161 2   Between the Lines paperback
ISBN   978 1 7837 1209 0   Pluto Press PDF eBook
ISBN   978 1 77113 163 6   Between the Lines PDF eBook
ISBN   978 1 7837 1211 3   Kindle eBook
ISBN   978 1 7837 1210 6   Pluto Press epub
ISBN   978 1 77113 162 9   Between the Lines epub

Library and Archives Canada Cataloguing in Publication
Wood, Lesley J., author
    Crisis and control : the militarization of protest policing / Lesley J. Wood.
Includes bibliographical references and index.
Issued in print and electronic formats.
ISBN 978-1-77113-161-2 (pbk.).–ISBN 978-1-77113-162-9 (epub).–
ISBN 978-1-77113-163-6 (pdf)
    1. Police. 2. Crowd control. 3. Intelligence service. 4. Demonstrations.
5. Protest movements. I. Title.
HV8055.W66 2014   363.32'3   C2014-900844-9
                                           C2014-900845-7

Between the Lines gratefully acknowledges assistance for its publishing activities from
the Canada Council for the Arts, the Ontario Arts Council, the Government of Ontario
through the Ontario Book Publishers Tax Credit program, and the Government of Canada
through the Canada Book Fund.

10   9   8   7   6   5   4   3   2   1

Typeset from disk by Stanford DTP Services, Northampton, England
Text design by Melanie Patrick
Simultaneously printed digitally by CPI Antony Rowe, Chippenham, UK
and Edwards Bros in the United States of America

To Sarah Vance, who wants my work to be useful,
and to Mac Scott, the most useful fellow I know

Contents

Tables and Figure

Acknowledgments

I must give my deep thanks to the stalwart research assistance of Tia Dafnos, Craig Fortier, Tim Groves, Stef Gude, Heather Hax, Sarah Hornstein, Mark Mansour, Choong Ho Park, Rehanna Siew, Rob Texeira, A.K. Thompson, and Milos Vasic. I know that building event catalogues isn't the best use of your energy. To those of you working to oppose police brutality in the cities I traveled to, thank you so much for sharing your documents, and wisdom. In addition to various activist defendants, these also include the legal beagles at the National Lawyers Guild, Movement Defense Committee, Law Union, New York Civil Liberties Union, Canadian Centre for Civil Liberties, Collectif Opposé à la Brutalité Policière, and the Partnership for Civil Justice. I'm also sincerely grateful for the editing help of Stefanie Gude and Kelly Burgess.

I've had the good fortune to be able to discuss the contents of *Crisis and Control* with activists determined to make the world more just, and with researchers and scholar/activists at various academic shindigs, including the ASA, CSA, ESA, ISA, SSSP and in York's Department of Sociology.

The project was funded in part by a York University Faculty of Arts Research Grant, a SSHRC Standard Grant ('Policing Protest: the diffusion of new tactics').

List of Acronyms

ACLU—American Civil Liberties Union
ACPO—Association of Chief Police Officers (UK)
APEC—Asia Pacific Economic Cooperation
CACP—Canadian Association of Chiefs of Police
CCLA—Canadian Civil Liberties Association
CCPC—Commission to Combat Police Corruption (New York City)
CCRB—Civilian Complaints Review Board (New York City)
CCTV—Close Circuit Television
CIA—Central Intelligence Agency (US)
COINTELPRO—Counter-Intelligence Program (US)
COMPSTAT—Comparative Statistics or Computer Statistics
COPB—Collective Opposed to Police Brutality (Montreal)
COR—Community Oriented Response (Unit) (Toronto)
CS (gas) —2-chlorobenzylidene malonitrile
CSE—Communication Security Establishment (Canada)
CSIS—Canadian Security and Intelligence Service
CSP—La commission de la sécurité publique (Montreal)
DHS—Department of Homeland Security (US)
DNC—Democratic National Convention (US)
FBI—Federal Bureau of Intelligence (US)
FIGs—Field Intelligence Groups (US)
FLETC—Federal Law Enforcement Training Center
FOP—Fraternal Order of Police (US)
FTAA—Free Trade Area of the Americas
HITRAC—Homeland Infrastructure Threat and Risk Analysis Center
IACP—International Association for Chiefs of Police
IAB—Internal Affairs Bureau (New York City)
INSETs—Integrated National Security Enforcement Teams (Canada)
ITAC—Integrated Threat Assessment Centre (Canada)
JTTF—Joint Terrorism Task Force
LAPD—Los Angeles Police Department
LRAD—Long Range Acoustic Device
MPD—Metropolitan Police Department (Washington, DC)
MPDC—Metropolitan Police of the District of Columbia (Washington, DC)

NATO—North Atlantic Treaty Organization
NIM—National Intelligence Model (UK)
NLG—National Lawyers Guild
NSSE—National Special Security Event
NSP—National Security Policy (Canada)
NTAC—National Threat Assessment Center
NYCLU—New York Civil Liberties Union
NYPD—New York Police Department
OC—oleum capsicum
OCAP—Ontario Coalition Against Poverty
OCCPS—Ontario Civilian Commission on Police Services
OPC—Office of Police Complaints (Washington, DC)
OPIRD—Office of the Independent Police Review Director
OPP—Ontario Provincial Police
OPS—Operational Police Service (Montreal)
OPSEU—Ontario Public Sector Employees Union (Ontario)
PERF—Police Executive Research Foundation
PBA—Patrolman's Benevolent Association (New York City)
POMS—Public Order Management Systems
PPU—Police Paramilitary Unit
PSA—Police Services Act (Ontario)
PSC—Public Safety Canada
PSU—Public Safety Unit
RCMP—Royal Canadian Mounted Police
RNC—Republican National Convention
SIU—Special Investigations Unit (Toronto)
SPVM—Service de Police de la Ville de Montreal
SQ—Sûreté de Quebec (Quebec Provincial Police)
SWAT—Special Weapons and Tactics
TPA—Toronto Police Association
TPS—Toronto Police Service
TPSB—Toronto Police Services Board
WTO—World Trade Organization

1

Introduction

It's the year 2010 and I'm standing in Allan Gardens, in the rapidly gentrifying east end of downtown Toronto, the evening before the meeting of the heads of state of the twenty richest countries (G20), later known as the "Austerity Summit." Hundreds of people from different student groups, community organizations, unions and diverse communities arrive in the park. There are women from domestic violence shelters, social workers and union members, student activists, parents and children, people from homeless shelters, punks, bike messengers, members of the South Asian Women's Rights Organization, Iranian refugees, migrant workers and various anarchist, socialist and social democrats. Entitled "Justice for Our Communities," the event is intended to bring local organizations and communities together, and to link the G20 summit to locally rooted demands for immigrant justice, environmental justice, affordable childcare, and an end to gender violence, police brutality and the marginalization of the poor, amongst other things. To say the least, the politics of the coalition coordinating the event are inclusive and complicated and we are marching without police permission.

I attended many of the planning meetings, but at this particular moment, I am helping with communications—relaying information about the police movements from a team of bicycle scouts circling the area to the activists attempting to lead the march into the streets of Toronto. The specific route around the downtown area is flexible, but the intention of the march is to stop at sites that represent the way that the austerity policies of the G20 impact our local communities—these include Toronto police headquarters, the Immigration and Refugee Board, a social assistance office and others. After visiting these sites, we will try to get as close as possible to the 3-meter-high fence surrounding the summit meetings. We aren't crazy. We do know that given the state of lockdown in the city, the police will block our path. So we intend to be flexible. We want this to be a peaceful event, one that parents and caregivers can bring their children. If the police start to act aggressively, and arrests seem imminent, our plan is to march back to Allan Gardens, where we will occupy the park overnight.

As people try to enter the park to begin the march, police search their bags. Protesters are only allowed in if they obey the police, and dispose of their bandannas, goggles and the sticks on which their signs were stapled. The heavily policed boundary is only one manifestation of the most expensive policing operation in Canadian history. The security for the combined G8 and G20 summits has topped $1 billion, and the results of this spending are on full display throughout the downtown core. Nonetheless, despite, and perhaps because of the police presence, the numbers swell and eventually, led by people with disabilities, many in wheelchairs—we head into the street. Then, the police commander tells the activist designated as a "police negotiator" that they have chosen this moment to bring the body of a soldier killed in Afghanistan directly across our path. We wait until the procession passes and move on. Our first stop is Toronto police headquarters. The crowd is packed tightly as people tried to hear what the speakers are saying. Suddenly a scuffle breaks out and police pull a Deaf man, Emomotimi Azorbo, from the crowd. When other activists try to intervene, the police beat them on the heads and arms with batons and push them with shields. Azorbo and another activist are arrested. Tensions increase. The police put their riot helmets on. Tensions increase more. Even the most placid demonstrator is becoming angry. I try to understand the big picture using my telephone and a small radio, and ask other marshals what we should be doing. No one knows. Our job of keeping people safe and reaching our destination seems somehow less important than taking a stand against the absurd police intimidation. Finally, we try to move the crowd along the street. Our negotiator tells us that the Toronto police commander says we'll be able to march down University Avenue, a massive roadway—towards the security fence. Then, all of a sudden, police form a line and block our path, helmets on and shields up. We are unable to keep marching. Obviously there is "a diversity of tactics" in the uniformed ranks. The Toronto commander we are speaking with yells into his radio and kicks a bottle of water in frustration. The crowd wants to keep moving and surges into the streets by the hospital, the only route available. A game of cat-and-mouse unfolds as protesters try to continue south, and the police continue to block us. Finally it becomes clear that we are outflanked. Frustrated, we return to the park to spend the night, undisturbed by the police.

In the morning, we receive news that in the early morning hours, police have arrested 17 key activists, waking some from their beds, and pulling others from vehicles. All are charged with conspiracy and kept in custody. Nonetheless, the large march planned for that day continues, with a section of the crowd breaking away to try to get to the fence surrounding the summit. When they are unable to do so, some protesters and passersby break the windows of shops and smash and burn three police cars. Over the following 24 hours, the police retake the city, surrounding and arresting over 1,100 people, making it the largest mass arrest in Canadian history (Mahoney and Hui 2010).

The over-the-top policing of the G20 launched frenzied media coverage, public hand-wringing, finger-pointing, inquiries, lawsuits and promises of "never again." Since that time, of course, Montreal police have arrested over 3,500 people in the 2012–13 wave of student-led protests against tuition increases, while police across the US and Canada have arrested hundreds of Occupy activists, and significant numbers of Idle No More indigenous sovereignty, anti-pipeline, immigrant justice and anti-police-brutality protesters. At these incidents, sometimes police surrounded protesters in "kettles" or "enclosures" and arrested them. Sometimes police Tasered, pepper sprayed, launched projectiles, and tear-gassed people. Sometimes police simply intimidated people out of protesting.

Clearly, the policing of protest in democratic, capitalist countries is now both more militarized and more dependent on intelligence gathering and pre-emptive control than in the past. This is a trend that has been observed in Europe, Australia, New Zealand and in North America, but this book highlights the emergence of this protest policing strategy in cities in the United States and Canada from 1995 until the present. It argues that this protest-policing strategy must be understood as a result of a neoliberal transformation of political, social and economic systems, and their effect on police organizations and decision-making. I seek to explain the incorporation of less-lethal weapons like pepper spray, tear gas and Tasers, and the use of barricades and riot control units into police forces in Canada and the US during this period, highlighting the conditions that have led to their increasing use against demonstrators.

Protest policing in both Canada and the US was different twenty years ago. The established public order management systems of the 1980s and early 1990s have been replaced by fortification, an escalation of coercive policing strategies, incoherent negotiation, generalized and indiscriminate information gathering, and intelligence-led and proactive policing (della Porta, Peterson, and Reiter 2006). In their studies of protest policing in the US since 1999, Noakes and Gillham (2007) label this approach "strategic incapacitation," noting how it attempts to pre-empt and contain protesters perceived to be threatening or disruptive. This restructuring of policing has taken place in tandem with neoliberal restructuring and converging economic, political (and climate) crises. By understanding how a strategy of limiting and responding to protest has emerged, we can better understand the limits and possibilities for dissent in the twenty-first century.

Some observers might argue that the job of the police has always been to beat, follow and arrest dissidents, and that little has changed in the past fifty years. Activists in both Canada and the US often reference state driven intelligence projects like the US COINTELPRO, designed to disrupt social movements, suggesting that the police are behind every internal movement division or failure. However, protest-policing strategies have changed significantly since the 1970s, and even since 1995 there have been serious changes in the way that police "deal with" protest and dissent. At the other extreme lies the argument that a new form of police state, in which the police are wholly unaccountable to political authorities or to the public, has emerged since 1995. Still other observers see militarized protest policing as a response to increasingly militant direct action movements in the Global North—and believe that the strategic incapacitation strategy of policing signals a growing polarization, with potential for revolutionary transformation. As an activist who has participated in demonstrations throughout the past twenty years, and as a sociologist frustrated by common-sense explanations of police strategy, I believe that in order to build the capacity of movements to resist state and corporate domination, we need to get beyond simplistic explanations and look squarely at police organizations, their decision-making procedures, and the forces that are influencing them.

This necessitates locating police strategy within the context of neoliberal transformation, a process characterized since the 1980s by an increased "marketization" of social life. In the 1990s, this transformation was accelerated by numerous free trade agreements and deregulation of the economy, and in 2008, the economic crisis furthered the transformation, especially in the United States. Neoliberal transformation has resulted in increasing deregulation and commodification of relations and practices of governance, education, sociality, and culture. In Canada and the US, governments have reduced social spending and avoided regulating large-scale investment and trade. Core cities in the Global North have become the domain of the "FIRE" sectors (finance, investment, and real estate), or the service sectors which support them. As a result, these cities have become increasingly populated by the rich and the poor, while any existing middle class has been displaced or disappeared. The manufacturing sector has fled to smaller cities or suburbs, while traditional public sector, health care, and education work has become unstable and precarious. Austerity policies have furthered income inequalities between rich and poor, and cities have been transformed accordingly. As Naomi Klein (2007) argues, elites have restructured the economy quickly, hitting the poorest and marginalized most directly. As corporations become more influential and states cut social spending, political and economic systems are transformed, including systems of policing. Increased privatization of policing, availability of new technologies, and the emergence of increasingly globalized policing networks have corresponded with a sometimes contradictory shift towards intelligence-led, community-oriented, and militarized policing strategies.

In the context of neoliberal transformation, and particularly since the attacks of September 11, 2001, symbols and messages of fear and insecurity dominate political culture in Canada and the US. Government spending is increasingly directed towards security, law enforcement and defense, distracting us from economic and political policies that facilitate the consolidation of wealth by the 1 percent. Despite falling crime rates, and ongoing distrust of the police, policing has taken on an expanded and altered role within government and economic systems.

In 1990, the Solicitor General of Canada produced a document entitled "The Future of Policing in Canada," which included predictions on the effect of neoliberal social spending cuts on policing. The report, written by criminologists Andre Normandeau and Barry Leighton, coolly describes the integration of the Canadian economy with the world economy, and subsequent "short term dislocations of labour." It notes that a "pool of poorly educated, unskilled unemployed people will grow in large cities, contributing to property crime and violence," and describes the downloading of services, the de-institutionalization of people, and the cuts to services (1990: 30). As a result, the authors conclude that there will be implications for police work: "more civil unrest may be anticipated, based on more groups in society seeing themselves as disadvantaged" (ibid.: 31) In response to these changes, the authors suggest increased privatization of law enforcement, collaboration, and the use of new technologies.

In the US context, David Bayley (1998) warned in the police publication, "Ideas in American Policing," that privatization and deregulation would provide new challenges for police, including increased group violence stemming from inequalities structured by race, class, and ethnicity. He claimed that such violence, when combined with increased criminal violence or terrorism, would encourage increased militarization and a "warfare mentality" by police. Indeed, as police researcher Peter K. Manning (2008: 30) explained, external political and economic pressures, including cuts to the budget, the collapse of the economy and, with it, the budgets of many large cities, forced change on US police agencies in the 1980s. Neoliberal response reforms within police agencies were similar to those facing other public institutions. These included the promotion of new management styles, the privatization, deregulation, and outsourcing of public sector operations, and a reliance on information technology and data analysis to facilitate the restructuring of these centralized institutions.

As the social safety net weakened under neoliberal restructuring, the police role became both one of "cleaning up" the results of damage caused by economic transformation and that of "securing a strong investment climate." The implications of both hit poor people and people of color hardest. As Neil Smith (2001) writes, the introduction of police strategies like zero tolerance and "broken windows" policies dramatically increased the role of police in eliminating any evidence of social disorder. Loïc Wacquant (2001: 81) noted that neoliberal transformation meant the "erasing of the economic state, the dismantling of the social state and the strengthening of the penal state."

Today, police operate within a context of ongoing social cleansing in which the legal, cultural, and political space for dissent has narrowed, facilitated by legislative tools like the PATRIOT Act, new laws against organized crime, bans on protest, anti-terrorism laws, and an increased state capacity for surveillance and border control. Police increasingly portray protest as a form of "threat," thereby justifying policing strategies, while new legal restrictions have meant that even legally permitted marches and rallies may now face an increasingly militarized police (Scholl 2013, Starr, Fernandez, and Scholl 2012).

As the policing experts anticipated, protest-policing strategies in this neoliberal era are influenced by those challenging the existing order. With the social amelioration functions of the state deteriorating, many of these movements are turning away from the potential offered by electoral politics. At the same time, social movements are increasingly globally connected, and this has allowed activist tactics, identities, and symbols to diffuse rapidly, facilitating waves of direct action protest. Diverse movements are more able to collaborate or coordinate in their struggles against neoliberal institutions and processes, through protest convergences against international institutions, global days of protest, and formal and informal electronic and face-to-face networking.

Context and Protest Policing

Despite these obvious connections, the relationship between neoliberal restructuring and policing is not a straightforward and unidirectional one. To understand the relationship between these processes and practices, we need to go beyond political rhetoric about the police as the tool of the elites, or as omnipotent masterminds. Instead, we must understand police institutions as complex and somewhat varied organizations with particular historical trajectories that contain active, relatively reflexive participants with changing strategies.

To understand the reasons why protest policing is changing, we need a general framework for understanding the connections between the social, political, and economic context and protest policing strategies and practices. The most detailed model for understanding the influence of context on protest policing styles is found in the work of Donatella della Porta and Herbert Reiter (1998) and that of della Porta, Abby Peterson and Reiter (2006). Both of these works argue that protest policing strategies are products of political systems, and police organization and culture, as filtered through police knowledge of protesters, and which evolve through interactions with protesters.

Della Porta and Reiter's 1998 work argues that protest policing is determined on the first level by:

1. organizational features of the police,
2. configurations of political power,
3. public opinion,
4. police occupational culture, and
5. police interaction with protesters.

All of these are filtered on a second level by "police knowledge, defined as the police's perception of external reality, which shapes the concrete policing of protest on the ground" (1998: 2). Policing knowledge is a product of the organization of police forces and political opportunities (della Porta, Peterson, and Reiter: 18). This model explains differences in protest policing styles as a result of the interactions between police, public, authorities, and protesters – while recognizing that the police themselves interpret the world and act on the basis of these interpretations. It is also used to explain the differences between protest policing strategies in Europe and the US, and to explain a gradual softening of protest policing in those regions during the 1980s and 1990s.

In more recent work, della Porta, Peterson, and Reiter note that, at least in the context of global justice summit protests in the twenty-first century, it appears that protest policing is becoming militarized. They explain this trend by examining the characteristic features of such events including complex police operations involving police from different nation-states, low accountability at the national level, and no accountability at the international level. Comparing protests in Genoa, Evian and elsewhere in Europe, they find that national traditions may moderate these effects, but observe an overall trend within the policing of such events. Adapting their national comparisons to the transnational context, they elaborate what they mean by the "configuration of political power," and argue that while in the 1990s in Europe, there was an expanding political opportunity for social movements, in the twenty-first century, this opportunity is absent, particularly for those trying to make change at the transnational level. Though there is support by civil society, potential allies who have connections to power may mistrust summit protesters, while international governmental organizations have low accountability to popular movements, and neoliberal institutions have even less. Police do not trust the protesters who gather at such events, perceiving them as confusing, with heterogeneous organizational structures, tactics and participation, including the presence of small, violent groups and a lack of interest in cooperating with the police. The combination of context, organizational dynamics and interaction with protesters has influenced protest control strategies and led to the fortification of summit sites, the escalation of coercive strategies, incoherent negotiation, generalized and indiscriminate information gathering, and "intelligence-led" and what is described as "pro-active" policing.

Della Porta and Reiter's initial model provides leverage for understanding the relationship between context and protest policing. Della Porta, Peterson and Reiter's subsequent work builds on this framework and shows how neoliberal restructuring has limited state responsiveness to the demands of social movements (2006: 187). Nonetheless, neither model can fully explain the effect of neoliberal globalization on protest policing.

This is not surprising. Della Porta and colleagues' models build on an understanding of state formation—one that is dominant in the social movement literature of Charles Tilly and Sidney Tarrow. This analysis, like Max Weber's, sees the state emerge out of struggles between competing power holders (Weber 1946). War making creates states, whose leaders then hold the monopoly on legitimate use of force within a given territory. In order to effectively wage war, and maintain power, leaders need resources. They extract resources in the most straightforward way possible (Tilly 1992). In some contexts, these resources can be extracted from natural resources easily; in others, power holders must build alliances with a capitalist class in order to obtain capital; in others, they need to extract taxes and labor from the population—sometimes through force. These differences are rooted in the ways their seizure of power is tied to different geographies, histories, and demographics (Tilly 1984). The ease with which power holders can extract the resources they need, and the manner in which they do so, influence the subsequent governing form (Tilly 1997). The governing regime may be dominated by the armed forces, Parliaments, or capitalist classes. For example, the processes that surrounded the emergence of the British state differ from the processes that surround the emergence of the French state, influencing the form and capacity of repressive institutions in both countries. This political process framework would see policing as part of this process, including the founding of the Metropolitan Police Force in London by Sir Robert Peel in 1829 as part of the establishment of the modern political order. Using a different approach, a government decree in France established the first uniformed police in Paris. Colonial policing can be traced to the Irish Constabulary Act of 1822, which established the Royal Irish Constabulary, whose first duties included the forcible seizure of land from the Catholic and Presbyterian population on behalf of the Anglican clergy.

These policing models emerged during the eighteenth and nineteenth centuries, when the British regime was frequently at war with its French equivalent—both in the colonies and on the European continent—and needed to obtain resources for these wars (Tilly 1995). These conflicts and the efforts to pay for them resulted in the growth of state infrastructure, and increasing burdens on ordinary people, as the growing state demanded labor, taxes and material goods. Accessing these resources transformed both politics and economics. The cost of building the nation state put unprecedented pressures on the local populations, and as the efforts to obtain monetary and human resources necessary for building this system increased, so too did popular resistance, urban poverty, and crime. Although military forces, government intelligence operatives, and private watchmen already existed, the public police force was proposed as one way for the power holders to maintain order, despite their founder's rhetoric to the contrary. As Sir Robert Peel explained, "The police are the public and the public are the police, the police being members of the public that are paid to give full attention to duties which are incumbent on every citizen, in the interests of community welfare and existence" (Anon. 1829). This explanation frames this innovation as simply an extension of good citizenship, ignoring both the repressive and often violent work in which the police were engaged, and the way wars and conquest underpinned their emergence.

As the British state developed, its economic and political infrastructure became more extensive. The processes of capitalization, proletarianization, and parliamentarization transformed politics, economics, and social life (Tilly 1992, Tilly and Wood 2012). An increasingly powerful capitalist class required an increasingly available proletariat. With the expanding reach of the state and the related communication and coordination between politics and economics, urbanization also flourished. Poor people flooded into the city and entrepreneurs attempted to take advantage of new technologies and populations, resulting in rising unrest, protest, crime, and disorder.

By the beginning of the nineteenth century, power holders in Britain faced a number of expensive challenges. Revolutionary movements appeared to be a threat after the upheavals in France in 1789 and in Ireland in 1798. Ideas about democracy were afoot. Alliances between a rising bourgeois class and the working poor in formal organizations established the social movement repertoire of marching, rallying, and petitioning. Such innovations pushed elites to partly democratize the Parliament, thereby expanding suffrage to wealthy men (in 1832) and Catholics (in 1793) (Tilly 1995/2005). At that time, security patrols were geographically limited, like the Bow Street Foot Patrol, or industry-specific policing, such as the Rotation Offices and Horse Patrol, established to protect gaming houses and tea rooms (ibid.). In cases of extreme disturbance or rioting, military forces like the Honourable Artillery Company were used. Until the early nineteenth century, most policing was done by informal security guards and watchmen (Williams 2007).

In addition to the model of Robert Peel's London Metropolitan Police—with its emphasis on public order, crime prevention, and control, and equation of uniformed patrol with images of welfare and service—continental and colonial models also influence contemporary policing in Canada and the US. Continental European policing is traditionally characterized by a centralized militarized force, counterbalanced by either a secondary or medley of local city forces (Mawby 2008: 22). In France, the centralized "gendarmerie" under the control of the Ministry of Defense pre-dates the state police force. Jean-Paul Brodeur (1983) explains that the task of "high police" such as the gendarmerie is to strengthen royal authority, using intelligence to forestall or disrupt challenges to power. While the goal of Peel's low police is the prevention and control of crime, high police may simply attempt to manage crime in order to maintain the status quo. Aspects of this dual model are particularly apparent in Canada, with the unique governance structures of the Royal Canadian Mounted Police (RCMP), or the approach of *Sûreté du Quebec* but are increasingly visible in both countries as intelligence and law enforcement institutions become more integrated, and more militarized. A third relevant template, the influence of which may still be seen, is that of the colonial police. Although French colonial traditions differed from British ones, colonial police shared the goal of extending colonial rule over territory and people, with the source of legitimacy coming from the colonial masters, rather than the indigenous population (Brogden 1987: 9, Mawby 2008: 24).

In all three varieties, it was within the process of state formation that the first police agencies emerged. The dynamics of state formation influenced the form of policing, identity, and the knowledge and culture of the police. In this vein, policing becomes a tool that the state offers to its supporters, in exchange for support. If the regime is relatively stable, so too will policing be stable. If the regime is undergoing rapid change, with unclear alliances and divisions, policing and policing knowledge may shift similarly.

This emphasis on political processes and competing authorities underpin della Porta and Reiter's explanation of how political context influences protest policing strategy, while de-emphasizing (but not rejecting the importance of) economic relations on state formation. However, without clearly understanding how changing relations of production influence political practices, a key dynamic in the development of the police is overlooked. The ways in which the structure and relations of political regimes are deeply influenced by the processes of wealth extraction and capitalization must be incorporated into any explanation of police strategy.

A historical materialist perspective sees the police as an innovation of capitalism, a tool the capitalist class uses against the working classes. For example, Peter Linebaugh's (1991) study of the repressive features of eighteenth- and nineteenth-century London explains how the Metropolitan Police emerged not simply to assist political elites to maintain order (which could have happened much earlier), but also to assist capitalists in the extraction of surplus value and protect the capitalist interests in a new economy. Emphasizing the centrality of the relations of production in social life, Linebaugh positions the struggle to impose wage labor as the dominant workplace relation in London.[1] He shows how workers tried to resist this shift through the ongoing pilfering of goods, using the defense of "custom" and "tradition." In order to stop this pilfering, and to increase the profitability of industries at the docks, the Marine Police Office was established in 1798. Until that time, there was no paid, centrally directed, and armed police force in London (Linebaugh 1991: 425).

Linebaugh emphasizes the links between colonialism, capitalism, and the police, noting that Patrick Colquhoun, a London agent for the planters of St. Vincent, Nevis, Dominica, and the Virgin Islands was central to developing the idea of the London police, testifying frequently to the Finance Committee on the subject of police, and drafting legislation on that subject (ibid.: 427). Colquhoun saw police as necessary to the growth of riches. He declared: "Police in this Country, may be considered as a *new Science*, in the PREVENTION and DETECTION OF CRIMES, and in those other Functions which relate to INTERNAL REGULATIONS for the well ordering and comfort of Civil Society" (Colquhoun 1797). Linebaugh (1991) explains that this conception of policing combines law and economics, the protection of property, and the protection of production. He argues that Colquhoun learned this from friends such as Adam Smith, "whose *Wealth of Nations* first appeared as 'Lectures on Police' (p. 428), and from people like William Robertson, who distinguished feudal from commercial societies by the presence of 'police'." Colquhoun describes how the London working class spins a "system of depredation," and is "disciplined in acts of Criminal Warfare," forming conspiracies driven by their unruly passions, rapacious desires, evil propensities, noxious qualities, and vicious and bad habits. As a result, this class needed the "humane improvement" offered by the police (ibid.). In his descriptions, Colquhoun clearly blurs the line between members of the working class and criminals. In his view, the police were established not to defend private property, but rather to create and sustain class relations in the production of private property. Linebaugh argues that the police wouldn't have emerged earlier because the relations of production were different. But during the early nineteenth century, with its transformation of social and economic life, those with access to money became active disciplinarians of the wageless through the police and, as the English Jacobins argued, the wages and rights of man became conjoined. It was liberals rebelling against the old aristocracy—that also resisted the formation of an organized, state-controlled force possessing repressive authority (Manning 1997: 86). Instead, the public police in the UK originated as locally controlled and were, in time, complemented by a national infrastructure that investigated "serious crimes," and evaluated and supervised local police forces (ibid.: 88).

Linebaugh's origin story shows the police as deeply tied to capitalism, and to a lesser extent, colonialism. Whereas Tilly sees the extraction of wealth as a tool for maintaining power, with the maintenance and growth of power as an end in itself, and policing a tool within the struggle for power, Linebaugh emphasizes the way capitalist transformations required police in order to accumulate capital. The question of whether police should be seen as a tool of the state or of capitalism influences how we understand the influence of neoliberalism on contemporary policing of protest in Canada and the US. By adopting Tilly's synthesis of political economy and political processes, in books like *Coercion, Capital and European States AD 990–1992*, the question of whether the police are a tool of the state or of capital may be partly resolved. Changes in the relations of production influence political relationships and the structure of power and contentious politics, including the emergence, capacity, and operation of repressive actors—including the police. While most Weberian descriptions of political processes bracket processes of capitalization, this approach would push us to pay attention to how the transformation of the economy has impacted contentious politics, including strategies for protest policing. The police need to be understood as an institution that is tied to both the state, which exists as a set of relationships for consolidating and maintaining power, and to capitalist relationships, competing for the extraction of surplus value. Both the political process theory of Tilly and the historical materialism of Linebaugh offer us ways to understand the emergence of the police as defenders of the status quo. By seeing the importance of the connection between both political and economic systems and the police, we can better understand the changes in policing.

This doesn't mean that the police are mere pawns in macro-level transformations. In order to understand their relative autonomy and its effect on police strategy more clearly, one needs to examine the interactions between the police and other actors, and the practices and discourses of the police themselves, as they enact and explain the changes within their own practices. Pierre Bourdieu's work on logic and strategy provide a useful method for investigating how the neoliberal restructuring of economic and political systems are enacted through struggles within the micro-contexts of police departments, civil liberties organizations, the media, and the courts and professional organizations. Like Bourdieu, I do not see strategy as the purposive and preplanned pursuit of calculated goals, but rather as "the active deployment of objectively oriented 'lines of action' that obey regularities and form coherent and socially intelligible patterns, even though they do not follow conscious rules or aim at the pre-meditated goals posited by a strategist" (Wacquant 1992: 25). In this vein, I will look at the practices, organizations, and discourses of the police themselves, as they struggle to enact strategies and justify tactics for responding to and pre-empting street protest. Such an approach moves beyond portraying police agencies either as tools of political and economic elites (although they may serve this function as well), or as the evil masters of the universe. By locating discourses around the use of force, the chain of command, threat, and the role of the police within an analysis of changing macro-political and economic contexts, I can better understand the logic of how and why OC spray, barricades, Tasers, and riot control units are increasingly used on unarmed protesters.

The Logic of Protest Policing

If we want to understand this logic, it is useful to remember that police agencies are socially constituted collective actors with identities and strategies about which they are both culturally constrained and relatively reflexive. The practices and strategies of the police, like any category of collective action are patterned and clustered into fields of interaction.

Bourdieu defines fields as "structured spaces of positions (or posts) whose properties depend on their position within these spaces and which can be analyzed independently of the characteristics of their occupants" (Bourdieu 1993: 72). Fields are structured by the state of power relations among the actors engaged in struggle over the definition and distribution of the field's specific form of capital (ibid.: 73). Different fields have different values for different forms of capital. In a settled field, participants agree on the values and rules of the game and how different forms of capital are measured and distributed (Steinmetz 2008: 596). However, at other times when the intensity of struggles within a field increase, new species of capital, new constituencies, or new fields or sub-fields may emerge (cf. Armstrong 2002, Bourdieu 1993, Steinmetz 2008, Hedström, Sandell, and Stern 2000).

As Janet Chan notes, the field of policing is a relatively low-prestige occupation in terms of economic capital, but enjoys a high degree of public and government support (political and symbolic capital) (2004: 330). Like other professions, police must defend their legitimacy, influence, expertise, and resources against challengers and opponents. To understand these defensive struggles, it is useful to recognize the history of the profession as one that competed and collaborated with military authorities. The institutional culture rewards and values bravery or toughness (also tied to masculinity) and an adherence to, and respect for, the chain of command. These institutional norms are internalized by police in ways that influence their logic and strategy. Bourdieu calls this internalized structure "habitus." He defines habitus as

> … [s]ystems of durable, transposable dispositions, structured structures predisposed to function as structuring structures, that is, as principles which generate and organize practices and representations that can be objectively adapted to their outcomes without presupposing a conscious aiming at ends or an express mastery of the operations necessary in order to attain them. (1990: 4)

The habitus of a police officer constrains the interpretation and evaluation of new interactions, and new information constrains police knowledge – and therefore police logics, justifications, strategies and practices. When we observe police attempts to establish, defend, justify, and change their strategy and tactics, we must ask what is being defended and obtained.

Often these struggles occur over the currencies of legitimacy, influence, and autonomy.

An analysis of the interaction between field, habitus, and capital produces an understanding of how police knowledge is constituted and changed, as a product of the organization of police forces and political opportunities (Chan 2004, della Porta, Peterson, and Reiter 2006: 187). Since the mid-1990s, the field of policing, the habitus of police decision makers, and struggles over the forms of capital have been transformed in significant ways. The field of professional law enforcement is merging with other fields, including that of the defense industry, military, and management consultants. In this transformed field, new actors are increasingly important, especially US-dominated, international, professional bodies, and multinational corporations. Their influence leverages the importance of cost-efficiency models, best practices, global integration, and public relations. This transformation has been observed in other professions within the same time period, with best practices certified by powerful expert consultants spreading rapidly to new users.

Where should I begin if I want to understand the changing forms of protest policing? Emphasizing the debates and conflicts amongst police and other players allows us to see changing protest policing strategy as networks of struggle among various players in policing organizations but also between politicians at all levels, the general public, security and defense industries, activists, judiciaries, and NGOs. Debates around the legitimate use of force against protesters, or debates around the appropriate level of security preparations, illuminate the logics at play in the struggles over policing decisions to barricade, Taser, and arrest disruptive protesters. Debates around such questions are considered within a field of policing that is increasingly globalized through international agreements and collaborations, increasingly profession-alized through conferences like those organized by the International Association of Chiefs of Police (IACP), increasingly integrated with private sector corporate interests, and through the establishment of regional and international policing organizations like the Police Executive Research Foundation (PERF). The growing density of these ties is creating new arenas, privileging shared professional identities, and facilitating the diffusion of best practices to new sites. If I examine the diffusion of these "best practices" in protest policing, I am more able to explain why and how police decision makers are increasingly adopting the logic and practices of strategic incapacitation.

Diffusion

According to Elihu Katz,

> Diffusion … [is] *defined as the acceptance of some specific item, over time, by adopting units – individuals, groups, communities*—that are linked both to external channels of communication and to each other by means of both a structure of social relations and a system of values, or culture. (Katz 1968, emphasis added)

Such an "item," innovation, or frame may come from another geographic area, another occupational group, another culture, or another planet. The vast majority of the time ideas do not diffuse. If they did, there would be no stability in practice, meaning, or technology. The successful diffusion of any innovation is dependent on the innovation itself, the transmitting context, the channels of communication, and the receiving context (Hedstrom, Sandell, and Stern 2000, McAdam 1995, McAdam and Rucht 1993, Myers 2000, Oliver and Myers 1998, Strang and Meyer 1993, Wood 2012). Highly visible innovations by legitimate transmitters are more likely to spread. Contexts where there are clusters of potential adopting actors also facilitate diffusion. Following social movement theorists Doug McAdam and Dieter Rucht (1993), conditions within the receiving context can aid those promoting or blocking the incorporation of a particular innovation. The acceptance or rejection of an innovation by these adopters may be influenced by characteristics of the innovation itself, namely, (1) the cost-benefit analysis of the innovation, (2) its compatibility or with existing identities and values, (3) the complexity of the program principles, (4) its ability to be tried, and (5) the demonstrativeness of its utility. Each of these involves processes within a receiving context. For example, the purchase of a flash-bang grenade that releases pepper gas into a crowd will be *evaluated* in terms of its cost and benefits in comparison to existing technologies. A police decision-maker, in *consultation* with other decision makers will look at earlier users of the flash-bang grenade and evaluate their reputation, prestige, level of success, and similarity to the force they work for. The decision maker will see whether he or she *identifies* with those previous users, seeing his or her own context as similar in some way to that of the earlier users. That decision maker will also compare the past uses of the flash-bang grenade and evaluate whether the needs of his or her agency are similar enough to justify buying the technology.

That decision maker, again, in consultation with others, both inside and outside the agency, will evaluate how the technology might be used and whether he or she will be able to promote the technology to others in their agency in such a way that they will see its value. If the flash-bang grenades are purchased, in order to incorporate the technology into the repertoire of a particular police agency, there will need to be an opportunity to experiment with the tool, adapt it, or its use if necessary, and certify its value. These different processes of comparison, evaluation, identification, promotion, incorporation, experimentation, adaptation, and certification may each involve competing or collaborative social relations within a field and are influenced by the past and present history of those relations in that particular site.

Within a field, innovations that are certified by opinion leaders in that field as useful and legitimate will be adopted by more actors more rapidly, following a general "S" curve, with early adoption leading to a period of rapid adoption and then tapering off (Katz 1999, Granovetter 1973). By understanding how struggles over innovations and their incorporation unfold, we get a better sense of how and why police decision makers incorporate barricading strategies, less-lethal weapons, riot control units, pre-emptive surveillance, and arrest into their protest policing repertoires.

Diffusion and Policing

In some ways, diffusion is a particularly important process in the field of policing. However, police agencies have characteristics that make diffusion difficult. Their role and history leads them to prioritize information from within their boundaries (Manning 1997). Their professional identity as knowledgeable, traditional, and effective, can also limit their openness to incorporating new ideas. Lingamneni (1979) and others argue that the hierarchical structure of police organizations resist the incorporation of innovations. Others have argued that because police organizations remain both largely autonomous from outside actors, and bounded by their political regime, they are less likely to consider ideas from outside themselves. Past research on the diffusion of computer systems and weapons found that police forces are more likely to incorporate innovations when they are connected to research communities (Weiss 1997, Weisburd and Lum 2005), or to policy communities (Weiss 1997). Police agencies are more likely to be influenced by other agencies seen as experts in a particular domain, especially if they are of a similar type, are geographically close, and have the same population size (Roberts and Roberts 2007). Looking at the incorporation of computer systems by police agencies, Manning found that certain factors increase the likelihood of incorporation, including

> … the active role played by the "evangelist" representing the host department; the fact that access to the system was free; and because it primarily empowered detectives—who enjoy a privileged position in policing—and did not challenge the traditional mission and organization of participating agencies. (Manning 2008)

Although it rarely happens, Lawless (1987) argues that successful incorporation of new technologies into police departments also necessitates surveying user needs and the active role of users in evaluating and giving feedback. Skogan and Hartnett found that

> … adoption and extent of utilization proved to be largely independent processes. Involvement in cosmopolitan networks, experience with using databases for law enforcement, and the human capital capacities of the organizations influenced the adoption decision, while organizational resources and experience in using the system drove the level of actual use … . (Skogan and Hartnett 2005)

Many of these conditions support diffusion by a wide range of actors. Della Porta and Tarrow (2012) found that innovations among both police and protesters were influenced by similar processes and conditions. Diffusion is more likely if a promoter actively promotes a particular innovation, and when potential adopters are able to assess and theorize the meaning and use of the innovation. In the current globalizing moment, they believe diffusion is an increasingly important process for both protesters and police. I agree, and believe the struggles of police for legitimacy and other forms of power within this crisis-prone system have encouraged the rapid diffusion of militarized protest policing tactics. This diffusion is facilitated by three conditions.

First, diffusion is more likely when potential adopters of an innovation perceive a crisis in their modus operandi. Over the past twenty years, police in Canada and the United States have faced repeated crises in legitimacy and capacity around public order incidents, including riots, protests, sports events, natural disasters, and terrorist attacks. These events can trigger periods of condemnation, public inquiries, lawsuits and sometimes, re-organizing or rethinking of past practice. For example, the Seattle protests against the WTO, the Rodney King riots in Los Angeles, the 9/11 attacks in New York City, and the G20 protests in London and Toronto have each stimulated tactical innovation, diffusion, and shifts in practice.

The second condition that facilitates diffusion is the increasing transnational integration of social relations. This means that information about new technologies and approaches flows increasingly easily. In these flows national boundaries are becoming less significant, integrating economies and political decision making. At the same time, the global integration of professional policing networks has integrated law enforcement bodies, both public and private, spreading both information on best practices, and providing venues for discussing the merits and drawbacks of best practices in different contexts.

The third condition that eases the diffusion and incorporation of new policing practices is the increasing importance of an internationally shared professional police identity. Facilitated by the increasing influence and integration of professional bodies, this is facilitating the process of identification or attribution of similarity. Potential adopters in the police need to see themselves and their context as similar to earlier users of an innovation. This process requires relatively open, reflexive conversation about the similarities between themselves and their context and previous users of a practice or innovation and that context (Wood 2012). Such a process is eased by organizational membership, training, and wider cultural understandings of protest, protesters, and the legal system – all of which are facilitated by the global integration of political, economic and police organizations and practices. In this context, practices promoted by actors who cut across organizational boundaries, like professional associations or defense industry lobbyists and corporations, gain legitimacy and influence—often reinforcing the influence of already powerful players in an increasingly integrated field.

Crises, integration, and the activation of shared identities each ease the spread of new, militarized protest policing tactics in the instability and consolidation of the current moment. But of course, the transmission, incorporation and use of these tactics vary. They are shaped both by the features of policing agencies, institutions and networks themselves and the varied interactions between police and their contexts.

Conclusion

Was police violence against protesters at the G20 in Toronto simply a product of an unraveling social system? The Commission for Public Complaints Against the RCMP (2012) found that despite the record number of arrests, beatings, and incidents of infiltration and kettling, the police acted reasonably. The provincial Ombudsman's inquiry found the opposite, arguing that police had violated many elements of the Ontario Policing Act in their treatment of protesters, and recommended that officers be charged (Marin 2011). In their After-Action Reports, both the Ontario Provincial Police and the Toronto Police Service defended their actions, but admitted confusion about communication and the chain of command. The OPP blamed the TPS, while the TPS complained that the intelligence officers hadn't provided adequate information (Ontario Provincial Police 2011, Toronto Police Service 2011b). It is clear that the current state of the policing of protest is still in flux and under scrutiny. The police weren't satisfied, nor were the public. Indeed, in the wake of the G20 protests, *Toronto Star* columnist Rosie DiManno demanded the resignation of Police Chief Bill Blair. The question becomes what will happen next? Will protest policing strategies continue to militarize and attempt to pre-empt and contain dissent?

In the following pages, I answer this question by examining the changing field and habitus of protest policing, the struggles over legitimacy, resources, and decision-making power, and the decisions of police as they act and justify their actions. In order to understand both about police practices and logics, I use newspaper accounts, the newsletters of regulatory bodies and the magazines of professional policing organizations. I analyze annual reports from police agencies and corporations, independent inquiries, my own field notes, intelligence documents obtained through information access requests, reports and analyses by social movements, police memoirs, court transcripts from trials, and other sources. I analyze the events, discourses, networks, and practices revealed by them. I look at when and how police agencies use militarized tactics against protesters in

Canada and the US, showing both overall trends and local variation, and how they justify these tactics to a range of audiences.[2]

Chapter 2 shows how waves of protest transform police organizations and their protest policing strategy using event catalogs of mass protests in Europe and North America from 1995 until the present. This will illustrate the shift away from negotiated management protest policing strategies that della Porta, Peterson, and Reiter (2006), McCarthy (1998), Rafail, Soule, and McCarthy (2012), Vitale (2005), De Lint and Hall (2009), Fernandez (2008), Starr, Fernandez, and Scholl (2011), Waddington (2007) and others have identified. In particular, I look at the emergence and spread of riot control units, less-lethal weapons, mass arrest, pre-emptive control and barricading strategies as tools against protesters.

In Chapter 3, I begin to explain why and how these tactics spread. Locating police agencies within a context of neoliberal restructuring, I analyze the trends in Canadian and US police organizations, and the spread of organizational and operational "best practices." In Chapter 4, I show how these trends intersect with the local relational context, arguing that divisions between police actors and other local authorities will affect protest policing decisions and the likelihood that police officials will turn to outside expertise. Chapter 5 uses the example of police use of pepper spray to show how dynamics in the local context facilitate the incorporation of a controversial protest policing tactic, including an analysis of the way pepper spray was transformed from a tool to be used only in life-threatening situations where a gun would otherwise be used into a tool for public order management. I show how a crisis in police legitimacy facilitated the use of pepper spray against protesters in Canada and the United States from its introduction in 1993 to the present, and I argue that a police agency is most likely to incorporate an already-controversial police tactic when that force faces a crisis and looks outside itself for solutions. Polarized local interactions between police and the public activate the boundary between police and civilian identity. This activation, combined with increased interactions and identification with professional policing associations and private security consultants, facilitates the ongoing incorporation of pepper spray and other less-lethal weapons.

In Chapter 6, I shift my attention to the role of professional policing organizations in an increasingly globalized field of policing to show how protest policing strategies are being influenced by the best practices promoted by the private sector through international policing conferences, trainings, and shared materials. Using the example of the policing of the Occupy movement in 2011, I examine the process by which "expertise" and "best practices" are generated, promoted, and shared, diffusing the protest policing approach of "strategic incapacitation," and benefiting the private sector.

Chapter 7 looks at the way that the attacks of September 11, 2001 restructured the logic of protest policing in both Canada and the US. Anti-terrorist initiatives funded the integration of intelligence gathering, border control, and law enforcement fields, and changed the way both the police and the public understood the terms "security" and "threat," bringing increased tensions between civil liberties and the right to protest. By analyzing police intelligence reports gathered during preparations for the 2004 protests against the Republican National Convention in New York City, the ways in which police see protest as threatening and requiring surveillance and control are illustrated.

In Chapter 8, I show how this new context has corresponded with police officials repeating stories about protesters, stories that rely on stereotypes and social taboos. Tracking the recurrence of "intelligence" that reveals that protesters are prepared to fill water pistols with urine and shoot them at police officers, I examine why such stories resonate with police, and are repeated despite a lack of evidence and the implications of such stories. I argue that intelligence-led policing, when combined with militarized policing, has contributed to the over-policing of protest, with mass arrests and violence becoming routine.

One of the unintended consequences of recent protests policing strategies is the emergence of new campaigns for police accountability and oversight. In Chapter 9, I explore the possibilities and limitations of such campaigns. Throughout both G20 protests, protesters faced innovations in less-lethal weapons, including vehicles that could emit high-pitched, loud sounds, riot control units, pepper spray, tear gas, smoke bombs, undercover officers, and high barricades. As a result of police abuses, numerous inquiries, investigations, and hearings were held, producing ensuing recommendations for more training, different weapons, clarification of the chain of command, etc. Nonetheless, such changes will not resolve the problem of brutal protest policing. Given the changes to political and economic systems, the patterns of interactions at the local level, and the diffusion of innovations that link them, protest policing is unlikely to become less repressive in the foreseeable future.

Indeed, police organizations are struggling for legitimacy and resources, as they simultaneously attempt to defend their power in an unstable system. Although demands for accountability and changes to policy are crucial to limiting the harm police do, deep change to the policing of protest cannot come while political and economic power continue to consolidate.

2

Policing Waves of Protest, 1995–2013

On October 1, 2011, New York Police Department officers arrested 700 Occupy Wall Street protesters as they marched from the streets of lower Manhattan onto the Brooklyn Bridge. Throughout the ensuing month, police in cities across the US, Canada, Australia, and Europe put pressure on hundreds of protesters who refused to leave their "Occupy" encampments. In a very public manner, these police operations illustrated how militarized policing protest strategies had become routine since the protests against the Asia Pacific Economic Cooperation (APEC) summit in Vancouver in 1997 and protests against the World Trade Organization (WTO) in Seattle in 1999. When police employed pepper spray and mass arrests to control demonstrators at these events, there was a massive outcry.

At the APEC protests, police pre-emptively arrested organizer Jaggi Singh, kept the protesters behind fences, and pepper sprayed them. Afterwards, a major inquiry ensued, into the RCMP's use of pepper spray, and the containment of protesters, and into whether police strategy was influenced by the Prime Minister's Office. The final 453-page report concluded that the police behavior "did not meet an acceptable and expected standard of competence and professionalism and proficiency" and blamed poor planning on the part of the RCMP (CBC News, August 7, 2001). It also found that the Prime Minister's Office's director of operations had directly interfered with security operations, challenging the independence of the police.

Two years later, the Seattle protests unfolded, between November 29 and December 2, 1999. Police had assumed they would be able to handle the large protests without disrupting the summit. However, when protesters set up blockades that disrupted traffic and access to the summit, the police became overwhelmed and pepper sprayed, shot rubber bullets and tear gassed the protesters (Gillham and Marx 2000). The mayor declared a State of Emergency and the governor called in the National Guard. After protests continued into the next day, the mayor declared 25 blocks of downtown Seattle a "limited curfew area." That was interpreted by both police and protesters as a "no protest zone." Police used less lethal weapons and arrested hundreds of people who entered the area.

The clashes between protesters and police were front-page news. After the summit ended, the Seattle Chief of Police Norm Stamper resigned, explaining, "I made major mistakes" (*Democracy Now* 2009). In the end, almost none of the more than 600 arrests led to convictions. Some protesters sued for unlawful arrest, winning over $1 million from various class action lawsuits (Young 2007). This confrontation at Seattle was seen as the launch of a new wave of protest for the global justice movement, and it was seen as a policing disaster, a "Pearl Harbor" that launched a period of re-assessment and justified the emergence of a new style of protest policing, especially in the US and Canada (Fisher 2001, cited in Noakes and Gillham 2007).

In this chapter, I will examine the new style that emerged with this wave of protest and track its associated tactics: less lethal weapons (pepper spray, Tasers, Long Range Acoustic Devices (LRADs), rubber bullets, etc.), barricades (security perimeters, kettling, protest pens), infiltration, and mass and selective pre-emptive arrests. However, I do not wish to suggest that the policing of protest has completely changed or imply that protest policing was not brutal in the past, nor that the policing of protest since the '90s has become completely militarized. To this day, the vast majority of protests in Canada and the US involve either little policing or "soft hat" policing strategies, whereby officers negotiate with protest organizers and facilitate their events using minimal police resources or confrontation. However, especially for activists who refuse to negotiate, or those seen as threatening, uncooperative, or unpredictable, police use a more militarized approach that Gillham and Noakes call "strategic incapacitation," due to its attempt to control and limit the effectiveness of protesters challenging the status quo.

The strategic incapacitation approach to protest policing recognizes the ways that police combine the intelligence gathering and analysis of intelligence-led policing in order to pre-empt protest through control or dissuasion of protesters. If police are unable to stop the protest, and protesters continue to appear "threatening" or "unpredictable," police shift their approach to one that uses mass arrest, supported by the use of less-lethal weapons and riot control units. John Noakes and Patrick

Gillham (2007) and Gillham, Edwards and Noakes (2013) argue that, since the Seattle protests of 1999, we are more likely to see police use the following tactics:

- the establishment of extensive no-protest zones, often by installing large concrete and metal fence barriers;
- the disruption of safe spaces, such as convergence centers where protesters would congregate to sleep, eat, and acquire information;
- the use of less-lethal weapons to temporarily incapacitate protesters so police could retake control of spaces of contention;
- the use of electronic surveillance technology to provide real-time information on demonstrators' activities to police, and
- pre-emptive arrests to re-organize leaders and large numbers of protesters.

Since 1999, Noakes and Gillham argue that these practices have become part of a model of militarized policing that has spread to new sites and contexts, along with increasingly modular understandings of when, where, and how to use it.

Donatella della Porta and her collaborators (2006) identify the combination of pre-emption and less-lethal weapons in their observations of the policing of international summits in Europe and North America in the early 2000s. But Alex Vitale observes the police use a particular version of strategic incapacitation against black nationalists in New York City beginning in late 1998. He argues that the protest policing style of New York's Police Department, called "command and control," is an extension of its broader policing model, known as the "broken windows" approach. This approach favors a rapid response to small offenses, with the goal of pre-empting larger ones. In the context of protest policing, this means maintaining full control of the streets, using the permit process, and rapid enforcement of laws through barricades and mass arrest. Vitale argues that after 9/11, the command-and-control approach was combined with militarized and intelligence-led strategies, in order to create the "Miami Model," a reference to Police Chief Timoney's actions at the FTAA protests in Miami in 2003 (Vitale 2007). This approach has established a joint, unified, multi-agency command/control network that treats protest activity as criminal. Repressive authorities respond to protest with militarized crowd control units, less-lethal weapons, barricaded areas, surveillance, pre-emptive arrests, and an intensive media and public relations strategy (Starr, Fernandez, and Scholl 2011).

Although there are variations in application, interpretation, and emphasis, these different explanations of the model of policing protest currently favored in Canada and the US each identify a strategy of intelligence gathering, in order to assess, predict and pre-empt protester activity, combined with the use of military formations, organizational forms, and technologies. While the roots of this strategy were in existence starting in the early 1990s, since 1999, the strategic incapacitation model of protest policing has become routine for the policing of large-scale, uncooperative protests in Canada and the US, including the use of less-lethal weapons, barricading strategies, pre-emptive arrests, intentional media spin, infiltration and specialized crowd control units. This chapter will highlight the introduction and spread of this model and these tactics over the past twenty years.

The Tactics

Less-Lethal Weapons

In the wake of the incendiary video capturing Los Angeles police beating black motorist Rodney King with batons in 1991, police sought weapons that could exert a level of force between that of the baton and the gun. That year, the National Institute of Justice hosted a brainstorming session to think about the possibilities of new non-lethal weapons technologies. Participants in this session were given a set of parameters for any new device under consideration. The device had to be inexpensive and improve on a present practice; it could not overburden the officer, or require extensive training or dedicated personnel; liability issues had to be manageable, and, of course, it had to work (Pilant 1993).

This discussion was also happening elsewhere in the post-Cold War context. Military strategists were exploring new options, and new technologies. General Anthony Zinni, Director of Operations for US troops in Somalia in 1992, was frustrated by the lack of options soldiers had in responding to rioting and demonstrations. He began experimenting and, due to experiments by him and others, in 1996, the US Congress created a Joint Non-Lethal Weapons Program, later providing it with an annual budget of approximately $25 million (Mihm 2004). Although coordinated by the Marines, each branch of the Armed Services and law enforcement officials plays a role in the program (ibid.). In 1999, a conference of National Armaments Directors advised NATO leadership on weapons procurement, and established the NATO Defense Capabilities Initiative, to explore the potential of such weapons and develop shared models of effectiveness (Institute for Non-Lethal Defense Technologies 2005). In 2001, Pennsylvania State University organized the first International Law Enforcement Forum on Minimal Force Options. In this forum and in law enforcement networks more generally, key decision makers agreed that such weapons were desirable tools and since the 1990s, have been encouraging their adoption. This includes pepper spray, conducted-energy devices like Tasers, LRADs, rubber bullets, concussion grenades, and tear gas. Military and police in South Africa and Israel, states with long-standing histories of state repression have used these tactics most extensively. In states without such nationwide conflict, it is regions or populations, such as indigenous populations in Canada (particularly if they offer an armed challenge to state legitimacy) that have been more likely to face such weapons than the population overall.

Private sector and public sector promoters promoted each new weapon as a tool for an "extraordinary circumstance," often justified by rulings or controversies that deemed existing weapons ineffective or legally problematic. Initial experiments with such weapons often triggered lawsuits and inquiries, research studies, and media attention. Indeed, it is such criticisms that have led critics to rename the category of "non-lethal weapons," as "less-lethal." Nonetheless, the weapons continue to diffuse, and be incorporated by new forces. Worryingly too, once adopted, the use of these weapons tends to suffer from a form of "mission drift," by which their use expands from its initial function, to its use for a broader set of tasks, and in a broader set of contexts. I review some of the most commonly used less-lethal weapons below.

Pepper Spray

Pepper spray, also known as OC spray (*oleoresin capsicum*) is derived from the capsicum plant genus, most commonly associated with cayenne. Initially used as a bear repellent in Canada, it began to be marketed as a personal security tool in the 1980s. The FBI endorsed it as an "official chemical agent" in 1987. OC spray appeared to fulfill all the criteria for an effective less-lethal weapon, and its use spread widely in both Canada and the US. The RCMP (Royal Canadian Mounted Police) began to use it for crowd control in Canada in 1992. By 1993, almost 70 percent of police forces in the United States had adopted the spray. It spread quickly as a tool to be used against combative suspects and by the end of the 1990s, pepper spray had virtually replaced the use of batons, Mace, or CS/CN sprays for this purpose. Police forces also began to use pepper spray as a tool for crowd control.

The gradual incorporation of pepper spray as a tool used for crowd control and in protest situations becomes clear after examining an event catalog of protests covered in the media between 1993 and 2012.[1] This data shows that OC spray was first used against protesters in both the US and Canada in 1993. On May 31, 1993, Ottawa police used pepper spray to break up fights between neo-Nazis and anti-racist activists. In September 1993, police in California used pepper spray to break up a Mexican Independence Day event protesting the lack of Chicano teachers and Mexican curriculum in local colleges and high schools. The *Orange County Register* noted police officials saying officers acted correctly when they used pepper spray to scatter the crowd, which was blocking traffic. "If it happens again, they're going to get sprayed again," said Fullerton Police Captain Lee DeVore. "We're not going to allow people to take over the streets and disrupt the community" (Shaffer, Davis, and Powell 1993).

Still, this was only the beginning. Police used pepper spray three times in Canada and the US in 1993, and five times in 1994. This increased by 1995, when police used pepper spray 14 times against protesters. Since then, the level of use has remained relatively stable. In 2011, police in Canada and the US used pepper spray 21 times against protesters. In 2012, it was used 28 times, although this increase was largely due to an intense period of student-led protests in Montreal. Despite ongoing use, the employment of pepper spray in protest policing continues to be controversial, often leading to lawsuits and inquiries. Said inquiries and additional research argue that its being sprayed can lead to ongoing health problems. In fact, guidelines for its use differ among different police agencies. Even during the preparations for the protests against the 2012 NATO Summit in Chicago, Police Superintendent Garry McCarthy explained that "each officer will be equipped with pepper spray, but ... it should be used only to thwart assaults on officers" (Associated Press 2012). There is further discussion about the diffusion of pepper spray as a public order tactic in Chapter 5.

Tasers
While earlier versions of "stun guns" existed, even used in crowd control situations, the use of "Conducted Energy Devices" (CEDs) increased rapidly

after 1999 when the company TASER emerged. Unofficially named TASER after "Thomas A. Swift's Electronic Rifle", for a character in a turn-of-the-century children's book, TASER developed a handgun-shaped device called the Advanced Taser (M-Series), which used a "patented neuromuscular incapacitation (NMI) technology." This model was replaced in 2003 by the Taser X26, and, in 2009, by the X3. Each modification resulted partly from criticisms of the weapon and its use. Beststungun.com describes the TASER in the following manner:

> It delivers a powerful signal that completely overrides the assailant's central nervous system and directly controls their skeletal muscles. Pull the trigger and it will shoot two small probes up to 15 feet to the assailant. A 15 foot range provides a great distance from you to the assailant. This can significantly reduce the chance of injury by avoiding a close confrontation.

TASER International explains that the devices are intended to provide

> ... solutions to violent confrontation by developing devices with proprietary technology to incapacitate dangerous, combative, or high-risk subjects who pose a risk to law enforcement officers, innocent citizens, or themselves in a manner that is generally recognized as a safer alternative to other uses of force. (TASER International 2009)

While the Taser was originally marketed as a tool to replace a gun, for the purposes of making an arrest, like the OC spray, its use has expanded to include obtaining compliance more generally. This use continues to grow, despite ongoing concerns about incidents where police have Tasered someone who subsequently died. According to Amnesty International, between 2001 and 2012, over 500 people in the United States died after being shocked by police Tasers. While most of the deaths have been attributed to other causes, medical examiners have listed Tasers as a cause or contributing factor in more than 60 deaths, and in a number of other cases the exact cause of death is unknown (Amnesty International 2012). Although TASER International continues to argue that there is no evidence that being Tasered causes death, increasing numbers of researchers and medical experts challenge this assertion.

Although high-profile deaths involving Tasers have slowed the adoption of Tasers by police, and often trigger modifications or increased rules around their use, new law enforcement agencies continue to adopt the weapon. Of the major municipalities in the US, only San Francisco has not adopted Tasers. Although the weapon is adopted as an alternative to a gun, it often begins to be used as a crowd control tool. Using a LexisNexis search of all media sources using the keywords "protesters," "protester," "demonstrators," and "Tasered," I found that Tasers are increasingly seen in protest contexts in Canada and the US. Before 2000, police or sheriff's department officers had only used Tasers twice against protesters, both already in custody. Between 2000 and 2005 inclusively, police used Tasers five times against protesters, usually to make an arrest or to force protesters occupying government offices to leave. In both cases of Taser use against sit-ins, the RCMP used the weapons against marginalized populations – Innu community members demanding housing and Algerian refugees trying to stop their deportations. At the FTAA protests in Quebec City, police used Tasers against protesters. The Public Inquiry into the RCMP's actions at that event found that "A high-voltage Taser was used to stun a protester who was on his knees and waiting to be arrested." The report adds, "The protester was not struggling and represented no threats to the members, to himself, to the public or to property" (Bourrie 2003). Between 2006 and 2012 inclusively, police used Tasers eleven times against protesters, to make arrests and to stop protesters from advancing. By 2008, more than half of all police agencies in the United States used some form of Conducted Energy Device (White and Ready 2010: 89). The decision to adopt them is usually bolstered by arguments that they reduce injuries in suspects. At Toronto's G20 protests, police brandished Tasers during a raid of an activist sleeping space, in order to intimidate demonstrators. During the 2011–12 Occupy wave of protest, Tasers were used against Occupy protesters in Washington, DC, and Olympia, Washington. I'll return to Tasers in Chapter 6.

Long Range Acoustic Devices (LRADs)

In response to an October 2000 attack on a US Navy boat, the USS *Cole*, in Yemen, security experts created the Long Range Acoustic Device (LRAD 2013). These "sound cannons" can broadcast police directives to the crowd but also can use "deterrent tones" to disperse crowds.[2] When used to its full capacity of 162 decibels, the LRAD can cause permanent hearing damage. LRADs were introduced to police domestic protests in the US in 2004, at the Republican National Convention in New York City. The "deterrence" function has been used in Honduras, Somalia, the Republic of Georgia and against domestic protesters in 2009 at the Pittsburgh G20 summit. The LRAD was displayed at Toronto's G20 summit, Occupy Wall Street protests in New York and Oakland in 2011, at the NATO summit in 2012 in Chicago, and in a "hand held" version at anti-austerity protests in Wisconsin in 2013, but was not used, other than as an extra-loud megaphone. A new tool, the LRAD is becoming part of the protest policing toolkit for large summit and convention protests in North America and elsewhere, with the manufacturer reporting five consecutive years of double-digit sales growth since 2006 (ibid).

Flash-bang Grenades
Some police forces are also increasing their use of less-lethal devices known as "flash-bang grenades," stun grenades or concussion grenades. Designed by the British military in 1969, these are rubber-encased devices that explode, creating a 175-decibel shock wave, while emitting a flash of light and releasing a charge of CS gas into the air. CS gas is a chemical irritant that burns the eyes, affects the respiratory system, and can cause vomiting (Christoff 2012). The weapon is designed to disorient people (referred to in promotional material as "enemies"). SWAT teams use the grenades during raids on homes. Such use has caused heart attacks and death from smoke inhalation. Police and military forces have long used the weapon as a public order tool in the Middle East, Europe and South Africa, but police in Canada and the US are increasingly incorporating the weapon into their public order repertoire, particularly at summit-type protests. Seattle police used them at the WTO protests in 1999. The RCMP then used them against protesters at the 2001 Summit of the Americas (Quebec City); the 2001 G20 Financial meetings (Ottawa); the 2008 RNC in Minneapolis/St. Paul; the 2009 G20 summit (Pittsburgh); the 2010 Oakland protests after a law enforcement officer was acquitted of manslaughter; the 2011 Occupy Oakland protests and 2011 and 2012 Montreal student protests, the 2013 Seattle Mayday protests, and the 2013 Oakland Trayvon Martin killing/George Zimmerman acquittal protests (Peel and Richman 2011, Rakobowchuk 2011). Three patterns are evident: 1) protests in Oakland and Montreal and large summit protests are the main contexts in which these weapons are used, 2) often in conjunction with other less-lethal weapons, and 3) once flash-bang grenades are used once in a particular location, they are more likely to be used again.

Tear Gas

Tear gas is a less-lethal chemical weapon that stimulates the corneal nerves in the eyes causing tears, drooling, a runny nose, burning sensations in moist parts of the body, difficulty breathing and temporary blindness. Although tear gas in warfare is banned by the UN's Geneva Convention, it is frequently used for crowd control by police on their civilian populations. There are different varieties of gas called tear gas, but it is composed of substances (most often CS and OC) that become gases through the use of propellants. CS gas contains a chemical named 2-chlorobenzylidene malonitrile. OC gas is a gaseous version of oleum capsicum, the same active ingredient in pepper spray. In the past, CN gas was used, but has been largely eliminated due to toxicity. CS gas can be used in different concentrations in grenades, and as a spray—in Britain, the spray used by the police forces contains 5 percent CS gas, whereas in the United States it contains 1 percent (Karagama et al. 2003). Different solvents may also have different effects. Research suggests that some effects of tear gas can be identified a month after exposure (ibid.). These effects are far more severe for those with ongoing respiratory problems. Tear gas was used at the Seattle WTO protests and since that time, used widely at global justice protests, most famously at the 2001 Quebec City protests against the Free Trade Area of the Americas, when police launched 4,700 canisters at protesters over the three-day period (Kolodner 2001).

Rubber Bullets

The term "rubber bullets" can be used to describe a large number of less-lethal projectiles, all shot from some sort of gun and designed to incapacitate but not penetrate nor kill the target. These include rubberized projectiles, plastic bullets, wooden pellets, and bean bag rounds. Most histories identify the British Ministry of Defence as inventing and first using rubber bullets against rioters in Northern Ireland in 1970. Tens of thousands of rounds were used during that conflict. Such projectiles are supposed to be shot at the ground, so the round bounces up and hits the target on the legs causing pain but not injury. Nonetheless, there were numerous serious injuries and three deaths from the police use of rubber bullets. As a result, police replaced them with the seemingly less-lethal plastic bullets (Jones 2010). However, between 1979 and 1985, a dozen people, mostly children, were killed by the plastic bullets. National Guards used rubber bullets against anti-war and civil rights demonstrators as early as 1970. However, a fatality in 1971 stopped their use until their reintroduction in the late 1980s. Since the Seattle protests, police in the US and Canada have used rubber bullets at summit-type protests, including the 2000 IMF/WB protests in Washington, the 2000 Los Angeles DNC, the 2001 Quebec City FTAA protests where police shot 900 bullets at protesters, and the 2003 FTAA summit in Miami (Pugliese and Bronskill 2001). Los Angeles police are relatively frequent users of the bullets, using them in 2007 against immigrant rights protesters—something that cost the city $13 million in subsequent lawsuits, and then again in the summer of 2013 against protesters upset with the acquittal of George Zimmerman, who had shot unarmed black teen Trayvon Martin. In addition, Montreal police used the bullets repeatedly against student protesters in 2012, shooting one woman in the jaw, causing her to lose several teeth.

Barricading Strategies

Police attempts to maintain control over the flow and movement of protesters are a central part of the strategic incapacitation police strategy (Scholl 2013, Starr, Fernandez, and Scholl 2012, Vitale 2012). Police used at least three techniques: protest pens, security perimeter walls, and kettling. Police in the US and Canada have used each of these on protesters over the past few years.

Summit Walls/Perimeter Fences

While there were fences surrounding the APEC summit site in 1997, they were relatively flimsy and clearly temporary. In 2000, the first solid, concrete, mounted perimeter fence was erected around the site of a major summit, the Organization of American States summit in Windsor, Ontario. That event was policed by 3,700 police officers, from forces including the RCMP, Ontario Provincial Police, Peel Regional Police Service, Toronto Police Service, Chatham Police Service, and the Windsor Police. Police After-Action Reports argued that the perimeter fence was one reason for the successful policing strategy at the event (Commission for Public Complaints Against the RCMP 2012). Although often attracting widespread public anger, perimeter fences were subsequently used at US and Canadian events including the FTAA Summit in Quebec City (2001), at Republican and Democratic Convention sites, and at the NATO summit in Chicago (2012). Perimeter fences were also used at the G8 summit in Genoa in 2001 and subsequent summit meetings, including Heiligendamm (2007) (Scholl 2013: 112).

Protest Pens or "Free Speech Zones"

These barricaded areas are spaces where permitted protest is allowed and regulated by law (scheduled times are sometimes assigned by lottery). They emerged as a result of First Amendment concerns in the United States. The first such pen was created in 1988, in Atlanta, Georgia, at the Democratic National Convention and became standard practice for large political conventions by the time the Republican Conventions in 1992 and 1996 and the Democratic Convention in 1996 took place. Often these pens incorporate CCTV cameras in their design, streaming images of would-be protesters into the summit area itself. Given the way these pens appear to render protest ineffective, many protesters refuse to use these areas.

Such pens are less well-known in Canada. In 1997, at the protests against the Asia Pacific Economic Community summit, the RCMP was accused of creating a fenced-in area for protesters far away from the delegates, although this accusation was deemed invalid by the public inquiry. In 2007, at a Security and Prosperity Partnership meeting in Montebello, Quebec, a similar pen was created, much to the disgust of protesters. In 2010, when the Integrated Security Unit planners for the G8 protests in Huntsville, Ontario, and the G20 protests in Toronto announced "designated speech areas" for both events, they faced extensive criticism. The Huntsville zone was 7 kilometers from the summit site, far beyond the "eyes and ears" of world leaders. Toronto's Queen's Park was labeled as such an area, attracting many protesters, many of whom believed that this would be a zone safe from police harassment. Contrary to their expectations, the park became surrounded by police, who ordered protesters to disperse and when they didn't, arrested, and sometimes assaulted them. According to an article in *Niagara at Large*, police accused 57-year-old retired farmer and amputee John Pruyn of "resisting arrest":

> ... they pulled his walking sticks away from him, tied his hands behind his back and ripped off his prosthetic leg. Then they told him to get up and hop, and when he said he couldn't, they dragged him across the pavement, tearing skin off his elbows, with his hands still tied behind his back. His glasses were knocked off as they continued to accuse him of resisting arrest and of being a "spitter," something he said he did not do. (Vallis 2010)

Clearly, the existence of protest pens or "free speech zones" did not protect protesters or their speech.

Kettling

Kettling is defined as the act of surrounding a group of protesters with barricades and holding them within the barricades (in a kettle) for an extended period. Sometimes protesters are later released, sometimes they are arrested, and other times they are photographed and/or searched, and then released. Police used kettling techniques in 1986 in Germany, against anti-nuclear demonstrators and in Britain in 1995, against disability rights protesters (Commission for Public Complaints Against the RCMP 2012). Kettling first came to widespread public attention in 1999, when London police kettled anti-capitalist and anarchist demonstrators protesting in solidarity with the demonstrations against the Seattle-based WTO summit. London police kettled protesters on May 1, 2001, containing thousands in central London's Oxford Circus. The use of kettles increased in tandem with increased counter-terrorism policing powers, and the endorsement of the kettling technique by the Association of Chief Police Officers, which further facilitated its use in the UK (O'Connor 2009, Commission for the Review of Public Complaints Against the RCMP 2012).[3] Kettling gained renewed infamy at both the London 2009 G20 protests and subsequent student protests, at which thousands of protesters were held. These events triggered a formal review of the tactic by Scotland Yard. In that review, Her Majesty's Chief Inspector of the Constabulary argued, "Kettling should … be used in moderation and only if and when deemed necessary."

In Canada, the kettling tactic is used infrequently and has not yet been reviewed by the courts. At the Toronto G20 protests, the Public Order Unit used kettling against demonstrators and faced criticism from Toronto Police Chief Bill Blair. Subsequent reviews of policing of these protests found that the use of kettling to be premature and contrary to established British guidelines on kettling. In Montreal, police had surrounded activists and arrested them en masse since the mid-1990s, but police use of this tactic has increased since 2011 (Poisson 2011). Police in US cities have used a technique similar to kettling since at least the year 2000. Sometimes called a "trap and detain" technique, Washington, DC police were sued for enclosing hundreds of protesters for hours during protests against the criminal justice system and the International Monetary Fund and World Bank in April 2000 (Cherkis 2011). In January 2002, the NYPD corralled protesters at the World Economic Forum meetings in New York for hours, gradually releasing them once their bags were searched. That same year, I was part of a group of protesters and passersby in Washington, DC, who were surrounded in Pershing Park. After not being allowed to disperse, all 400 of us were arrested, charged, and held for approximately 24 hours. Despite the controversy surrounding kettling, it continues to be used, most visibly by the NYPD against Occupy Wall Street protesters in October 2011, when they arrested 700 people on the Brooklyn Bridge.

Pre-emptive Arrests

Pre-emptive arrests have also become part of the strategic incapacitation strategy, as a way to limit public protest before it becomes disruptive. This strategy has three variations. The first is to pre-emptively arrest organizers of protests, as was done at the following meetings: the Minneapolis RNC (2008), Vancouver's APEC (1997), and the Toronto G20 (2010). In Toronto, 17 individuals accused of masterminding disruption were arrested early in the morning before the protests began. The second approach is to raid and arrest protesters at convergence spaces before protests begin. This was done at the Republican National Convention in Philadelphia in 2000, when the police raided a building where activists were constructing puppets and protest signs. The third is to arrest a rallying or marching crowd in anticipation of their future activity. This happened on the eve of the IMF/World Bank protests in Washington, DC, in 2000 and 2003, and at the Republican National Convention protests in New York City in 2004. Montreal police pre-emptively arrested hundreds in anti-G8 protests in 2002, and student demonstrations in 2012–13. In Canada, the charge of "breach of the peace" (not a criminal offense) is frequently laid in order to hold protesters without charge for up to 24 hours. These pre-emptive strategies have become a common occurrence at large protest events, in many cases triggering expensive class action lawsuits for wrongful arrest. Indeed, when the Republican National Convention released its budget for the 2012 event, they included the cost of such lawsuits and their settlements in their security budgets.

Infiltration and Conspiracy Charges

While the focus of this research is the visible police strategy for managing and controlling street protest, I want to briefly note the role that police infiltration and conspiracy charges play in controlling protest. Infiltration is not a new police tactic. Used by both police agencies and intelligence services, its primary goal is to gain intelligence about the threat posed by protesters. However, other tasks are increasingly combined with information gathering. In both Canada and the US, laws directed explicitly against organized crime are being used against social movement organizing. In this context, infiltration is being used more frequently in Canada, the US and the UK (at least) in order to obtain the information necessary to charge social movement organizers with conspiracy. Conspiracy charges are agreements that two or more people will commit a crime in the future. Such charges can turn minor charges of mischief into far more serious charges. In what was known as the "green scare," US police infiltrated radical environmental and animal rights networks in a more intentional fashion after 2002, resulting in over 35 activists convicted of conspiracy charges, and more than 30 others charged, but not convicted (Crimethinc. 2013). By 2005, John Lewis, an FBI deputy assistant director and top official in charge of domestic terrorism argued that "The No. 1 domestic terrorism threat is the eco-terrorism, animal-rights movement" (Schuster 2005). Infiltration and conspiracy charges are also used to demobilize movements outside North America. A massive series of arrests in which conspiracy charges were laid were due in part to infiltration by British authorities, resulting in 114 people being accused of conspiracy to commit aggravated trespass and criminal damage (BBC, 13 April 2009). Initially such charges were used primarily against those accused of being involved in interfering with environmentally destructive facilities, hunting, or vivisection. However, since 2008 the police are using to those involved in organizing public protests. Organizers involved with the 2008 RNC protests in St. Paul, Minnesota, the 2012 NATO protests in Chicago, the 2010 G20 protests in Toronto, and Occupy Cleveland protests in 2012 have each been infiltrated, resulting in conspiracy charges. Prior to the Toronto G20 protests, at least two police officers infiltrated organizing networks leading to charges of conspiracy to riot and conspiracy to commit mischief (Groves 2011). In the end, through collective negotiations, eleven of the activists had their charges dropped and the other six were jailed for periods up to two years for the lesser charge of counseling to commit mischief and counseling to obstruct police (O'Toole 2011).

Public Relations and Media Spin
An under-acknowledged element of contemporary protest policing is the extensive public relations campaigns engaged in by police before the protests even begin. This aspect of protests policing was noted

by Alex Vitale in his analysis of the "Miami Model" of protest policing of the Free Trade Area of the Americas protests in 2003. This strategy includes intentional efforts to de-legitimize protesters and justify police strategy. Police decision makers are well aware of the importance of a "good communication strategy." Such a strategy is intended to illustrate preparedness to political and business leadership, discourage and intimidate potential protest participants, particularly those who might engage in disruptive behavior, and build morale among police forces, and potentially the public.

These pre-event media campaigns may highlight new equipment, such as the LRAD or pepper spray launcher, preparations such as the building of a security perimeter, or they may focus on potential threats and the way police will be preparing for them. Before the 2002 World Economic Forum summit, police held repeated media conferences about their preparedness, and many media outlets broadcast images of police, armed with large guns, patrolling in front of Starbucks cafes, Gap stores, and the hotels where the event and its delegates would be located. As the CBC documentary feature about the police response to the 2010 G20 protests in Toronto title: "You should have stayed at home!" suggests, the message sent by such coverage of militarized policing is definitely one that discourages protest.

Militarized Units

The militarization of protest policing is part of a larger militarization of policing in Canada and the US, the most visible face of which is the more frequent use of militarized units (Williams 2011). These include SWAT teams, crowd control units, and riot squads. These units are used for different tasks—armed standoffs, and in anti-gang units, developed as part of policing during the War on Drugs, in addition to public order or riot control units. While such units are composed of regular police officers, who are selected or who volunteer for the unit, these participants in such units have undergone specialized training, tend to wear more protective equipment, and utilize additional specialized weapons. Surveying all police departments in the US serving cities of 50,000 or more, Kraska and Kappeler (1997) find an increase in the number of Police Paramilitary Units (PPUs), an escalation in their activity, a normalization of these units in mainstream policing, and a direct link between PPUs and the US military. PPUs are increasingly used in protest policing contexts and provide both less-lethal and regular weapons that ordinary officers don't use. The use of paramilitary units increased rapidly in the 1990s, with 538 percent increase between 1980 and 1995 (Kraska and Kappeler 1997: 7). In 1980, only 300 deployments of such forces took place; by 1995, there were 30,000 deployments (Kraska 2001: 142). By the 1990s, 90 percent of small- and medium-sized American police forces and 65 percent of small American jurisdictions had SWAT teams.

In general, police agencies developed specialized units for public order later than the SWAT teams developed for policing in the War on Drugs, or for armed standoffs. In the context of public order or crowd control, such units are only deployed for a small percentage of protest events overall. The 2008 Richmond, Virginia Crowd Management Team (CMT) manual explains that the team should be used

> … in situations in which large crowds have formed where a propensity for violence is present and may require the use of specialized personnel … Factors that will be considered include but are not limited to:
>
> - Estimated size of crowd
> - Propensity for violence
> - Group involved
> - Type of operation
> - Officer safety. (Richmond Police Department 2008: 3).

This team maintains equipment including riot shields, less-lethal chemical agents, cutting tools, helmets, body protectors for the chest, arms and legs, cameras/videos, batons, gas masks, mass arrest kits, and flex cuffs (ibid.: 5). Such "Darth Vader" units are widely employed to police summit protests and convention protests in Canada and the US. However, over the past few years, PPUs have been increasingly criticized by the public for the way their approach may escalate tensions with the public. Some security operations try to keep such units hidden in order to limit this dynamic, while other operations display the units in order to dissuade potential "troublemakers."

Repertoire of Repression

Militarized forms of repression are being used much more frequently against protesters who are designated uncooperative or threatening. Police and intelligence agents are much more likely to label protesters from poor or racially marginalized communities, ideologically oriented protesters, and youthful protesters in this way. Summit protests of international financial institutions and similar events—partly because they bring together such a variety of protesters in a high-stakes context, with massive security budgets, with protesters, some of whom refuse to negotiate with police—tend to be perceived as threatening. Political conventions in the US and Canada, European Union summits, NATO summits, and other major events or episodes of protest such as the Occupy protests or the Quebec student protests also trigger a strategic incapacitation strategy by police. However, militarized police action and mass arrest do not unfold at every summit. At the past twenty G7/G8 and G20 summits, seven saw no arrests at all, two others saw less than ten arrests, and only nine saw more than a hundred arrests take place. Similarly while some included street battles involving less-lethal weapons and specialized units, others involved only routinized protest and "soft hat" policing.

What determines whether an event becomes a major militarized clash between police and protesters? The most dramatic clashes at such summits since the Seattle WTO protests took place in Genoa (2001), Gleneagles (2005), Heilingendamm/Rostock (2007), and Toronto (2010), the policing of which was characterized by numerous arrests, barricades and the use of less-lethal weapons. However, these demonstrations were not the only large protests, nor were they the only ones to feature property destruction. They didn't have the largest security budgets, nor the largest police details. Looking at the policing of the Republican and Democratic National Conventions, we see significant variation (see Table 2.1).

Table 2.1   US political conventions—police tactics and arrests

	DNC arrests	DNC police tactics	RNC arrests	RNC police tactics
1996	14 (Chicago, IL)	Raids, pepper spray, protest pen	27 (San Diego, CA)	Protest pen
2000	194 (Los Angeles, CA)	Rubber bullets, protest pen	400 (Philadelphia, PA)	Pre-emptive arrests, raids
2004	1 (Boston, MA)	Protest pen	1,800 (New York, NY)	Barricades, kettling
2008	100 (civil disobedience, Denver, CO)	Protest pen	800 (St. Paul/ Minneapolis, MN)	Conspiracy charges, pre-emptive arrests, raids, concussion grenades, teargas
2012	27 (Charlotte, NC)	Perimeter fence	1 (Tampa Bay, FL)	helicopters

So how do we understand the use of less-lethal weapons, barricades, and pre-emptive tactics against protesters? Later chapters will examine the ways struggles within the local political field and the field of policing more generally are influential on police decision making, but the explanation also depends on the context of waves of protest. Like the changes in police logic and practice themselves, these cycles of protest are in themselves partly a response to the neoliberal restructuring of political and economic systems, the increasingly aggressive approach of elites in this context, and the spread of new technologies of communication and coordination. These undulations help to trigger new waves or cycles of protest.

Waves of Protest

Policing strategies have been repeatedly transformed by waves or cycles of protest. Understanding this means recognizing the ongoing interactions amongst police and protesters, as well as amongst protesters and amongst police (Scholl 2013). Protesters, like police, struggle with questions of strategy and tactics, jockey for legitimacy and influence, and are constrained by their internalized logic, and the ongoing and shifting structure of the activist field. During periods of increasing mobilization, protest activities will become more frequent and larger. New tactics will be invented and adapted. Coalitions will form more easily, diffusing symbols, ideas, and tactics through their networks. New actors with new ideas will find it easier to become engaged, as pre-existing routines are broken down. As a wave of protest accelerates, it will gain more attention from the public, political, and repressive authorities (de Lint and Hall 2009, Tarrow 2011). Police attempts to control a movement, thereby increasing the costs of protesting, may halt the wave or do the opposite. Movement cycles may transform public policy, personal biographies, and social relationships, but they also influence police strategies and the organization of the police (Morgan 1987, in Tarrow 2011).

The undulations of waves of protest are tied to protester innovations and police response (McAdam 1983). When protesters perceive and articulate their concerns that existing strategies are ineffective, and suggest a new technique, a new protest wave may escalate, leading to increased and less predictable interactions between movements and police. The process of diffusion plays a key role in such changes for both protesters and police. Adoption of a new technique or technology is then driven by the availability and evaluation of alternatives. As della Porta and Tarrow argue, the availability of information about a new technology is affected by "the proactive intervention by a sender actor aimed at deliberate diffusion of an innovation." An innovation is then assessed through an analysis of past events and their definition as successes or failures, and a theorization of the tactic which leads to its adaptation for new sites and situations (della Porta and Tarrow 2012). Once a new status quo is established, it will tend to become routinized until a new wave of protest/repression and its attendant crises emerge.

Waves of Protest and Reorganizing Repression
Historical perspective provides a deeper understanding of the influence of interactions between waves of protest and police. After a period of relative quiescence between the 1930s and the 1960s, the wave of student, black power, anti-war, gay and lesbian protests unfolded in the late 1960s in the United States, which amongst other things, called existing protest policing strategies into question (McPhail, Schweingruber, and McCarthy 1998: 51). The level and range of street protest seemed to threaten the social system. Police attempted to contain and limit these protests using the escalated force strategy. This meant that they used whatever means they had available, for example, officers clubbing protesters with batons, along with tear gas. Widespread coverage of events like the policing of the 1968 Democratic National Convention in Chicago, the police turning fire hoses on civil rights protesters in the southern states, and tear gassing demonstrators during protests against police brutality and racism led to large numbers of arrests and increased anger, but it did not effectively establish order. As McCarthy and McPhail (1998) note, controversy about this approach to public order led to a number of federal commissions in the United States. All found that police actions against crowds often exacerbated and, in some cases, provoked the civil disorder. All advised a number of changes to the policing of demonstrations (Williams 2011). During the same time period, condemnation of the use of escalated force by police in the US had a significant influence on police response to protest in Canada (de Lint and Hall 2009). In discussions that took place at sites such as the Canada Association of Chiefs of Police (CACP) and the International Association of Chiefs of Police, police officers reassessed and reorganized their protest policing strategy, prioritizing a negotiated

management approach. At the same time, the grassroots movements of the 1960s and '70s were in decline. Many radicals became burned out, while others were in prison or dead. Some social movements stayed in the streets, while other organizations that had historically provided movement infrastructure formalized, institutionalized, and professionalized, seeking non-profit status, funding, and paid staff (Scholl 2013). Still others were ready to find the means to stay in the streets in ways that would limit the financial and legal costs to their organization and movement. Simultaneous discussions among police leadership in both Canada and the US also highlighted the desire to reduce political and economic costs of protest policing, while still maintaining order (de Lint and Hall 2009, McCarthy and McPhail 1998). Increasing value was placed on intelligence gathering regarding what protesters were doing, thinking, and targeting. Different tendencies emerged, but in the US, Canada, and Europe, negotiation and communication were prioritized as a way to limit the costs of visible repression. These strategies went by different names, including "negotiated management," "public order management systems," and "liaison policing" (de Lint and Hall 2009). However, for devalued populations deemed threatening or unpredictable, including immigrant, racialized, or indigenous populations, escalated force remained the dominant strategy.

McPhail and his colleagues (1998) list five key dimensions within what they call "Public Order Management Systems" (POMS): This model was intended to make protest less disruptive through establishing and maintaining clear lines of communication between police and protesters. Such lines of communication were to facilitate the channeling and control of protest activity. Some police hoped this strategy would maintain and regain their legitimacy with political and economic decision makers, by establishing a professionalized, less dramatic style of protest policing, aspects of which would include:

1. Policing is centrally concerned with protecting the rights of demonstrators to protest.
2. Community disruption is an inevitable by-product of protest, and the role of the police is mainly to limit the extent of the disturbance.
3. Negotiation between police and protesters is emphasized before and during a protest to limit conflict.
4. Arrests are rarely utilized by police, and when they are used, they are selective, orderly, and often planned in advance through negotiation,

taking place only after several warnings; only protesters that break the law are arrested.

5. Force is only used as a last resort to protect the safety of persons or property.

Willem de Lint and Alan Hall (2009) track a similar trajectory in their study of the development of liaison policing in Canada. Police increasingly framed labor protests as "civil conflicts" between private bodies. In this context, police framed their job as one of acting as neutral liaison between the parties, only engaging once the courts had passed an injunction enforcing police engagement. This new approach emphasized de-escalation and trust-building and, despite some opposition among police forces, spread widely in Canada. Such an approach was welcomed by labor leaders interested in directing the movement away from unpredictable street protest and picket lines, and towards the bargaining table. By the early 1990s, many police forces were attempting to use aspects of this approach, not only for strikes, but for a wide range of public order situations in the US, Canada, Europe, and other democratic states. While this model limited the costs of protesting to social movement organizations, and facilitated large-scale actions, it also made social movement protest less threatening and newsworthy, limiting the leverage of the less powerful (McCarthy and McPhail 1998).

The Wave of the Global Justice Movement

By 1998, the limitations of the routinization of the relationships between protesters and police were being assessed by activists, and a new wave of protest was emerging globally. Stories of creative and effective direct action by the Zapatistas in Mexico taking over land, Reclaim the Streets blocking highway construction and occupying the streets with dance parties in the UK and elsewhere, anti-free trade and anti-neoliberal protests globally, anti-fascists in Europe, and anti-clearcut logging blockades spread across the West Coast of North America were all facilitated by digital networking. In the US and Canadian representatives of these movements, increasing numbers of protesters refused to negotiate with the police and cooperate with the police using POMS system of negotiated management. This refusal was due in part to increasing momentum within anarchist movements, emboldened by the recent collapse of state socialism in the Soviet Union. In North America, some anarchist protesters cited Ward Churchill's *Pacifism as Pathology*, arguing that pre-arranging arrests with the police in an orderly fashion was a losing strategy, constrained the power of protest, limited media coverage, and de-emphasized the urgency of the crisis at hand (Churchill 1998). In Canada, protests against neoliberal restructuring, as well as police use of pepper spray at the 1997 APEC protests, underscored the narrow boundaries of acceptable protest, and called into question the legitimacy and utility of negotiation. At the Seattle protests in 1999, increasing numbers of protesters stepped outside established protocols of negotiation with the police and successfully disrupted both the WTO summit and the city at large. The "Battle in Seattle" was heralded as a success by many protesters, and refusal to fully cooperate with police became a known tactic employed by parts of the global justice movement. Using the protests in Seattle as justification, the US and Canadian governments promoted or established training programs in more militarized tactics and the strategic incapacitation approach. As Noakes and Gilham report, in the year following the WTO protests in Seattle, US police forces invested heavily in new riot gear and sent representatives to seminars sponsored by the International Association of Chiefs of Police and the US Department of Justice designed to provide public safety agencies with (the) skills, knowledge, strategies, and tactics necessary "to control a new breed of protester" (Beasley, Graham, and Holmberg 2000, Noakes and Gillham 2007). The Ontario Provincial Police reviewed its operational planning because of new and aggressive tactics being used by protesters to confront police and disrupt summits (OPP 2006). A report written by the Canadian Security and Intelligence Service (2000) cited "the anti-globalization threat" as a reason to re-organize protest policing. The shift towards a more militarized strategy around protest consolidated after September 11, 2001, manifesting as more generalized "major incident training [or] … major event training." There is more about this change in Chapter 6.

Despite the inclusion of protest events into a broader policing category, 13 years later the Seattle protests are still cited as the transformative moment that justified a shift in protest policing strategy. In 2011, ex-NYPD chief Howard Safir wrote:

> Lessons learned in Seattle from the chaotic and damaging street riots at the 1999 WTO Ministers meeting have greatly improved both the pre-event intelligence, incident prevention strategies and response tactics that law enforcement in the United States can utilize to minimize casualties, injuries, damage and disorder. These include tools

and methods to anticipate the volume, nature and dynamics of protests; policy, communications and other strategies to reduce the likelihood of violent incident and patrol, designating safe areas for protest, and barrier design methods to control crowds while protecting freedoms. (Safir 2011)

From 1999 to 2004, as a wave of global justice protest facilitated the diffusion of disruptive tactics and the refusal to cooperate with authorities, police used the increased confidence of the movement to justify borrowing and adapting militarized tactics and intelligence gathering from other policing, security, and military settings, to re-establish order and reduce the disruptiveness of the protesters.

Convention and Summit Protests
Strategic incapacitation remains the dominant model for policing protest at international summits and political conventions in Canada and the US. While justified initially as a supplement to negotiated management, to be employed when protesters refused to communicate or cooperate with police, the militarized aspects of the model have appeared with increasing frequency. Restructured, globalized, and increasingly privatized networks of policing have heralded the use of such tactics as successful responses to protesters threatening to engage, or engaging, in property destruction, or to protesters who simply refuse to cooperate with authorities and are thus perceived as threatening.

This is most obvious when we look at the policing of political conventions, mass protests, and summits held by international financial institutions. Such events are perceived as particularly complex security challenges, involving relatively long lead times, high visibility, protected persons, and significant professional stakes for hosts, police chiefs, political leadership, and social movements. Protesters at summits are perceived as particularly unpredictable and threatening, despite the fact that in no summit or convention protest in Canada nor the US have protesters attempted to physically harm either delegates or passersby. Mass protests of movements that mobilize quickly, and without clear, institutionalized leadership trigger similar reactions, being perceived as similarly unpredictable. Examples of these include the immigrant rights protests in the US in 2007, the Occupy protests of 2011, or the Quebec student protests of 2012.

Since 1998, political conventions in the US have been identified as "National Special Security Events" by the federal government. This designation generally means that security becomes the responsibility of an FBI Joint Terrorism Task Force (JTTF), a partnership between the Federal Bureau of Investigation, components of the Department of Homeland Security, and state and local law enforcement. The use of these task forces blur the line between "domestic terrorism" and protest activity (Good 2008). In Canada, operations for National Security Events are integrated, most recently through Public Safety Canada.

Best Practices for Worst-case Scenarios
When the site of a political convention or summit is announced, police and local decision makers experience intense uncertainty about the innumerable pieces that must come together for such an event. As a result, one of the first things the police do is consult with experts in major events planning. In the late 1990s, this expertise was offered informally, and police planners experimented and adapted their existing approaches and routines, drawing on local expertise. Gradually, however, expertise has consolidated, contributing to an increasingly modular response to large-scale events that attract protesters in Canada and the US. This modularity depends on the accumulation and use of a set of processes and documents that include:

1. Federal intelligence threat assessments and reports (US Department of Justice, Federal Bureau of Intelligence, Canadian Security and Intelligence Service, Royal Canadian Mounted Police);
2. Best-practices documents from professional policing and security organizations, including the International Association of Chiefs of Police, the Canadian Association of Chiefs of Police, the Police Executive Research Foundation, Police Chief Magazine, etc.;
3. "After-Action Reports" about similar or related events issues;
4. Reports from collaborators, including Joint Intelligence Groups and Integrated Security Units, and
5. Reports issued by private sector analysts, trainers, and consultants, many of whom are ex-police or military.

Each of these sources has advice on what threats the event may include, and how to respond to those threats. As security officials at the 2008 Denver DNC explained, police have been watching tapes of their opponents in action, protests from around the world, analyzing tactics and developing responses.

> One of the big concerns, is [protesters] setting fire to junked cars, or using cars to block traffic that would prevent delegates from getting where they need to go … Locking to hotel doors … This is the kind of tactic the police are preparing for downtown—parking or abandoning cars near airport … If a tactic was used in the past, security forces in Denver will be prepared to see them used again … They have ordered 1000 protective suits to 1000 person field force to protect against chemical or biological weapons. (Maas 2008)

One highly placed security expert said, "For anything protesters might try, we'll have a counter attack. We are prepared for anything" (CBS News, August 13, 2008).

The accepted "best practice" surrounding preparations for such events consistently argues for increased spending, preparation, intelligence gathering, and access to the latest technologies. The way this planning process has dovetailed with a wider reliance on threat assessment frameworks and militarized, technical solutions to policing problems helps to explain current model of protest policing. I discuss this further in Chapter 6.

Since the 1999 Seattle protests, the coherence of this repertoire of police tactics has meant that it is not unusual to see large numbers of arrests, less-lethal weapons, surveillance, and barricades at relatively small summit or convention protests where no property destruction takes place. Despite successful and expensive lawsuits, and ongoing public criticism, the strategic incapacitation model continues to be used—with the goal of eliminating disruptive protest. The fundamental assumptions of the model remain unquestioned:

- Uncooperative Protesters = criminals = threat
- More money = more security
- Intelligence-led policing = better policing
- Pre-emptive arrests are an effective and appropriate way to limit protest.

There is some variation between national contexts on the spread of this model. Mass arrests, and subsequent class action lawsuits, are much more routine in the US. The use of pepper spray, tear gas, and Tasers is more common in Canada. It seems that once police have a tool, they are more likely to use it. Once they use it, they are more likely to use it again. If this is true, the policing tactics employed at high-octane summit or convention protests may be influencing policing of other types of protests. It may be that militarized police tactics trickle down from summit to street, and that the opposite is also true: militarized tactics of SWAT teams and anti-gang policing trickle up from street policing to the policing of protest (Wiliams 2011).

Policing Occupy Movements
The Occupy Wall Street protests of 2011 and 2012 are significantly different than summit protests. Largely local and stationary, the "Occupy" protests spread from Wall Street, New York City, across the US, Canada, and, to a lesser extent, Europe, Asia, Australia, and beyond. Particularly during the first few months, Occupy activists across North America occupied public and private spaces for extended periods. These occupations often attracted large numbers of people. The protest tactics and broad participation seen at the original New York City Occupy Wall Street protests were explicitly non-violent, but often also non-cooperative: the refusal to apply for permission for occupations and non-permitted marches. The initial NYPD response was muted, but became dramatic on September 24, 2011, when mass arrests and police use of pepper spray and kettling took place. However, ensuing public outrage was widespread when footage of NYPD Inspector Anthony Bologna pepper spraying three young white women trapped within a barricade went viral, leading Bologna to be disciplined, and attention and sympathy with the Occupy movement to rapidly increase. It was within this context, that the strategy of "Occupy" spread rapidly. Response by both municipal authorities and police to the growth of the Occupy movement was mixed. In some locations, particularly where there were left-leaning local authorities, Occupiers were left relatively alone for the first month. In other cities, police evicted the protesters quickly. In his lovely comparative study of the repressive strategy of the police against the Occupy movement, Alex Vitale (2012) finds no evidence of widespread militarization or coordination amongst authorities. Instead, he reminds us that most police departments still attempt to use a negotiated management style of policing. But he also notes that there was variation in police strategies in different cities. While Seattle, Dallas, Washington, DC, and San Francisco police were relatively

restrained, New York police micro-managed Occupy Wall Street. When I was there during March and April 2012, after Zuccotti Park had been cleared, Occupy protesters were trying to maintain an ongoing presence at an alternate location, Union Square, with frequent meetings, feedings, information tables, and "think tank" sessions. Every night at midnight, those who remained would be forced to remain standing and moving, or otherwise be arrested. Ongoing Occupy Wall Street protester presence on Wall Street was kept under surveillance, restricted behind barricades, and steadily harassed. Those who tried to hold political signs in the area were strictly channeled and controlled, and every day, small numbers of protesters were arrested. In contrast, Los Angeles and Oakland police used negotiated management approach to begin with, and then turned to a more militarized approach, after the evictions of OWS encampments in each city. In Oakland, police used concussion grenades, tear gas, pepper spray, and batons to subdue protesters and end their occupation. The policing of the Canadian encampments was relatively undramatic, with few arrests, outside of the final evictions.

In both countries many occupations remained in place until late November 2011. Despite only a few broken windows, 7,765 arrests were made at 430 Occupy events as of September 2012 (Occupy Wall Street 2012).[4] The use of concussion grenades and ongoing harassment were an attempt to control and constrain the movement.

Occupy movements in all their variations were policed differently than the global justice movement, the anti-war protests of 2002–04, the Quebec student protests in 2012–13, or immigrant rights protests across the US and Canada in 2007. Despite the visible longer-term shifts in policing, police in different jurisdictions employed the strategic incapacitation repertoire differently, due to local history, patterns of interaction among police and protesters and among policing networks, and other organizational and institutional dynamics discussed in Chapter 3.

Conclusion

Since the mid-1990s, police in the US and Canada have changed the way they police protest. Before that time, police didn't use pepper spray, Tasers, LRADs, and kettling against protesters. Mass arrests were made *after* protesters engaged in civil disobedience or rioting, not before. But today, the use of pre-emptive arrests, spatial control tactics including barricades, pens, and walls, less-lethal weapons, surveillance, conspiracy charges, and police media campaigns are unsurprising.

The use of this repressive repertoire cannot simply be seen as the result of rational choices by police decision makers in response to protester innovations. Instead, a connection exists between waves of protest and changes in the protest policing repertoire, whereby the interactions between protesters and police are structured. When waves of protest successfully disrupt the status quo, they surprise authorities, challenging their legitimacy, and convince them that existing strategies aren't effective, leading to a period of reflection, experimentation, assessment, promotion, and adoption on the part of the police and state. When global justice protesters demonstrating at events in 1997 and 1999 created a crisis in policing, the police in the US and Canada tried to respond. They turned to their increasingly responsive, integrated, and powerful professional networks for advice. In these spaces, police managers, professional organizations, and the private sector were able to certify and promote particular tactics and techniques and construct a more militarized status quo. The following chapters will seek to understand how the processes that underlie diffusion operate, so the increasing spread of and use of less-lethal weapons, barricading strategies, and pre-emptive control by some, but not all, police forces can be explained. I'll turn now to the role of international trends in policing, and the effect of national and local contexts on the incorporation of these militarized tactics.

3

To Serve and Protect Who? Policing Trends and Best Practices

Cops are cops are cops, right? We expect certain behaviors from police officers and are perfectly comfortable with stereotyping this "armed gang," given that their power puts them outside ordinary social life. These stereotypes vary, but especially if we are members of racial minorities, are young, or engage in street protest, we are likely to distrust the police. As the last chapter showed, police agencies are barricading, pre-emptively arresting and using less-lethal weapons against protesters more than ever before. But their approach to protest policing is only part of the changes that police and their organizations have undergone. Police organizations have been transformed by some of the same trends that have affected other professions: new managerialism with its emphasis on results, an emphasis on private/public partnerships within community policing, increasing use of information technology, and the attendant gathering of information in order to direct decision making.

However, these trends have played out differently in different countries and different cities. Different forces have incorporated organizational trends, and protest policing practices, differently, and at different rates. This has affected the protest policing strategy of different forces. The adoption of a model of decentralized management, and the importance of quantifiable success in the NYPD means that as a protester, one is more likely to get arrested in New York than in Toronto. The highly visible (rhetorical?) commitment to community policing and relationship building with the community by the DC police department helps to explain why you would be more likely to be pepper sprayed in Montreal than in Washington DC. If we are to understand the way that strategic incapacitation approach has spread widely but with local differences, we need to understand the context of, and sources of this variation.

The backstory to these struggles is neoliberalism. In some ways, police agencies face the same pressures as other public institutions. With a shrinking public sector, police agencies are under pressure to justify their funding and to display their effectiveness. As Naomi Klein (2007) has pointed out, neoliberal politicians seeking power are prone to emphasize the ineptitude of existing leadership to handle social and economic crises. The rhetoric they use condemns inefficiencies as both economic and moral failings. In response, they propose to cut social services that are "soft" and that foster the "dependency" of the poor and marginalized, with a celebration of "tough on crime" policies—that rely on law enforcement bodies to take on an increasing range of tasks. Police agencies are seen as an increasingly necessary and central part of maintaining the social order. This, in combination with powerful police unions and an increasing reliance on high-tech solutions has shaped the restructuring of police agencies and meant that despite cuts to social spending, the costs of policing continue to rise. A 2012 *Globe and Mail* editorial reported that the cost of policing in Canada had risen for 14 consecutive years, even after adjusting for inflation. In 1995, the cost of policing was $6.6 billion (constant); by 2010, it had increased to $10.8 billion. Translated into per capita spending; in 1995, policing cost each Canadian $226, increasing to $318 in 2010. Similar to countries including the UK, Australia and Japan, the number of officers per person has risen—in 1995 there were 187.7 officers for every 100,000 people—by 2010 there were 203.2 (Stats Can. 2011). In the US, a similar increase has occurred during the past 25 years. More than half of US police agencies grew in size between 1996 and 1999, with the others maintaining their current size (Koper 2004: 5). There were also rising personnel costs and greater demand for policing services. According to the Department of Justice, local police departments cost 55.4 billion dollars in 2007 (fiscal year), a 14 percent increase since 2003, even after adjusting for inflation (Gascon and Foglesong 2010). Since the economic crisis of 2008 began, however, many US police forces have cut salaries and slowed their growth, while their Canadian equivalents did not (*Globe and Mail* 2012).

Analysis confirms that the increasing costs of policing in that province were also due to the neoliberal strategy of downloading costs onto municipalities:

> Municipal police services are undertaking federal and provincial law enforcement and correctional services tasks such as border security, counterterrorism, embassy/consulate protection, peacekeeping on First Nations lands, public order maintenance in response to federal or provincial decisions (e.g., G20), prisoner transportation and court security. (Ontario Association of Police Services Boards 2012)

In this, and other jurisdictions, police organizations are also increasingly the main institution dealing with tasks like school safety, victim assistance, mental health interventions, crime prevention education, etc., due to absence of other resources for these tasks or regulation (ibid.). This is in a context of austerity economics, privatization and deregulation which correspond with spikes in inequality, unrest and crime—with the police mandated to solve the problem as cheaply and quickly as possible.

In many ways, police organizations appear to have been successful. Violent crime rates are down across the Global North. However, the legitimacy of, and trust in, the police is declining. This is particularly so for people of color. A 2013 Gallup poll (US) found that only 42 percent of non-whites and 60 percent of whites had a great deal or quite a lot of confidence in the police. This has declined significantly from 2006, where 48 percent of non-whites and 68 percent of whites had such faith. The response to the question of "do you have a great deal or quite a bit of confidence that police can protect you from violent crime?" was perhaps even more surprising, given the decline in violent crime. In 2005, only 61 percent of US respondents and 67 percent of Canadian respondents concurred.

Best Practices in Professional Policing

Placed in the position of managing all manner of social crises using the blunt weapons of policing, police leadership figures must maintain their legitimacy, influence, and funding. At the same time, there is a great deal of confusion about how to proceed. In response to such challenges, police leadership increasingly turn to professional policing networks, the private sector, and civilian authorities and the "best practices," a term adopted from business management frameworks to designate industry standards that are widely accepted. These networks frame policing as a profession that can be effective, cost efficient, service-oriented, and scientific. The hegemonic actors in these networks certify particular technologies, tactics, and strategies as legitimate and valuable. Since the 1990s, these experts have certified many of the militarized tactics discussed in the last chapter, but also organizational trends including new managerialism and community policing with its attendant emphasis on public-private partnerships, as well as an increasing use of communication and information technologies for directing decision making. Each of these trends corresponds with a decentralization of the command structure, while maintaining the possibility of strong central management.

New Managerialism

The International Association for Chiefs of Police (IACP) first notes in a 1976 report that a military model is unsuited to police-citizen relations (IACP 1976: 270). They note that the military has different sources of motivation and control, and different patterns of work and working environments. Instead, they note that the police have more in common with business. As cited in De Lint (1998), the IACP report states, "[B]oth police and business exist to deliver a service or a product to the same market—the public." The framing of policing as a business, and police chiefs as managers, accelerated during the 1990s. As Ross McLeod, CEO of the private Canadian security company Intelligard put it:

> I have fairly good relations with senior police officers. Their role is in some ways comparable with mine as a private sector CEO. They have reporting relationships to police boards and authorities; they are assigned program goals; they have to devise business plans that are consistent with the goals laid out for them by their governing boards or authorities; they have to operate within a budget; and, they face the hostility of unions who try to restrict their area of managerial discretion. (McLeod 2002: 75–6)

Further, Peter K. Manning (1995) shows how Total Quality Management (TQM), a broad trend in American management, within the new managerialist approach, spread from budget and planning officers and professional associations to police. TQM framed policing as a business with a "product" or "service" offered by police forces to their "customers." It was in this context that police chiefs were initially called "Chief Executive Officers" (Manning 2008: 31). An Australian review of NYPD reforms notes that it was in the context of the TQM trend that NYPD

Commissioner Bratton reformed the organization, with the belief that modern business theory and practices could lift a low-performance organization to higher levels of accomplishment. Bratton described the process as one of moving from "a micro-managed organisation with very little strategic direction to a decentralised management style with strong strategic guidance at the top." Bratton's approach entailed the following:

- Seven crime control strategies and a strategy for dealing with police corruption were established and publicly released; Precinct commanders were granted far greater latitude to initiate operations and run their own precincts; Weekly crime statistics became the indicator of performance with computer pin mapping and other analytic techniques used to identify crime and corruption patterns; Re-engineering teams were established to reform the organizational systems of the NYPD;
- A cultural diagnostic was conducted to determine the obstacles to change in the culture of the NYPD; COMPSTAT (computer statistics), a key accountability measure, was established, whereby meetings are held twice a week to question precinct and squad commanders about their performance in crime prevention. These are meetings of more than a hundred of the most senior officials of the NYPD, and are used to positively reinforce good performance and to expose and correct poor performance. (Corruption Prevention and Education Unit 1997).

Bratton's transformation of one of the world's most high-profile police forces created a new model of policing, linking management techniques to community policing, crime mapping, and an emphasis on technological analysis, customer service measures, and specialized units to determine priorities and pre-empt social disorder.

Community Policing
The US Department of Justice describes community policing as "a philosophy that promotes organizational strategies, which support the systematic use of partnerships and problem-solving techniques, to proactively address the immediate conditions that give rise to public safety issues such as crime, social disorder, and fear of crime" (US DOJ 2013). Emphasizing partnerships between police and the community, business, government, and non-profit organizations, community policing evolved as

a response to a crisis in police legitimacy and to neoliberal restructuring in both the US and Canada. In the US, President Clinton's law-and-order initiative created the federal Department of Justice's community policing program, which spent billions of dollars to establish regional training centers, fund the training of 600,000 police officers, and to organize anti-gang, anti-drug, school, and neighborhood-based programs. This initiative promised to increase the number of police officers "on the street" by 100,000, while also making police agencies "lean and efficient" (Manning 2008: 35). This approach was shaped by an influential 1994 monograph produced by the Community Policing Consortium, made up of the IACP, the National Sheriffs' Association, the Police Executive Research Forum (PERF), and the Police Foundation (Bureau of Justice Assistance 1994). This body certified the approach as valuable and effective, facilitating its spread throughout US police networks.

Community policing initiatives also became more central in Canada. As Canada's Department of Justice explains, by the 1990s, virtually every police force in Canada had incorporated the term "community policing" into their written mandates (Horne 1992, in US DOJ 2013). There was a great deal of variation in how the term was interpreted and, likewise, implemented. Rhetorically at least, across the country, community policing signaled a shift away from "traditional policing," oriented by crime control, towards an approach that "incorporates a mixture of order maintenance and community service" (Wood 1996, in US DOJ 2013). Decentralized authority and an emphasis on "problem solving" reliant upon information gathering, awareness of context, the actions of relevant actors (victims, offenders), and the responses and perceptions of citizens and private/public institutions, are generally understood to be characteristics of community policing in Canada (Bala et al. 1994).

Ken Menzies (2004) argues that there are two different versions of the (at least rhetorical) turn to community policing in both the US and Canada. First, there is the neoconservative version, which emphasizes zero tolerance for small offenses, implemented by use of force (that is, "broken windows" policing); secondly, there is the neoliberal version, which highlights the use of partnerships with the community, to pre-empt disorder, minimize risk, and implicate the police in a wider set of social relationships. We see different versions of community policing in the four police forces examined in this chapter. But while the definition of community (or neighborhood) policing can vary widely, in all cases it corresponds with an increasing involvement of the police in processes of social regulation. All four cities discussed here; Toronto, Montreal, New York, and Washington, DC, have also adopted some version of community policing, reintroducing the focus on local patrols and commanders who were responsible for the crime rates in those areas.

Information Technology

The evolution and decentralization of community policing corresponded with an increased reliance on information technology. The clearest example of this is the much-studied introduction of Compstat (comparative statistics) in New York City in 1994 (Manning 2008). This approach used computer mapping of thefts, assaults, drug-related activities, property destruction, murders, and other crimes to look for patterns, with the ostensible intention of strategic use of resources. It dovetailed with the approaches of New Managerialism, with its emphasis on efficiency and the display of measurable results. A central element of Compstat was large, sometimes public, meetings, at which local commanders would have to justify their response to crime in their area. Crime mapping and analysis spread widely through professional associations and informal police networks. As NYPD Deputy Commissioner Mike Farrell explains, "CompStat is about performance measurement and performance management, accountability, and creating an opportunity to focus everybody's attention, provide that sense of urgency, and share best practices" (PERF 2011b). This information technology facilitated a decentralization of operational authority to unit commanders, while keeping pressure on these actors to be accountable to the central leadership. In some ways, such demands also put new pressure on street cops to conform to agency-wide directives. Compstat diffused widely. By 2006, 60 percent of police departments with 100 or more sworn officers had implemented Compstat or a similar program (Weisburd and Lum 2005; Willis et al., 2010). While its diffusion has not been as widespread in Canada, there is increased value given to the use of statistics and computerized mapping.

Intelligence-led Policing

This was also the case with "intelligence-led policing," a central policing trend during the last decade. Ratcliffe defines intelligence-led policing as:

> … a business model and managerial philosophy where data analysis and crime intelligence are pivotal to an objective, decision-making framework that facilitates crime and problem reduction, disruption and

prevention through strategic management and effective enforcement strategies that target prolific and serious offenders. (Ratcliffe 2008: 89)

This approach shifts the task of policing as one of "reacting" to crime and disorder to one that "pre-empts" it, through an emphasis on systematic intelligence gathering and analysis, and the strategic use of resources to channel and disrupt potential disorder. The formal adoption of intelligence-led policing has organizational implications, making the intelligence function of policing, and its detectives or investigators far more central to decision making and operations. I'll discuss this in much more detail in Chapter 7.

These trends of new managerialism, community policing, information and communication technologies, and intelligence-led policing made police organizations more attentive to media portrayal, community relations, and widely shared "best practices"—influencing the approach to protest policing. However, a shared reception and incorporation of these policing trends didn't eliminate local variation. I'll turn now to the way national and local histories mediate the broader transformation of protest policing.

Canadian vs. US Policing

Some have summed up the difference between Canada and the US in their respective mottos—Canada's "Peace, Order and Good Government" vs. the US's "Life, Liberty and the Pursuit of Happiness." The differences are trivialized in such a comparison, but the phrases do reflect aspects of the dominant narratives of the two states. As Bayley (1992) explains, historical structures of policing reflect histories of political power, changing little after they emerge. If this is the case, the US is a nation-state whose formation story speaks about brave independent rebels struggling against unjust authority, and settling the West. In the nineteenth-century US, especially in Eastern settlements, the police were a tool of local political authorities. In the urban centers of the US's East Coast, police organizations more often resemble their British public antecedents, but police were less tied to the national government and were more dependent on local political authorities for legitimacy, authority, and funding (Mawby 2008: 19, 31). Unlike the English police, US police were often required to be residents of their local communities (Smith 1940; Fogelson 1977, in Mawby 2008: 31). They were almost immediately issued firearms, but only later donned uniforms, after resisting them for their association with the British military (Miller 1977). Often the police commissioner or Board of Commissioners were appointed by the mayor, creating a context where corruption became endemic. There were federal marshals, and later the Federal Bureau of Investigation—but the purview of these bodies included only criminal matters when federal laws were broken such as in mail robberies (Beahen 2008).

In contrast, the history of Canadian policing is rooted in a national story of competition between colonial powers, and gradually increasing autonomy. Because of the ongoing occupation of indigenous lands under the auspices of the British Crown, and the more recent history of colonization, Canadian policing has emerged as much more of a mélange of British metropolitan policing, French continental policing and French and British colonial policing. The influence of French models remains visible in Quebec through its ongoing use of the Napoleonic code within its legal system, the militarized approach and governance of the Provincial Police the *Sûreté du Quebec*, and British colonial policing remains significant through the largest police force in the country, the federally organized and regulated Royal Canadian Mounted Police (RCMP). This force emerged out of the North West Mounted Police who were authorized by Parliament in 1873 to pacify the North West of the country, including what later became the provinces of Alberta and Saskatchewan, and defend the country against settlement from the United States (Beahen 2008). This was a paramilitary force, armed for combat and intended to dominate the territory and its indigenous population. It remains uniquely accountable to the federal government, although the level of autonomy of the RCMP remains contested and controversial. Despite the case of the RCMP, policing is supervised provincially, and regulated through Provincial Police Acts. However, other than Ontario and Quebec, most provinces and territories contract their policing services to the RCMP.

If we were to caricature policing in the two countries in a crude way, we might say that US policing is more locally oriented, heavily armed, and decentralized; while Canadian policing is more professionalized, and centrally (both federally or provincially) controlled. Exacerbating these differences are some basic differences in the profile of policing in the two countries. In Canada, there are approximately 250 police agencies, whereas in the United States, there are more than 40,000, most of which have a complement of less than ten officers. The US population overall is more heavily policed. There are also important differences in the structure and processes of the legal systems of the two countries, meaning that formal complaints of the police take different forms. In the US, class action lawsuits against the police are more common, while in Canada, public inquiries in Canada are a typical response to controversy. In addition, different labor laws mean that police unions are more powerful influences on police practice in Canada than they are in the US. Influential police unions correspond to higher pay and benefits. The more active unions in Canada ensure that a first-class officer in a big city earns $80,000–$90,000 a year on average—before overtime and benefits (*Globe and Mail* 2012). In contrast, in May 2011, US police officers earned $56,260 (US Bureau of Labor Statistics 2012). Police in Canada also tend to have more education and training than their US equivalents—facilitating the emphasis on science and formality in professionalized police.

There are also national differences in the historical conception of appropriate police-governance relations. The articulated goal by professional policing experts of such relations is to avoid having either a police who are a tool of political leaders, or a police who are unaccountable to anyone but themselves. Instead, the ideal type is one where police are both apolitical and autonomous (Sossin 2004). While police in both countries have gained autonomy over the past twenty years, Canadian police have traditionally been more detached from elected local authorities than in the US, where chiefs of police are often appointed by the local mayor. Instead, in Canada, police forces are regulated by provincial and national government bodies whose interests, while defending the political and economic status quo, will not be as partisan.

The differences between Canada and the US have influenced the histories of policing in the two countries, and their current practices. The organizational trends of new managerialism, and community policing with their celebration of private-public partnerships and quantifiable results emerged in the neoliberal US context, and are most influential in that regime, while the British roots of intelligence-led policing has had a longer-term and more widespread effect on Canadian police strategy and practice. These differences in organizational trajectories have been tied to differences in protest policing. But variation is also significant within nation-states, which I turn to below.

Local Variations of Protest Policing

Cities and their histories vary by population, by their economic context, their political governance, their location, history, geography, and their culture. No one expects that the policing in New York City will look like the policing in Moose Jaw, Saskatchewan. Amongst even similar cities, police forces vary in their interactions with the local population. There are clear differences in the style of protest policing in Montreal, New York, Toronto and Washington, DC. There were 2,195 protests reported in the major papers in the four cities from 1995 until the end of 2005. These include both conventions and summit protests, and day-to-day pickets, marches, rallies and sit-ins.[1] Perhaps surprisingly, this meant that similar numbers of protest events were reported in each of these large cities, averaging 50 events per year. The year with the largest number of protests was 1995 and the year with the smallest number was, unsurprisingly, 2001—the year of the attacks on the World Trade Center. Each city has different periods of intense protest activity and periods of relative calm, with the most dramatic vacillations seen in Toronto, where yearly counts of events range from 25—112 (a range of 87). The least variation appears in DC whose quietest year (2001) saw 31, and its most active year with 64 protest events (a range of 33), which likely results from the city's consistent destination for protesters from across the country.

Table 3.1   Percentage of protests that included arrests, 1995–2005

	DC	NYC	Toronto	Montreal	Total average
1995	20	9	4	4	9.25
1996	12	22	13	3	12.5
1997	22	10	5	0	9.25
1998	15	14	11	5	11.25
1999	19	40	16	13	22
2000	20	54	13	11	24.5
2001	16	17	32	5	17.5
2002	31	18	10	12	17.75
2003	23	20	15	9	16.75
2004	18	26	24	9	19.25
2005	13	14	10	18	13.75
Average	20.90%	26.40%	15%	9%	

At these events, police arrested protesters 15,236 times. A dispropor-tionate number of arrests in cities occurred in years where there were summit protests (DC 2000, Montreal 2002), or political conventions (New York 2004), but they are not the only sites of conflict. Although we must bracket variation in media coverage styles in each publication and city, it appears that there is significant variation in the frequency that police arrest at demonstrations. Whereas only 9 percent of protests in Montreal resulted in arrest, over 26 percent of those in New York City did so during this period.

There is also variation amongst the four cities in other aspects of protest policing. Police in Montreal use pepper spray far more frequently against protesters than in any of the other cities. If we do a comprehensive search of all media sources for incidents when police used pepper spray against protesters from 1995 to the end of 2012, we find that Montreal police pepper sprayed protesters 29 times, including 17 during the student protests of 2011–12. In contrast, Toronto's and Washington's police only used pepper spray 8 times against protesters over the 17 years. New York City police doubled this rate at 16 times. Particularly if we were to adjust these figures for the sizes of the city and their police forces, it is clear that Montreal police rely much more frequently on pepper spray than the other forces.

Barricading strategies are more difficult to track, given that they are often so routine—but the NYPD is well known for its tendency to surround protesters with wooden "workhorse" barricades, or more recently, interlocking metal barricades. According to the New York Civil Liberties Union's (NYCLU) report "Arresting Protest," the NYPD's policy of using pens at permitted demonstrations emerged out of two separate events in 1996: a celebration at City Hall to commemorate the winning of the World Series by the Yankees, and New Year's Eve at Times Square (Dunn et al. 2003). The pens were introduced more widely at that time in order to more easily control the crowd and to facilitate the extraction of those who wanted to, or needed to leave. Since that time, police have used barricades to separate large and small demonstrations from vehicular and pedestrian traffic, allowing only one or two small openings for people to enter and exit the demonstration. This approach emphasizes the importance of "minimizing community disruption and maximizing police control" (ibid.). Although other cities use barricades on occasion, no other major city did so during the numerous anti-war marches and rallies on the weekend of February 15, 2003 (ibid.). Since the protests against the Republican National Convention of 2004, orange snow fencing has also been used to surround and arrest protesters. As NYPD's Chief Smolka testified for the hearings around a civil suit launched by the NYCLU, it is generally true that "the standard practice [of the NYPD] in Manhattan South when it knows of a demonstration almost regardless of size is to use pens of one sort or another," and that "when pens are set up, it's expected that that is the area where participants in the demonstration will assemble" (*Stauber and the NYCLU* vs. *City of New York*. 03 Civ. 9162 (RWS) Smolka Dep., at 71). This approach is justified by the NYPD as a requirement for managing protest in the busy city of New York. In Washington, DC, police use barriers less frequently, and Toronto and Montreal police, almost never.

Tear gas and Tasers are rarely used in public order contexts, but of the four cities considered here, police in Washington, DC have been most likely to do so. There is clearly local variation in the use of different tactics within the strategic incapacitation strategy. Explaining why Montreal police use pepper spray and flash-bang grenades, while the NYPD relies on barricades and mass arrests complicates the story of a uniform shift in protest policing. Police handle protest differently in different cities, and different countries. Police in New York City and Washington share a particular history of policing, a legal system and cultural norms, as do the police in Toronto and Montreal.

Explaining Local Variation
Even within a nation-state with a shared history of policing, local conditions and interactions contribute to differences. We need to understand the workings of police at the local level and how police forces make their strategic decisions. Municipally, police officers incorporate legal and institutional conceptions of public space and use their discretion to shape restrictions actually imposed on public spaces (Bourdieu 1990). Further, police strategy is never developed outside of social relations. The decision to adopt a new technology or to push beyond existing practice is often subject to influences from outside the local environment. I'll discuss these influences further in Chapter 6. But police leadership is also influenced by relations amongst sections of law enforcement, and relations with political authorities, and broader publics. Certainly, the relative influence or significance of these different players is always in flux; in order to understand police decisions to incorporate or use particular tactics or strategies, we must consider how the leadership, structure (management and unionization), oversight, allegations of corruption, key protest incidents, and associated litigation influence the way legitimacy, resources (budget and police strength), and autonomy are defended, maintained, and increased. In the next chapter, I'll use these differences to explain

the variation between police agencies in the four cities—Montreal, New York City, Toronto and Washington, DC—and how this affects the way they incorporate strategic incapacitation.

4

Local Legitimacy and Struggles for Control

Given the state of the world, local police agencies regularly engage in public order policing. However, they are often ambivalent about it, given that it isn't central to their professional identity of crime control. Indeed, P.A.J. Waddington (1994: 379) finds that police are wary about protest policing, given the trouble that often ensues. They distinguish between "on the job" and "off the job" trouble. "On the job" trouble is that which comes during deployment in the streets—through confrontation with protesters. "Off the job" trouble is that which comes before or afterwards, with inquiries into brutality and errors in judgment, media coverage and accusations of brutality. The combination of both sorts of trouble can provide leverage for critics of the police who may challenge police legitimacy, political capital, and access to resources. The likelihood and impact of both sorts of trouble for the police are partly tied to the transformations of Canadian and US policing. In both countries, there is a trend towards increasingly militarized protest policing, with an increasing use of pre-emptive arrests, less-lethal weapons and barricading tactics. But there is also national and local variation, tied to the pattern of relationships and resources in the local political field. In some cities more than others, police will be more likely to risk accusations of brutality, and repress protesters in a dramatic fashion. This chapter explains this local variation by examining the way that fluctuations in local political relationships either increase police autonomy, or facilitate the power of critics of the police. This approach builds on the insights from studies of political opportunity that argues authorities may be more vulnerable to challengers when they are divided or in flux, and more autonomous when they have strong alliances with other powerholders (Tilly 1995). In this vein, I'll consider the way two sets of interactions influence police autonomy. The first source of variation is the interaction amongst the police themselves—struggles amongst leadership, rank-and -file officers and police unions. The second source of local variation is the interaction between police agencies and other power holders and local challengers, including local mayors, ethnic and racialized communities, city councils and oversight bodies. These two sets of interactions with police influence their ongoing struggles to defend their own legitimacy, resources, and influence. When a police officer shoots a young black man, or even more dramatically, a young white man, or when a police department is revealed as corrupt, it will face criticism, and questions about the effectiveness and legitimacy of its leadership and practices. How the agency responds to such moments depends partly on the broader role and legitimacy of the police, and partly on the local relational context. Sometimes police agencies can easily deflect criticism. At other times, when a political opportunity, or gaps between themselves and other power-holders emerges, they may be forced to acknowledge a need for change, or to reach out to potential allies inside or outside of the local regime. Protest policing can trigger such moments. If a police department arrests hundreds of people without apparent cause, or an officer is filmed beating or Tasering a protester, a crisis may emerge, facilitating or blocking the incorporation of new tactics or strategies. This chapter will look at the characteristics of four police agencies (Montreal, New York City, Toronto and Washington, DC), and their relational dynamics in order to consider the role of local political opportunities on the incorporation and use of militarized tactics in protest policing.

Montreal—Service De Police De La Ville De Montreal (SPVM)

The SPVM is the second largest police force in Canada, with 7,126 employees, over 4,200 of which are uniformed officers (from SPVM website 2009). Between 1995 and 2013, there were five chiefs of police. The current chief, or *director du service*, is Marc Parent, appointed in 2010, replacing Yvan Delorme (2005–10), who had, in turn, replaced Michel Sarrazin (1998–2005). The previous chiefs were Jacques Duchesneau (1994–98), and briefly, Claude Rochon (1998). The history of the force has been shaped by both local and provincial politics. In recent years, the force has been hounded by accusations of corruption, ineffectiveness, and brutality. Like other Quebec institutions, the agency engages with but sometimes ignores larger trends from Anglophone North America. Sylvestre notes that in the past, some high-ranking SPVM officers traveled to the United States to observe how the "broken windows" model and related legislation was being implemented and to learn from the experiences of their counterparts, they subsequently chose not to fully incorporate that model, instead slightly adapting to their existing practices (Sylvestre 2010: 807). Since 1997, it uses a neighborhood or community policing approach, with a network of *Plans de Quartier* or neighborhood hubs supported by four operational centers. The force has been frequently reorganized (2002, 2004, 2006, 2008) and this flux is tied to ongoing tension between a desire for decentralized responsiveness and the need for coordination (SPVM 2008). The SPVM explains this frequent reorganization as tied to the "city's constantly changing political (municipal organization, ministerial directions, etc.), legal (legislative changes, etc.), economic, social, demographic and criminal landscape" (ibid.).

As a result, the SPVM, like Montreal itself, has an unusual and changing governance structure. The force is overseen by a number of political bodies at the municipal level, including a body of elected officials, La commission de la sécurité publique (CSP), which is also responsible for approving each service's annual budget and strategic directions. The CSP has nine members, comprised of eight municipal politicians and a representative from the provincial government. The CSP itself answers to the city's agglomeration council *(counseil de l'agglomération)* and its executive committee *(comité executive)*, presided over by the mayor.[1] Notably, the relationships between the police, the mayor's office and City Hall more generally are not always harmonious. In February 2013, the police raided City Hall, as part of larger anti-corruption operations. The mayor was replaced, and then his replacement was arrested in June 2013 on charges including fraud, conspiracy, breach of trust, and corruption in municipal affairs (Panetta and Blatchford 2013). Although policing is a municipal responsibility in Quebec, the provincial government exercises considerable influence over the SPVM through the Ministry of Public Security (Ministère de la Sécurité Publique), and other ways. For example, as a matter of course, it is the ministerially supervised provincial police force, the *Sûreté du Québec*, that investigates fatalities involving SPVM officers. Unlike in Toronto, New York, and Washington, Montreal police have no formal civilian oversight body. The provincial ministry also has the authority to hold individual SPVM officers accountable for their actions, via its police ethics committee *(comité de déontologie policère)*.[2] In fact, the committee's scrutiny over SPVM activities has become closer since March 8, 2000, when an amendment to the Police Act *(Loi sur la police)* came into effect, requiring SPVM chiefs to inform the Minister of Public Security, without delay, of any allegation of criminal wrongdoing committed by an officer (See SPCUM 2001: 15). Finally, perhaps the most important example of ministry oversight is a tacit political tutelage between SPVM chiefs and sitting ministers, a relationship which past inquiries into corruption argue has been problematic. Another central player affecting policing in Montreal is the police union. Since the 1960s, with the notable exception of the RCMP, police unions have become an important influence on Canadian policing in urban contexts. The *Fraternité des policiers et policières de Montréal* is no exception. In the past, this "Police Brotherhood" has often successfully and publicly contested management decisions, including the then-chief's intended dissolution of the riot squad in 1981 (Forcese 2002: 70). The *Fraternité* is also visible around contract negotiations. In 2008, after two years of contract negotiations, the union organized its members to refuse to wear their standard-issue uniform below the waist, instead wearing shorts, camouflage, and other gear (Chung 2008). They also wore red baseball hats during union-led marches and rallies, the attire meant as a challenge to anyone perceived to be against the interests of the police. In 2013, *Fraternité* President Yves Francoeur called for the firing of City Manager Guy Hebert over a report that Hebert had tried to get Chief Marc Parent fired. At other times, the head of the *Fraternité* has himself worked to remove the SPVM police chief. For example, in 2008, Francoeur publicly criticized Police Chief Yvan Delorme for failing to support officers, after a number of police shootings of young men of color.

The SPVM budget has risen consistently over the past twenty years, with an average increase of 4 percent a year (SPVM 2013). In the years after the 9/11 attacks, there was additional money available, and various anti-terrorism initiatives were established. Since that time, the city council has made regular attempts to reduce the police budget. In 2010, more than half the Montreal police force marched with their union, in opposition to a $35 million budget cut (Curtis 2010). The police chief at the time threatened to sell police services to corporations in order to raise extra funds. Although the funds allocated to police were formally reduced, for six years, overtime costs kept the public spending on police high. Then in 2012, while funding for other public services was cut, the police budget was increased by $28 million, making public safety (police, civil security, and fire) 20.7 percent of the city budget (Montreal 2012: 21). The force continued to receive the second highest amount of funding in Canada, despite criticism that it operates with impunity, and is less effective at reducing crime and closing cases than other forces.[3] This funding and especially the overtime expenses are often explained as the cost of protest policing.

Montreal—Protest Policing

Montreal has a long history of militant street protest, sports riots, and raucous street festivals. The SPVM website explains that they regularly police 1,500 public events per year, 97 percent of which do not involve arrests. Nonetheless, there exists perhaps the highest level of distrust between left-wing social movements and the police among the four cities studied herein. Public order operations have been repeatedly reorganized. Before 1994, such operations were organized by the local commander, with little specialized training, nor information sharing. In 1994, retired judge Albert Malouf was commissioned to analyze police operations in the wake of the July 1991 shooting of Marcellus Francois. The final report analyzed this and other shootings, and the police response to the Guns and Roses riot of 1992 and the Stanley Cup riots of 1986 and 1993. Malouf found that the police had no crowd control plan, nor did they have a systematic way of communicating between regular forces and the specially trained "tactical squad." He recommended a number of changes, including the development of a broader Public Order Section that coordinated resources and established strategy for the tactical "Intervention Group" and closer supervision of officers. He noted too that the police union was a disruptive influence, and undermined the authority of the chief of police. On 3 February 1994, Chief Roland Bourget publicly stated, "My experience has been that the police chief is in a position to manage when the brotherhood gives him permission to do so" (Contenta 1994).

Following the Malouf Report, there was a reorganization of protest policing, but the new unit quickly faced a great deal of public criticism about their treatment of protesters. In 1995, police repression of protesters opposing the right-wing organization Human Life International spawned the formation of the Collective Opposed to Police Brutality (COPB), which holds annual demonstrations on March 15, the International Day Against Police Brutality. These events frequently end with large numbers of arrests (Dupuis-Deri 2013). The number of arrested protesters in Montreal has drawn the attention of international observers. The United Nations International Committee on Civil and Political Rights noted that close to 2,000 protesters were arrested by Montreal police between 1999 and 2005, more than in any other Canadian city during the same period (O'Hanley 2005).

The organization of protest policing within the SPVM is a complex affair that has become visible partly through repeated challenges in the streets and in the courts by the COPB. Testimony by police in court transcripts from trials against the COPB in 2003 found that the different actors active in policing the COPB's Day Against Police Brutality protests in 2002 included: the Operational Planning Service (OPS) which is responsible for coordinating the personnel for an event; the Intelligence Division of the SPVM, which directs OPS, and uses threat assessment frameworks to evaluate sources of public information, such as the media, and more surreptitious sources, including wiretaps or informants. This same operation is done for both terrorist threats and protest events. The Intelligence Division gives some of this information to the Security Liaison Division which has in the past taken the following steps for organizing protest policing for a permitted event: attempting to contact the organizers of the event, trace the profile of invited participants, look at the history of past events of the actors, and estimate the potential threat of disorder posed by the group. On the day itself, the Tactics Section, or Intervention Group, is the specialized crowd control unit engaging with the protesters. This unit was in existence until April 2002, when its participants were merged into the intervention units in each section of the city. Throughout the operation, the Investigations Section is operational, identifying law breakers and law breaking within the crowd.

The months of demonstrations by student protesters in 2012–13 were a significant challenge for the Montreal police. After months of demonstrations that were escalating in size and militancy, the provincial government passed Bill 78 in May 2012, with the ostensible purpose of ensuring that no student is denied the right to receive education at the school they attend, and preventing anyone from impeding the school's ability to provide that education. The law restricted protest or picketing on or near university grounds. The law further required that organizers of a protest consisting of 50 or more people in a public venue anywhere in Quebec, submit their proposed venue and/or route to the relevant police force for approval in advance. The municipality of Montreal also passed Municipal Bylaw P-6, prohibiting the holding of any demonstration with an undisclosed route or one considered by the police to be inappropriate. Sergeant Jean-Bruno Latour, SPVM spokesperson, went so far as to say, "The Charter [of Rights and Freedoms] protects the right of expression, but there is no right to protest." (*La Presse*, 22 March 2013) During a recent presentation on policing major events, Alain Bourdages of the SPVM explained how during the student-led mobilization of 2012, the agency had policed 711 protest events including 117 night-time protests, leading to 71 injured officers over an eight-month period, remarking how the protests "tested all our experience and our models."[4]

It is in this polarized and highly mobilized context that the Montreal police became the most frequent users of less-lethal weapons—including pepper spray, flash-bang grenades, and rubber bullets—against protesters, of any police force in either Canada or the US. In professional law-enforcement publications, the force promotes its expertise in countering anarchist and student demonstrators (Winfield 2012). Its experiments with militarized tactics are critiqued by social movement organizations like the COPB, but the lack of civic oversight of the force, a relatively unstable municipal governing body, and the strength and autonomy of the Montreal police union combine to allow only rare opportunities for public input into tactical decision making by police. When the opportunity exists, as it did around the expanded use of Tasers, those critical of police militarization are able to have influence in this divided regime. However, those moments are very rare.

New York City—New York Police Department (NYPD)

The NYPD is the largest police force in North America, with 34,450 uniformed officers and 7,000 civilian staff, who police the five boroughs of New York City. In December 2011, just after the NYPD had faced criticism for its pepper spraying of Occupy Wall Street protesters, Mayor Bloomberg boasted, "I have my own army with the NYPD, which is the seventh biggest army in the world" (*Daily Mail*, December 1, 2011). Indeed, the NYPD currently has 4.18 police officers for every 1,000 people, almost double the police/population density of Los Angeles (Ganeva and Gottsbiener 2012).

The current commissioner of the NYPD, William Bratton, was appointed by Mayor Bill de Blasio shortly after de Blasio's election in November 2013. One of the most high-profile police leaders in the US, Bratton helped to transform both the NYPD and US policing during the 1990s. He will replace Ray Kelly who had been the longest serving commissioner—working under Mayor Bloomberg from 2002 through 2013, and between 1992 and 1994. Kelly was preceded by Bernard Kerik (2000–02),

Howard Safir (1996–2000), and William Bratton (1994–96). The NYPD underwent dramatic reforms during the late 1990s under the leadership of Bratton and Mayor Rudolph Guiliani, who had appointed him. The NYPD is accountable to the mayor of New York City, who makes the appointment of commissioner, the top civilian role. The commissioner, in turn, appoints the chief, the top uniformed officer. This system has been blamed for a 20-year cycle of repeated corruption scandals. As a result, an extensive anti-corruption infrastructure has been put into place (Corruption Prevention and Education Unit 1997). In 1993, the NYPD reorganized its Internal Affairs Bureau (IAB) and established an independent Civilian Complaint Review Board (CCRB). This body has the formal power to investigate, make findings, and recommend disciplinary action to the NYPD commissioner on complaints against police involving excessive or unnecessary use of force, abuse of authority, discourtesy, or offensive language (ibid.). This body is staffed with a hundred investigators and comprises its own city department. Nonetheless, it is seen as ineffective. In July 1994, the Mollen Commission, investigating police corruption in the force, reported that police engaged in the drug trade, was the most prevalent form of corruption in the NYPD. It made recommendations for change in police culture and management, command accountability, internal investigations, sanctions and deterrents, community outreach, and independent external oversight. As a result of the recommendations in that report, the IAB and CCRB were strengthened, the mayor established a Commission to Combat Police Corruption (CCPC) to oversee the oversight bodies, and there was a new emphasis on training. An anti-corruption expert was appointed to the police academy, and drug testing was introduced for new recruits; in 1995, 18,000 police officers undertook a mandatory ethics training (Corruption Prevention and Education Unit 1997). However, there are ongoing criticisms of these oversight bodies. In 2011–12, the CCRB closed 2,518 cases, only 27 percent of which were full investigations that involved known officers and complainants, and only 74 of these 671 (3 percent) were found to be substantiated (CCRB Report 2012). The New York Civil Liberties Union testified that the CCRB doesn't work because its work is not fully supported by the mayor—who appoints the chief of police—nor does the City Council (NYCLU undated). Despite these multiple bodies, there are ongoing concerns that the oversight bodies are not truly independent. In 2013, there were renewed calls for federal oversight, perhaps by an inspector general. But both Mayor Bloomberg and NYPD Commissioner Kelly rejected this suggestion. Kelly argues,

"We have plenty of oversight in place right now. We have five District Attorneys, we have two US Attorneys, we have the Committee to Combat Police Corruption and we have our own internal oversight" (Gines and Heat 2012). Interestingly, Kelly doesn't mention the CCRB. Some have argued that the weakness of the CCRB complaints process has contributed to the explosion of lawsuits against the NYPD and New York City. Between 2006 and 2010, the number of lawsuits increased 70 percent per year. There were 8,882 suits filed against the NYPD from July 1, 2010, through June 30, 2011 (Moore 2012). Over the past decade, lawsuits and other claims against the NYPD have cost New York City taxpayers more than $1 billion. These numbers are significant. Whereas Los Angeles residents pay $14 per capita per year in police-generated lawsuits, NYPD lawsuits cost residents an average of $81 each (Robbins 2012). The proportion of these that are tied to protest policing is unclear, but the ongoing attention to the issue suggests the figures are significant. The overall NYPD budget is similarly enormous. In 2012, Commissioner Kelly requested $4.6 billion from the municipal government, 15 percent of the total city budget. While overall budget cuts are currently under way, the police budget remains relatively untouched.

The strength of the police budget has more to do with the relationship between the mayor and the NYPD than a united workforce. The force is represented in contract negotiations by multiple unions—including the Patrolmen's Benevolent Association, the Benevolent Association, the Detectives' Benevolent Association, the Captains' Endowment Association and others. None of these organizations, individually or collectively, have the equivalent influence that the Toronto or Montreal police unions hold.

The NYPD is a much-respected innovator and leader in the policing field, particularly in the US, but also internationally. When Mayor Rudy Guiliani was elected in 1994, he made "cleaning up" the city, using the police a key element of his program. The city was in a financial crisis, with large numbers of homeless people and significant levels of street crime. He charged Police Commissioner Bratton with the task. As discussed earlier in the chapter, Bratton cracked down on visible disorder (the "broken windows" approach), blanketing the city with police, with the goals of transforming the city in order to improve "quality of life" for those working or visiting. Bratton hired significant numbers of new officers, established the Compstat program to track crime "hot spots" and monitor police performance, and encouraged the building of partnerships between police and other institutions. This reorganization, and the removal of visible homelessness and a simultaneous drop in crime rate, bolstered the reputation of the NYPD both locally, within the broader field of policing and beyond. Compstat was recognized by the Kennedy School of Government at Harvard University and received praise from former Vice President Al Gore (Weisburd et al. 2004). However, the increased oversight of officers and ongoing performance evaluations displeased many rank-and-file NYPD officers, and their union, the Patrolmen's Benevolent Association, criticized such initiatives and Guiliani during the late 1990s. Nonetheless, the model spread widely across the US (Weisburd et al. 2008).

During the same period, the NYPD faced increased public criticism for both racism and brutality after a number of high-profile incidents including the 1997 torture of Abner Louima in a police precinct, the 1999 shooting and killing of Amadou Diallo, and the 2000 shooting and killing of Patrick Dorismond. These events and the lack of charges against these police officers triggered widespread protests and outrage and, for many, called into question the strategies and leadership of the NYPD. The attacks of 9/11 overshadowed these concerns, and led to renewed public support, augmented budgets and more interventionist policing, with an emphasis on intelligence gathering (this is further examined in Chapter 6). But police legitimacy faced new challenges ten years later in the wake of evidence that the NYPD engages in routine racial profiling through its policy and practice of "stop and frisk." After findings revealed that the vast majority of those stopped and frisked were young men of color, a federal judge recommended another new level of oversight, an inspector general. Shortly thereafter, the policy of "stop and frisk" was declared unconstitutional. Despite these reforms, the tight relationship between the NYPD commissioner and City Hall means that the NYPD operates with a great deal of impunity and authority. The way the elected city leadership values this tight relationship was made clear when longtime critic of the police de Blasio was elected, and appointed William Bratton as his commissioner. This relationship means that divisions between City Hall and the police are minimized, allowing significant police autonomy. Partly as a result of this autonomy "New York's Finest" have been able to become innovators in the use of barricades to control pedestrian traffic, and in the use of pre-emptive arrests that have become central to the strategic incapacitation strategy. Although they face ongoing criticism for their approach, it has limited influence on the police, except when it allies with significant federal or judicial actors.

The NYPD and Protest Policing

The NYPD has built a reputation among police forces across the US as being a leader in crowd control (PERF 2011). Many of the innovations developed there have spread elsewhere. Before the 1960s, a small number of officers were summoned from many precincts and often lacked coordination. Beginning in the 1960s, the department trained large forces of officers and supervisors who practiced crowd control together and were called up as a unit when unexpected demonstrations occurred. In 1968, a Special Events Unit was formed to respond to daytime student demonstrations and parades. In addition, a tactical patrol unit was formed to patrol high crime neighborhoods in the evenings, and could be mobilized for demonstrations as well. However, the Tactical Patrol Force became well-known for its brutality, and, in 1984, it was eliminated by then Commissioner Ward and replaced with six smaller units, permanently assigned to a patrol command covering all or large sections of a borough. In 1992, a year after three days of rioting in Crown Heights, a Disorder Control Unit, reporting directly to the chief of police, was created. Rather than being a specialized unit comprised of officers who take the streets en masse, this unit is more of a preparatory team with a mandate to prevent and suppressing civil disorder, whether planned or spontaneous (Holden 2009). To this end, it conducts readiness exercises and develops response plans.

The NYPD requires potential protesters to apply in advance for a permit to march or to rally, and to apply for a separate permit in order to use amplified sound. This process puts the weight of responsibility on protesters, and the power and information into the hands of police. Permits are often refused or adjusted, meaning that protesters without sound permits, or those who disrupt traffic, may be quickly arrested. If the police do issue a permit, they are able to withdraw it for any reason, at any time. Alex Vitale (2005) argues that this NYPD approach of "command and control" regulates every element of protest activity as an extension of the "broken windows" approach. Disorder or potential disorder is thereby quickly pre-empted or managed through arrest and control (Vitale 2005: 292).

The attacks of September 11, 2001, and surges in police legitimacy, public fear and federal funding emboldened the force to more tightly contain and constrain public demonstrations, monitor activists and infiltrate organizations (Boghosian 2007). During the World Economic Forum protests in New York City at the end of January 2002, the summit site was barricaded, bag searches became routine, and every Starbucks,

McDonalds, Gap, and Nike store in midtown Manhattan was patrolled by NYPD officers. Thousands of protesters were corralled in pens for hours, despite intense cold and holding permits allowing them to march. Two years later, the NYPD refused to give permits to anti-war activists for a demonstration on February 15, 2003, to rally in Central Park, or to march on city streets. Chief Michael Esposito said that neither would be permitted. He denied the organizers from United for Peace and Justice a permit to march due to concerns that the organizers had not provided concrete guarantees of the size of the crowd, and the police's concerns that the crowd would be unruly, admitting that although there was no known terrorist threat connected to the march, general concerns about terrorism influenced the decision (NYCLU 2003). Instead, the police insisted that the rally be held on First Avenue, where police contained protesters in metal pens. When large numbers of arriving protesters were unable or unwilling to enter into these barricaded areas, police attempted to clear the streets with horses, as well as pepper spraying protesters (against NYPD policy) and arresting 350 people. Further concerns about the NYPD's protest policing strategy emerged around the Republican National Convention in 2004, when police engaged in significant infiltration of grassroots political movements, and pre-emptively arrested over 1,800 protesters and passersby during the Republican National Convention, holding them for up to three days. The NYPD were sued by movement lawyers for both incidents, leading the NYPD to claim that they would change their treatment of protesters. However, the NYPD continued to intervene quickly to arrest, and control protest in the city. Although Occupy Wall Street was not immediately cleared by police at the site of Zuccotti Park, ongoing harassment, monitoring and enforcement of minor offenses led thousands of participants to be arrested during the first two months.

The NYPD clearly manages to control protester activity more intensively than the police in other cities studied here, and it shares a resistance to oversight, criticism and substantive change, due to its strong support by the mayor's office, and the weakness of its oversight bodies. This autonomy has allowed it to become an innovator in the use of barricades, and pre-emptive arrests to limit protest activity. Despite a great deal of criticism, it has been able to promote its approach internationally. However, in situations like the massive arrests at the 2004 Republican National Convention, or the pepper spraying at Occupy Wall Street, concerted challenges by advocacy organizations such as the Center for Constitutional Rights (CCR), the National Lawyers Guild (NLG), the New

York Civil Liberties Union (NYCLU), progressive critics in city council, the judiciary and the media, combined with lawsuits, can shake the legitimacy of the police with a wider public. However, the autonomy of the NYPD allowed the force to avoid any significant consequences. When 29-year veteran NYPD Deputy Inspector Bologna pepper sprayed Occupy Wall Street protesters, a police spokesman and the mayor initially defended his actions, but as the controversy continued, Bologna was cast out, docked vacation pay, redeployed to Staten Island, and denied payment of his legal costs by the city. Bologna had instead to depend on the support of the police union. However, this "punishment" had its limits: when the CCRB wanted to investigate Bologna's behavior, the NYPD allegedly undermined the process, allowing Bologna's attorney to ignore requests to participate in hearings. In a context where a force holds such influence, crises are more likely to be resolved by the punishment of a few officers than any widespread shifts of the NYPD's approach.

Metropolitan Toronto Police Service (1995–98)/Toronto Police Service (TPS) (1998–present)

The Toronto Police Service (TPS) is the largest municipal police force in Canada, with 8,292 personnel, including 5,629 police officers and 2,417 civilian staff (TPS 2011). The current TPS chief is William Blair, who replaced Julian Fantino who served 2000–05 (Mike Boyd served briefly as interim chief between them). Fantino took over from David Boothby (1995–2000), who was preceded by William McCormack (1989–95).

The TPS, like all police forces in the province of Ontario, are governed and regulated by the Police Services Act (PSA).[5] The Act became law in 1990 as a means of defining the role of all police services in Ontario (excluding the RCMP). In addition, civilian oversight of the TPS has been in place since the establishment in 1957 of the Metropolitan Toronto Board of Commissioners of Police, when 13 separate municipal forces were amalgamated to form the Metropolitan Toronto Police. The chief is directly responsible to the Toronto Police Services Board (TPSB), composed of seven civilians, including three city councilors, but the board has a limited mandate. It notes, "The Board shall not direct the Chief with respect to specific operational decisions or with respect to day to day operations of the Service … The role of the Board is to establish, after consultation with the Chief, overall objectives and priorities for the provision of police services" (TPSB n.d.). After widespread criticism of the policing of the G20 protests, and of the limited role the TPSB had taken, the TPSB became somewhat more interventionist, but it remains loyal to the sitting chief, who it appoints.

In addition to the TPSB, there are three other civilian-based oversight/investigative bodies that have provincial jurisdiction in Ontario. The Ontario Civilian Commission on Police Services (OCCPS) is a quasi-judicial body whose role includes conducting investigations into police chiefs, officers, and members of police service boards. The OCCPS can also, on request from complainants, conduct reviews of decisions made by police forces on public complaints. Since 1997, individual police forces in Ontario have been responsible for handling all public complaints made against the force and/or its officers. The second civilian investigative body is the Special Investigations Unit (SIU). The SIU emerged from recommendations from the hearings of the 1988 Task Force on Race Relations and Policing. Established in 1990, the SIU is composed of civilian investigators who investigate incidents where police actions have led to serious injury or death.[6] Ian Scott, the director of the SIU from 2008 through 2013, complained that the police did not cooperate with investigations. He sent nearly 125 letters to the chief of police alleging that officers repeatedly violated their legal duty to cooperate with the unit by "failing to notify the unit, destroying their notes or refusing to answer material questions" (Kane 2013). The chief of police didn't respond to any of these letters. In 2009, in response to ongoing concerns about police impunity, the Office of the Independent Police Review Director (OPIRD) was established. This role of this agency is described on its website as "to make sure that public complaints against police in Ontario are dealt with fairly, efficiently and effectively" (OPIRD 2013). Despite this emphasis on independence, complaints about police conduct are generally sent from the OPIRD to the relevant police chief to retain or take action (ibid.). This lack of enforceable direction limits the effective influence of the OPIRD. Of the 1,600 complaints about police conduct sent to the OPIRD in 2011–12, only 121 were retained for investigation (ibid.). The Toronto Police cite different numbers in their 2011 annual report, arguing that from 501 complaints of police misconduct, only nine formally identify misconduct (TPSB 2011a).

Although the relationship between the TPSB and the police chief are relatively friendly, the relationships between the chief, the mayor, and the Toronto Police Association (the TPA, or police union) have gone through periods of strain. Like Montreal, in 2013, the Toronto police have been conducting a criminal investigation that involves the city's mayor, Rob Ford. The tensions between police chief and mayor have a history: there was significant animosity between the previous Chief Fantino and the social democrat mayor at the time, David Miller. Nonetheless, given that the mayor has little control over the police, except through the budget committee in City Council, it has little impact on police practice. However the relationship between the TPA and the police chief, and the force more generally, is particularly noteworthy. The police union is a powerful political influence in the city (Forcese 2002). In the 1980s and 1990s, it explicitly "took on politicians" seen to be critics of the police, using private investigators to dig up dirt on these politicians, and raising funds to this end through the sales of pro-police stickers, the displaying of which was rumored to help motorists avoid tickets (ibid.). Although the Canadian Civil Liberties Association (CCLA) criticized this "True Blue" campaign, the TPSB was reluctant to intervene. In 2000, Mayor Lastman declared the Association "completely out of control" (Forcese 2000: 73). That same year, Craig Bromell, president of the TPA was interviewed on the CBC television show, *The Fifth Estate*. Bromell explained his strategy; "I think if you found somebody who is an enemy of the police, we don't want him around. So you try and get him kicked out of office. Pretty simple … All the other loudmouths, they're going to keep their mouths shut … [We're]going to target our enemies" (Barber 2000). Even the chief of police could be a target of the TPA. Bromell spoke of Chief Boothby: "He doesn't have any power over us" (ibid.). If a chief sanctioned officers for misconduct, the TPA fights back; it did so against Chief Julian Fantino, arguing that he was "harming the reputation of the Toronto police," and mobilizing a non-confidence vote (Forcese 2000: 75). This pressure may have contributed to the refusal by the Police Services Board and the new mayor, David Miller, to renew Chief Fantino's contract. Clearly, despite the oversight bodies that hold formal control over the Toronto Police Service, they have less influence than the Toronto Police Association.

The funding for the Toronto Police Service is established by a vote of the Toronto City Council. Year after year, the police budget continued to increase and also became a larger proportion of the city's gross and net budgets. In an example of the budgetary heft carried by the TPS, in 2009, the Toronto Police Service Board instructed the police to cut their spending by 5 per cent; instead, they received a 4.8 percent increase. There was no increase in the police budget in 2013, but at that point, the

TPS claimed more than 10 percent of the city's operating budget (City of Toronto 2012).

Toronto Police Service—Protest Policing
In 1988, the Toronto police's specialized crowd control functions were established prior to the G7 summit (Harman 1995). To prepare for this event, the Toronto police went on a "fact-finding mission" to Britain and to the US to learn about the best practices of other forces. The British visit, in particular, reshaped protest policing in the city. The Toronto force formed a Public Order Unit and embraced a proactive approach of preventing disorder, rather than reacting to it. Initially, according to the original commander of the unit, there was a reluctance on the part of other units to support it with their own resources, but it eventually obtained its own budget. While the Public Order Unit was kept in the background during the 1988 summit, it became increasingly visible and was eventually perceived as successful, drawing officers from other Canadian agencies to the Toronto Police Services for training. In 2001, the Ontario Adequacy and Effectiveness of Police Services Regulation was enacted. The Regulation requires police forces to have either a Public Order Unit, to enter into an agreement with another police force to have public order functions provided, or to develop a regional or cooperative arrangement regarding public order with other forces.[7] The Regulation requires that mechanisms be in place specifying when the unit is to be used, distributing public order procedures to members of the unit in the form of a manual, ensuring members are appropriately trained for the unit's requirements, and establishing specific procedures in relation to labor disputes.[8]

In Toronto, the unit responsible for fulfilling this requirement is the Public Safety Unit (PSU), which falls under the Operational Services of the Specialized Operations Command. The unit was formed in 1996, when the Emergency Planning Unit (disaster management) merged with the Public Order Unit, responsible for dealing with issues of crowd control.[9] The Public Safety Unit emerged partly in response to criticisms of policing during the OPSEU strike in 1996. Given its location at the Provincial Legislature, the Ontario Provincial Police (OPP) were responsible for public order. At that event, the OPP riot squad violently suppressed the demonstration. Metro Toronto Police Association President Paul Walter informed the media that OPP officers boasted before the attack that they would "whack 'em and stack 'em" (Rapaport 1999: 219). One high-ranking

Metro police officer described the OPP to a reporter from the *Toronto Star*: "They were like animals" (Mascoll and Rankin 1996).

Shortly after Julian Fantino became chief, in 2000, there was a major clash between the police and protesters. Influenced by the heat of the global justice movement, an anti-poverty protest in Toronto organized by one of the city's most visible social movement organizations, the Ontario Coalition Against Poverty (OCAP) marched on the provincial legislature building. When the protesters were refused entry, they attempted to push through the police line. Intense fighting between police and protesters unfolded, with numerous injuries on both sides. Dozens of protesters were arrested, and charged. Three OCAP organizers were charged with inciting a riot. After a lengthy trial, mistrial, and second set of hearings, these charges were dismissed. But it was a game-changing event for the Toronto police, led at that time by Chief Fantino. In July 2000, following this protest and subsequent meetings between the OPP (Emergency Management Bureau), and the TPS (Public Safety Unit), the current form of the Public Safety Unit was established—consisting of four subsections: Public Order Unit (crowd control), Emergency Management Unit (disasters), Industrial Relations Liaison (deals with strikes, picketing, and any labor-related conflict), and the Community Oriented Response Unit (COR). The COR Unit is a "high-visibility" specialized support unit that assists other units as required, in cases of "disorders, emergencies, searches and high demands for police service" (TPSB 2000). Members of the COR Unit are trained in crowd control and public order policing techniques (*Toronto Police Services Board* v. *Toronto Police Association*, 2004). In addition to the Public Safety Unit, crowd control is also a responsibility of the Mounted Unit. Bicycles are also used in crowd situations, as they are in all four cities.

Following the establishment of this expanded unit, the first OPP/TPS command course for senior officers was delivered in March 2001, and the new public order model first used in April 2001, to police the OAS Finance Ministers summit in Toronto (OPP 2006). The shift in the style of protest policing was notable for its display of heavily armed officers, displaying less-lethal deployment guns, and the presence of helicopters. When Fantino's contract was not renewed in 2005, and Bill Blair gained command, he differentiated himself by his emphasis on negotiated management. In 2009, Tamil protesters occupied University Avenue (a major street in downtown Toronto) for days and marched onto the Gardiner Expressway (a major artery). Blair was able to negotiate a strategy that cleared the roadways with minimal arrests and escalation.

Toronto police faced a significant challenge in 2010, when the location of the G20 summit was announced as the downtown financial district. The federal government took little heed of police needs or capacity in deciding to host the summit in the financial district, a decision made mere months before the summit. A multi-jurisdictional force was assembled, made up of 53 agencies, but most of the city remained formally under the control of the Toronto Police Service. However, there was confusion and division amongst police forces, including the OPP, now under the command of ex-Toronto Chief Julian Fantino. When the summit was over, police had arrested over 1,100 people after kettling in the rain, and charging others with conspiracy. Protestors smashed shop windows and destroyed three police cars. Initially, the city congratulated the police on maintaining order, and pollsters found widespread public support of police actions. But as the stories of raids, arrests, and intimidation became more well-known, the tide turned, and the *Toronto Star* called for Chief Blair's resignation. Toronto's mayor initially supported the chief and his operation, but footage of police beatings and hostility led Mayor Miller to become more circumspect. Chief Blair initially argued that there was no evidence of abuse, and that those making complaints were self-interested agitators.

Widespread calls for a full public inquiry continued. While neither the resignation nor the full public inquiry occurred, there were multiple, smaller inquiries into the policing of the G20 summit, including an investigation by the Commission for Public Complaints Against the RCMP, the Toronto Police, the OPIRD, and the Toronto Police Services Board each released an "After Action" report on the policing of the event. Their conclusions varied, although all cited problems with the chain of command and communication between the Toronto Police Service and the Integrated Security Unit, and between analysts compiling intelligence and police decision makers. Although initially the SIU dismissed accusations of police abuse, evidence from cellphone and video cameras led the police chief to obtain permission from the Toronto Police Services Board to lay charges against a small number of Toronto police, one of whom has been convicted and sentenced as of December 2013. After the results of various inquiries were released, the chief conceded that "things could have been done differently and therefore better" (Gee 2012). He subsequently declared he would no longer allow "kettling" to occur at demonstrations and announced a review of public order strategies that would "enhance capacity" (TPSB 2012). The policing of the G20, and additional, consistent accusations of corruption, brutality, and racism have challenged the legitimacy of the Toronto police. Nonetheless, they remain a powerful agency, whose influence is maintained through the way the chief carefully manages the various pressures from oversight bodies such as city council, the public and the Police Association. This maneuvering has been relatively successful: the force retains its resources and is considered a leader in professional policing and negotiated management. It arrests fewer protesters, uses less-lethal weapons more rarely, and faces fewer lawsuits and public condemnations than the NYPD, the SPVM and the MPDC.

Washington, DC—Metropolitan Police Department of the District of Columbia (MPDC)

The Metropolitan Police Department of the District of Columbia (MPDC, also known as the DC Police, DCPD and MPD) is the municipal police force of Washington, DC, comprised of approximately 3,800 sworn officers and 600 civilian support staff (MPDC 2011–12). Police operations in Washington, DC are unique for a number of reasons. First, as a Federal District, the DC Council is not in charge of its own budget, which is overseen by the Federal government. Secondly, as the nation's capital, the city has numerous policing agencies operating within its boundaries. The Metropolitan Police Department is the main police force in DC, but operating within the US Capitol area, are also US Capitol Police, the US Park Police, Federal Marshals, and the US Secret Service. During many protests at the US Capitol, these forces must coordinate.

As in New York, the chief of police in DC is appointed, or renewed, by the mayor. There have been four DC mayors between 1995 and 2013, but only three police chiefs (Larry Soulsby 1995–97; Charles Ramsey 1998–2006; Cathy Lanier 2007–present), which is less turnover than the other three cities. However, both Soulsby and Ramsey left the job amidst controversy—Soulsby around accusations of corruption, and Ramsey after major lawsuits tied to his decisions. Chief Lanier was mentored by Ramsey during a period of reorganization and described the culture of the force in the 1990s as "just bad from the top on down." After making sergeant, a superior officer harassed Lanier to such an extent that she sued the department (Buntin 2012). The relationship between the mayor and the police chief in DC is a close one. In 2007, Mayor Fenty delegated his authority regarding all provisions of collective bargaining between the District of Columbia and the DC Police Union to Chief Lanier, stopping any increase to compensation for rank-and-file officers (Jayson 2012).

In his in-depth study of the agency between 2000 and 2002, Peter Manning shows how the complex and competitive relations among different cliques and teams within the force made the introduction of Compstat-style innovation by Chief Charles Ramsey extremely difficult. Different players had different interests and distinct relations to federal or municipal politics, others had loyalties and ties to past police chiefs. Cumulatively, the structure of these relations meant that any attempt to alter information management and control was extremely politicized (Manning 2008: 143–5).

Because the District has unique governance structures, the MPDC is formally and informally scrutinized by an extraordinary number of bodies, including Congress, the elected city council, the mayor, and ad hoc supervision (a control board and city financial officer) who have fiduciary responsibility for the force (ibid.: 133). It has the highest density of officers per capita of any US city, and is often used to showcase various federal law enforcement initiatives.

Despite the number and complexity of structures overseeing the MPDC, the department has faced repeated and frequent corruption scandals over the past thirty years (Kappeler, Sluder and Alpert 1998, in Manning 2008: 135). Its leadership has repeatedly resisted actual oversight and evaluation. A New York City-style CCRB was abandoned in 1995 as ineffective and replaced, in 2001, by the DC Office of Police Complaints (OPC), an independent agency, with one MPDC officer on its five-member board. In 2012, 579 formal complaints about police conduct were closed during the fiscal year. Of these complaints, none led to criminal conviction of the officer, 14 were adjudicated, 321 were dismissed, and 154 were referred back to the MPDC or to another police agency. Perhaps not surprisingly, the Annual Report of the OPC complained that the MPDC exonerated those officers who did not cooperate with the complaints process noting, "MPD is—again—effectively undermining the legitimacy of the OPC's investigative process" (OPC 2012).

The sergeants and officers of the DC police are members of the District of Columbia Police Union, Fraternal Order of Police (FOP), and the Metropolitan Police Department Labor Committee (FOP). The current head of the DC Police Union Kris Baumann was elected under a banner of challenging Ramsey and is now an outspoken critic of Chief Lanier, calling her achievements, "all smoke and mirrors" (Buntin 2012). This tension between Chief Lanier and the union reached a high point in 2012, when the police union sued her because there had been no increase in compensation for five years (Jayson 2012). As Manning notes, the fragmented nature of the agency, in a context of repeated scandal, has made innovation and organizational change difficult in the MPDC. This extends to the arena of protest policing.

Washington, DC—Protest Policing
As the US capitol, Washington, DC is the site of numerous national, as well as local, demonstrations, with national demonstrations mostly targeting national sites like the Capitol buildings or national parks, where protest policing is the purview of the US Park Police or other federal agencies. However, when protesters hit the streets of DC, the MPDC's Special Operations Division manages their impact. Like the agencies in the other cities examined here, there has been repeated reorganization and transformation in the way that protest is managed in DC.

The massive May Day 1971 anti-war demonstrations in Washington led to two major lawsuits against the District based on charges of wrongful arrest and police overreactions (DC City Council 2004). These events led to the issuing of a handbook on how to handle demonstrations, and increased training for officers. These changes seem to have had some effect, as there was no litigation against the city around the policing of protests between 1978 and 2000 (ibid.: 22).

When the WTO protests took place in Seattle, the DC force paid close attention. The idea that the context had radically changed was repeated several times by other MPDC officials, including Chief Charles Ramsey, who used anti-globalization activists' threats to "shut down the city" as a justification for why anti-globalization demonstrations in recent years have demanded preemptive treatment from the MPD. Indeed, the Council investigation suggested that this belief justified the controversial crowd-control decisions that the MPDC made between 2000 and 2003. In 2000, four-and-a-half months after the Seattle protests against the World Trade Organization, the International Monetary Fund and the World Bank held their annual meeting in Washington DC on April 16–17. The police strategy was driven partly by local concerns and partly by a desire to avoid the "mistakes" of the Seattle protests, where the summit had been disrupted. The MPD used Fire Department officials to inspect the Convergence Center, ordering it closed for violations and then, the night before the protests against the IMF began, 700 people protesting the death sentence of Mumia Abu Jamal were surrounded and pre-emptively arrested. The following year at the inauguration of US President George W. Bush, a group of activists formed a "black bloc," in an attempt to maneuver and disrupt more easily; MPD Detective Jed Worrell and MPD Investigator Patrick Cumba, dressed as part of the bloc, wearing black hooded sweatshirts and bandannas, beat and pepper sprayed people in the crowd (ibid.: 35). On September 2002, the MPD surrounded protesters and passersby in Pershing Park at the same time as anti-war and global justice demonstrations, and arrested 400 people.

In the wake of these events, subsequent lawsuits, and the reticence of the MPD to justify their actions, the DC Council was concerned enough to launch an investigation. Led by Kathy Patterson of the Judiciary Committee, the DC Council attempted to gain a clearer picture of the patterns of police decision making and practice in regards to protest policing. In 2004, their report, *Report on Investigation of the Metropolitan Police Department's Policy and Practice in Handling Demonstrations in the District of Columbia* was released (ibid.).

Throughout the period, the MPD justified pre-emptive arrests on the basis of intelligence that protesters would plan to disrupt the streets and institutions in the city. The Patterson Report notes that when asked why he had ordered the arrests that day, Assistant Chief Newsham's deposition before the Committee explained:

> Another thing that was weighing heavily on my mind when I made that decision was the intelligence that I received that this particular group was intent on doing destructive things. I felt that if they were able to leave the park I think they would have gone out and done some of these things because of their behavior before entering the park. (Ibid.)

The DC movement law firm, Partnership for Civil Justice, launched a number of class action suits around these incidents, targeting both the policies and the practices of the MPDC and the US Park Police. The MPD avoided cooperation with the lawsuits and the DC Attorney General's office has been accused of destroying and hiding relevant evidence. The DC Council also became involved, particularly after Chief Ramsey avoided answering the questions of the City Council about these events. In 2004, the DC City Council passed the First Amendment Rights and Police Standards Act, largely in response to the 2002 arrests (Cauvin 2007). These lawsuits have cost the District significant resources, as it is responsible for compensation when the police are at fault. In 2007, the City agreed to pay $685,000 to settle a lawsuit whereby protesters at the 2001 Bush inauguration were pepper sprayed by police (ibid.). In 2010, $14 million was offered to those arrested at the 2000 demonstration against the death penalty for Mumia Abu Jamal. In 2011, the City settled the Pershing Park suit for $8.25 million dollars, after a 22-year veteran of the force, Detective Paul Hustler, quoted Ramsey as saying, "We're going to lock them up and teach them a lesson." This challenged the earlier testimony of Assistant Chief Newsham who had claimed responsibility for the arrests, and the assurances from Ramsey that he wasn't involved in that decision. What led Ramsey to consider pre-emptive arrests reasonable? What forces were at play?

The answer to these questions may lie in the fractured agency, and a fractured and shifting local context. More so than the other three forces considered here, the MPDC is divided by multiple loyalties, histories, and interests. The tensions within the force between those loyal to past and current chiefs, to various departmental initiatives, and to the union leads to low morale and difficulty adopting and incorporating new ideas, as Manning (2008) documents. In addition, the complex external political context, with the fluctuating priorities of mayors in an embattled and relatively powerless environment, who may in turn be collaborating or challenging sections of DC Council or Federal initiatives and control over the budget, all of whom use law-and-order policing as a football, plus the presence of non-local and thus relatively unknown protesters, puts pressure on the police chief and the MPDC as a whole. In such a context, the effort of the chief to maintain a united face against critics may inadvertently lead the chief to activate a particularly strong boundary between police and outsiders, thus exacerbating two problems: a resistance to oversight, and a reliance on widely certified, Federal intelligence assessments that portray protesters from outside the local context as threatening.

Comparing the Forces

There are many similarities among policing in the four cities. Between 1995 and 2012, all four police forces experienced significant crises in legitimacy. All four forces have been accused of corruption, brutality, and racism. None of them have complaints procedures that are seen by outside observers to be effective. In the face of criticism, all four police forces work to maintain their autonomy, legitimacy, and the economic capital included in local budgets. They do this using four different mechanisms:

1. resisting the influence of oversight bodies,
2. limiting internal divisions,
3. building alliances with external sources of legitimacy, and
4. introducing innovations certified by high-status policing experts.

The use of these mechanisms depends partly on the local context and partly on the position the agency has in the larger field of policing. The profile of the NYPD in policing circles and the alliance between the NYPD commissioner and the city's mayor make it particularly resistant to oversight and critics. While that force may lose legitimacy in the eyes of sections of the public, it retains significant political capital due to this relationship, and as a result, has been more of an innovator in strategic incorporation than an adopter of tactics and practices from elsewhere. The high level of autonomy that the force possesses has limited the importance of internal divisions and meant there has been less need of external sources of legitimacy. Despite massive lawsuits and widespread controversy around the policing of protest, in recent years, only federal and juridical decisions have forced the NYPD to change its policies.

In contrast, the fragmentation of police/government relations, and internal divisions especially in the less influential municipalities of Montreal and Washington, DC lead police leaders to both leverage their local legitimacy and to limit the effect of internal divisions by adopting and using practices certified by outside experts. These include intelligence-led policing, and the use of less-lethal weapons such as pepper spray, Tasers, and other less-lethals, as well as barricading strategies, pre-emptive control, and infiltration. There is some variation here—Montreal's police agency is more unified, has less oversight, less government support, and a more mobilized population than Washington, making it both more autonomous and militarized.

We can see these differences in the way local context affects the police incorporation of a new tactic if we look at how Tasers are proposed as a solution after controversial police shootings. In all four cities, such shootings have led both to public outcry and have been exploited by the producers and promoters of less-lethal weapons such as pepper spray, and various versions of Tasers, and other conducted energy weapons. In some cities, the decision to adopt was relatively simple, and in others the resultant struggle is ongoing. In New York, the police shooting of Sean Bell on his wedding day in 2006 generated a public outcry. In response, the NYPD commissioned the RAND Corporation to evaluate the Taser. In 2008, a pilot project was launched, with 520 sergeants wearing Tasers on their belts, leading to thousands of sergeants carrying the weapons in 2009.

The process was slower in Montreal and Toronto. After the police fatally shot two men in Montreal in 2008, the Montreal police force gradually increased the number of Tasers available to its officers, raising the number from 42 to 57 in 2011. Although the weapon became part of the SPVM toolkit in 2010, the agglo city council limited when and how the Taser could be used, but police continue to argue for their expanded use. (For explanation of "the agglo council," see Note 1.) Similarly in Toronto, in 2004, O'Brien Christopher-Reid died after police pepper sprayed him. The following year, after an impressive public relations campaign by TASER and its allies, the Toronto Police obtained a hundred Tasers. Ontario police chiefs and associations and coroner's inquests also encouraged the government to expand the use of stun guns, but the Province refused. Then in 2013, the police shooting of Sammy Yatim led the Province to alter the Police Act, allowing all front-line officers to carry Tasers. Weeks later, the Toronto Police Services Board allowed Toronto police to adopt them, despite significant public opposition, but denied them the money to pay for them. In each of these cities, a crisis of legitimacy triggered by a police shooting was resolved with the further incorporation of the Taser.

By 2014, police are only occasionally using Tasers on protesters. However, the pattern seen for the introduction of pepper spray seems to hold true. Publicly recognized brutality leads to crises of legitimacy, creating opportunities for both the recommendations of critics and experts, judicial reviewers and political authorities that facilitate the introduction of, or expanded use of Tasers. These opportunities often trigger the police to adopt new practices, tools, technologies, and training. Sometimes it seems that when a protest policing strategy results in lawsuits, angry media blasts, and public inquiries, there is increased motivation on the part of the police to adopt a new strategy or tactic. This observation supports both the insight of political opportunity theory, that division amongst authorities correlates with increased opportunities for influence from outsiders, and a mainstay of diffusion theory, that the local incorporation of a new tactic is often triggered by a perceived need for change (Rogers 2003, Tilly 1995). In the case of protest policing tactics, the trigger is often a visible example of police brutality or false arrest. In Canada and the US, such excesses, especially when they involve protesters that are seen as victims and are publicly visible through media coverage, can lead to challenges of police legitimacy and prompt changes to police strategy. This sequence leads to openness to outside influence—which doesn't always mean militarization—it can also mean critics push for oversight bodies or an elimination of kettling.

Local patterns of relations affect the incorporation of, adaptation, and/ or experimentation with new protest policing tactics. Sometimes, police unions fight the police leadership. Sometimes, they fight the mayor. These conflicts may facilitate or stop changes to policing tactics. When a mayor and police leadership cooperate, it may mean they become less accountable to other actors. If these alliances break down, there may be opportunity for change. The struggles for legitimacy, influence, and resources influence local fields of protest policing. These struggles are part of the story of changes in protest policing, and help to explain the variation in the shared trajectory towards strategic incapacitation.

5

Officers Under Attack— The Thin Blue Line, Pepper Spray, and Police Identity

As examined in the last chapter, the incorporation of a tactic is tied to attempts by those in power to maintain their legitimacy, autonomy, and resources. The result of these attempts influence police decision making. When power-holders, lawsuits and the public push police agencies to alter their strategies and tactics, police increasingly look to best practices that are certified in the broader field of policing. The dynamic between a regime and its police force can, for example, begin to explain the rapid spread of strategies involving less-lethal weapons and new methods of barricading. This chapter will specifically take up the use of pepper spray, one such less-lethal weapon, to illustrate. We know that the spread of an innovation often follows an "S-curve," wherein initial adopters slowly increase in number, followed by a surge in adoptions, until a high proportion of potential adopters have incorporated an innovation, at which point, the rate of adoption will slow (Rogers 2003). Various processes underpin this S-curve. The adoption of an innovation, especially for early adopters, involves theorization, during which potential adopters individually or collectively consider the utility and appropriateness of an innovation by theorizing its use in a relatively abstract manner. The innovation may also be adapted to new contexts and users, who experiment with the adapted innovation. Each of these processes involves feedback loops, which may influence whether and how an innovation is adopted. Common sense and past research would suggest that when experiments are deemed successful, incorporation is more likely; inversely, when experiments are deemed disastrous, incorporation becomes less likely.

It seems, however, the diffusion of the use of pepper spray as a crowd-control tool was not stopped by negative feedback. Early experiments by police agencies using pepper spray as a crowd-control tool were widely criticized. Nevertheless, police continued to adopt the spray, and to use it for crowd control. Why is this the case? This chapter considers this question and finds that the persistent diffusion of pepper spray among police forces is tied to two factors. The first is the certification of pepper spray by powerful actors in the defense industry, consultants, and trainers in the field of professional policing, naming it as an appropriate weapon to be used on protesters. The second factor is the "thin blue line" of police identity, which pushes police to see themselves as similar to other police, despite and perhaps because of the public criticism that they may face.

Both certification and identification are key mechanisms within the diffusion process. Certification is the mechanism by which respected experts argue that the innovation is a useful one. Identification is the process by which potential adopters of an innovation see themselves as similar to previous users in some way. The certification of pepper spray by police leaders, and identification of new adopters with earlier users of pepper spray, facilitated the diffusion of pepper spray as a crowd-control tool, despite two policing incidents in 1997 that generated intense criticism. The first incident took place when the RCMP pepper sprayed people protesting the Asia Pacific Economic Community (APEC) in Vancouver, BC. The second occurred when police pepper sprayed anti-logging protesters in Humboldt County, California. Police forces were widely condemned on both occasions, and lawsuits, inquiries, and public opposition occurred. Nonetheless, police across Canada and the US continued to adopt and use pepper spray as a crowd-control tool.

Pepper Spray and its Use

As discussed in Chapter 2, pepper spray, also known as OC spray (*oleoresin capsicum*), is derived from the *capsicum* genus of plant, most commonly associated with cayenne. Although pepper in various forms has long been used as a weapon, during the 1970s and 1980s, the spray format was used by mail carriers as a weapon against dogs, and as a personal security device. It wasn't until 1987 that the FBI endorsed it as an "official chemical agent", largely on the basis of research done by Special Agent Thomas W. W. Ward at the FBI Academy that showed that the spray was an effective and relatively safe way to subdue aggressive individuals. In that year, pepper spray became the most widely used spray munition, replacing Mace sprays that faced increasing criticism (Law Enforcement Training Network 2004). In the wake of the incendiary video of the Los Angeles police beating of Rodney King in 1991, police forces showed a renewed desire to find weapons that exerted force between that of the baton and that of the gun. That year, the National Institute of Justice hosted a brainstorming session on new types of "less-lethal" technologies. Participants in this session were given a set of parameters with which to consider any new device: the weapon had to improve on a present practice; it could not overburden the officer; it had to be inexpensive; it could not require extensive training or dedicated manpower, and the liability issues had to be manageable. And, of course, it had to effectively achieve the goals of the users (Pilant 1993).

OC spray appeared to fulfill all the criteria, and its use subsequently spread widely, in both the US and Canada. By the end of 1991, more than 3,000 local law enforcement agencies in the US had added it to their arsenals (Habernero 2000). By 1993, the use of pepper spray had been adopted by 70 percent of county police forces in the United States, 69 percent of the municipal police, 66 percent of the sheriff's departments and 63 percent of the state police (US DOJ 1993). Pepper spray was initially promoted as a tool for "preventing violence" and subduing agitated individuals who appeared to be threatening (Law Enforcement Training Network 2004). The RCMP began to use it for crowd control as early as 1992 (Draaisma 2007). Its use spread quickly across Canada, but other forces used it mainly for individual suspects, rather than crowd control.

From the beginning, there were concerns about the effects of pepper spray, especially after a number of in-custody deaths following its use. A report issued by the US Army in 1995 argued that, administered in high doses, pepper spray use could cause a variety of dangerous side-effects, including cardiovascular and pulmonary toxicity, and that there was "a risk in using this product on a large and varied population." (CCRB 2000). In response, the National Institute of Justice in the US funded studies throughout the decade that reached favorable conclusions about the spray's effectiveness and associated health risks (Davison 2007: 22).

By the mid-1990s, police use of pepper spray faced increasing controversy. In 1995, the International Association of Chiefs of Police (IACP) released its Pepper Spray Evaluation Project, a project funded by the US National Institute of Justice (NIJ), evaluating the effectiveness of pepper spray. The study examined pre- and post-introduction assessments of assaults on officers, subject injuries, the number of use-of-force complaints, and implementation/process issues, including product selection, training, and operational considerations. In 1996, Thomas W. Ward, the FBI's primary expert on less-lethal weapons, pled guilty to fraud after receiving $57,000 from Capstun, the second largest manufacturer of the spray, and ensuring approval of its use by police throughout the US (Phillips and Godfrey 1999). He was convicted and sentenced to two months in jail. In 1997, the Department of Justice released additional information from a study related to the IACP report, evaluating effectiveness of pepper spray policies, implementation training, and the use of pepper spray. In 1998, there were various publications issued about the toxicological impacts of the use of pepper spray, as reports of injury and death began to increase.

Nonetheless, by the end of the 1990s, pepper spray had virtually replaced police use of the baton, Mace, and CS/CN sprays on combative subjects (Adkins 2003: 14, Pilant 1993).[1] Despite ongoing, damning research, or perhaps because of it, two things happened. First, specifications on how and when to use pepper spray become more explicit. Secondly, the use of pepper spray continued to increase, and police experimented increasingly with OC spray as a crowd-control tool.[2]

According to media coverage, Canadian police, specifically the Ottawa Police Service, first used pepper spray for crowd-control purposes on May 31, 1993, to counter anti-racist activists trying to disrupt a neo-Nazi rally. Projectiles were thrown at the neo-Nazi members of Toronto's Heritage Front, gathered on Ottawa's Parliament Hill. A number of anti-racists then broke through police lines to further confront the racists, prompting police in riot gear to use pepper spray instead of batons to disperse protesters. The first use of pepper spray against protesters in the United States occurred a few months later, in Orange County, California, on September 15, 1993, Mexican Independence Day, when 300 Chicano high school students walked out of school calling for more Chicano teachers and diverse curriculum. They marched onto the streets, disrupting traffic. A joint operation by five police forces cordoned the crowd under an overpass and sent in squads to arrest suspected leaders. When they did so, the crowd attempted to protect those being arrested, and the police responded with pepper spray and batons. The third time police used pepper spray against protesters that year was on October 23 in Victoria, BC, when anti-racist activists attempted to disrupt an election rally of a right-wing candidate, Preston Manning. Police used pepper spray to subdue protesters and make an arrest. These early uses are illustrative of how it began to be used as a crowd-control tool; by the end of 1995, police forces in 22 locations did use it for this purpose.

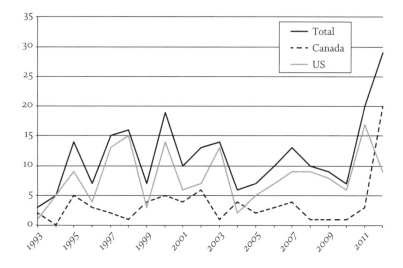

Figure 5.1   Use of pepper spray as crowd-control tool, 1993–2012

The data collected in the aforementioned search indicates fluctuations in the use of pepper spray, and shows how they follow waves of more transgressive protest, between 1997 and 2003, and again between 2011 and 2012. By 1997, police had used pepper spray a groundbreaking 15 times against protesters in Canada and the US. These incidents included: one scuffle in January in Seattle, Washington between officers and Critical Mass bicycle activists; an incident in April in upstate New York where state troopers used pepper spray against indigenous protesters from the Cattaraugus Indian Reservation, blocking a highway in protest of increased state taxation; DeKalb County, Georgia police officers who sprayed animal rights activists storming a barricade in April; two days later, police at the University of California, Berkeley sprayed pro-affirmative action student protesters occupying an administrative building. In June, police in Eugene, Oregon used pepper spray (and tear gas) against environmental activists who attempted to stop the cutting of 40 large maple trees by sitting in their branches. A few days after that, police in St. John's, Newfoundland sprayed rowdy fishing union members fighting an increase in fishing license fees and changes in fishing regulations. Later that month, police in Arlington, Virginia pepper sprayed animal rights activists occupying a McDonalds restaurant and arrested 16 of them.[3] In September, police in Saginaw, Michigan used pepper spray to stop anti-racist activists from attacking several neo-Nazis. In October, police in San Diego pepper sprayed anti-police brutality activists attempting to occupy a police station. In November, animal rights activists confronting scientists who use animal experimentation were sprayed by police in Anaheim, California. Later that month, indigenous anti-colonial activists in Plymouth, Massachusetts were sprayed and beaten by police for marching against a Thanksgiving Day celebration without a permit. And in Milwaukee, Wisconsin, anti-racist protesters confronting a KKK rally were pepper sprayed by police. Most of these events, with the exception of the Plymouth indigenous protest, received little attention and the use of pepper spray went largely unchallenged.

However, that same year, two incidents of pepper spray use against protesters led to widespread condemnation. They raise questions about the particular features of the diffusion and incorporation of the spray as a crowd control tool amongst police agencies. The first took place in Humboldt County, California, where, in three separate incidents, officers from the Eureka Police Department and the Humboldt County Sheriff's Department sprayed anti-logging protesters involved with the longstanding campaign to defend the Headwaters Forest. During the first incident, the activists occupied the head office of the Pacific Lumber Company; during the second, they blocked logging equipment; and during the third, they occupied a congressman's office. Each time, activists locked their arms into devices or to equipment in order to stop their removal. During the third event, police held back the hair of four young women and applied cotton swabs soaked in pepper spray directly to their eyeballs. When the women did not unlock themselves, the police sprayed pepper spray directly into their faces (Denson 1998). Once arrested, the activists were offered no medical attention. The police videotaped these actions and when the footage was seen more broadly, there was an outcry. Editorials in the *San Francisco Chronicle*, *San Francisco Examiner* and *Los Angeles Times* all condemned the practice as torture (nopepperspray.org). Calls by the American Civil Liberties Union and Amnesty International to ban the use of pepper spray followed suit. A letter from Amnesty International to the sheriff's office argued, "The sheriff's department and possibly the police department's actions during the protests also appear to have violated international standards set out in the UN Basic Principles on the Use of Force and Firearms by Law Enforcement Officials." An amicus brief shortly after the Humboldt incident argued that the "use of pepper spray as a kind of chemical cattle prod on non-violent demonstrators resisting arrest constitutes excessive force and violates the Constitution." Margaret

C. Crosby, an ACLU-NC staff attorney who wrote the brief with Police Practices Director John Crew said, "Certainly, a jury should be afforded an opportunity to evaluate this new experimental use of a chemical *weapon*. The single most important consideration in assessing the reasonableness of the use of force is whether the suspect poses an immediate threat to the safety of the officers or others." Crosby also noted that "the Humboldt authorities arrested peaceful demonstrators, seated, linked and locked into a metal device. They were dramatizing their commitment to protecting old-growth redwood trees. They were not menacing anyone" (ACLU 1999). Even the state's Attorney General Daniel E. Lungren, who had introduced pepper spray to the state's law enforcement arsenal, said that the use in these cases was not in accordance with state policies (Denson 1998). Nonetheless, a federal judge refused to ban the use of pepper spray on protesters (ibid.). In addition, following the incidents in Humboldt County, the California Commission on Police Officer Standards and Training (POST) changed the state-wide standards on the use of pepper spray, removing the distinction between active (violent) and passive resistance to arrest (such as going limp or using a lockdown device), going so far as to label passive resistance "an oxymoron" (Nopepperspray. org 2006).

The Humboldt County incidents led to multiple lawsuits and three jury trials, the last of which was finally settled in 2006, when a federal jury verdict confirmed officers had used excessive force (ibid.). The incidents generated a huge amount of media attention. A Factiva search using the keywords "Humboldt," "pepper spray," and "protesters" produced 380 headlines. In 2000, law enforcement researchers argued that police use of OC on non-violent activists in Humboldt County, California in 1997 raised concerns about the potential for misuse of chemical irritants by law enforcement officers, as did other encounters that year (Anderson, Hirschmann, and Jones 1998). As a result of this concern, citizens' groups have attempted to restrict law enforcement use of pepper spray (ibid., Kaminski, Edwards, and Johnson 1999).

The second event that triggered a wave of opposition to the use of pepper spray as a crowd control tool was at the Asia Pacific Economic Community (APEC) Summit of world leaders in Vancouver, British Columbia in the same year. At that event, world leaders gathered at the university, behind a security fence, far from the eyes of protesters. When some protesters tried to break down part of the security fence, RCMP officers sprayed them, catching some members of the media as well.

Shortly afterwards, the police also pepper sprayed a number of protesters engaging in civil disobedience, and others blocking the road (Desai and Taylor 2007). After the video of the pepper spraying was televised and a reporter found evidence that the Prime Minister's Office had promised the Indonesian prime minister that he would not be faced by protests, there was widespread public outrage. Despite this reaction, then-Prime Minister Jean Chretien tried to brush off the incident, responding to a reporter's question by infamously saying, "Pepper? I like it on my steak!" Editorials in national newspapers called for the prime minister's resignation. Over fifty protesters filed formal complaints and a federal inquiry was launched into the RCMP's policing of the event. When their findings were finally released in 2001, the Commission for Public Complaints Against the RCMP concluded that the police actions "did not meet an acceptable and expected standard of competence and professionalism and proficiency" (CBC 2001). They also found that the use of pepper spray by at least one officer, Staff Sgt. Hugh Stewart (known in the media as Sgt. Pepper), was unnecessary and could not be justified (Draaisma 2007). Indeed in Canada, the police use of pepper spray became associated with this incident, nicknamed "Peppergate." The event triggered a high volume of media attention and public debate. A Factiva search of news media using the keywords "APEC" and "pepper spray" yielded 496 headlines.

Given the high-profile, widespread public outrage, and taxpayer expense generated by these two events, one might expect that police use of pepper spray against protesters would decline. While the controversies in California and British Columbia did prompt additional research into the health effects of pepper spray, in 1998, the Canadian Police Research Centre reviewed the technical and health issues associated with OC spray (Ruddick 1998).[4] Police agencies in the US and Canada did not cease adopting and using pepper spray against protesters. In 1998, police used it at roughly the same rate as the previous year, 15 times in the US and once in Canada. Clearly, the incidents in Humboldt and in Vancouver did not have a dramatic influence on the frequency of pepper spray use against protesters. In fact, in some cases, police appeared to be imitating the officers facing condemnation. One such case took place in Minneapolis, Minnesota, a few months after a judge had dismissed the Humboldt protesters' claims of excessive force by the sheriff's officers. It was to be the first time pepper spray was used against protesters in Minnesota. On December 20, 1998, armed with automatic rifles, billy-clubs, and pepper spray, 802 Minneapolis police officers, state police, and officers from the local sheriff's department raided a 15-month-old encampment of about fifty non-violent Native and environmental protesters trying to halt the construction of a controversial Minnesota highway (Bayly 2006). The protesters had occupied seven houses that were due to be bulldozed to make way for the highway. It was the largest police operation in state history, and one that was haunted by the shadow of the FBI assault in Waco, Texas. Politicians wanted the site cleared without any deaths, and were spooked by stories that the activists were stockpiling weapons, and running gas lines between the houses (Losure 2002).

During the raid, the police used tactics that were strikingly similar to the police procedures employed in Humboldt County. They held protesters' eyes open, spraying them directly (Solstice 1999). As one officer later testified, "I sprayed the product on my glove hand and I wiped it across the face, the entire facial area, from forehead to chin, ear to ear" (Losure 2002: 44). Protesters argued that police were using "pepper gel on some protesters not only as a way to get them to unlock, but even after they were handcuffed and in custody" (Solstice 1999). Months later, District Judge Stephen Aldrich dismissed charges laid against the two activists who had been pepper sprayed, citing a "lack of probable cause and outrageous police conduct" to justify his decision (Bayly 2006). The judge noted that the activists had suffered "extreme pain, blindness, vomiting, uncontrollable crying and drooling—not only for the hours in custody, but the after-effects lasted for days" (Losure 2002: 58).

The controversy around pepper spray in Humboldt may have increased the profile of OC spray, and facilitated its incorporation by Minnesota police seeking federal expertise about new tools. Existing users of an innovation simply maintained the status quo. The controversy may also have lead existing users of the spray to reinforce their decision to use the product. In July 1992, the Metropolitan Toronto Police began a field study of OC spray by training and equipping 500 members with this specialized product. Results were encouraging and, in 1995, the Metropolitan Toronto Police Service Board approved the service-wide use of OC (Toronto Police Service 1998). According to Toronto Police Services Board guidelines established at the time, pepper spray could be used by police in four instances: to prevent police from being overpowered when violently attacked; to prevent a prisoner from being physically taken from police custody; to control a violent situation when other use-of-force alternatives are not viable, and to disarm an apparently dangerous person armed with an offensive weapon. The vast majority of such situations do not involve crowd control situations or protesters. The first time any protesters were sprayed by police in Toronto was on September 27, 1995, when the OPP sprayed anti-poverty and union protesters opposing a 21 percent cut to social assistance rates at the Legislature. Then in March 1996, the OPP used pepper spray to disperse striking public sector workers at Queen's Park. This event led to a Commission of Inquiry by Willard Z. Estey, a retired Supreme Court of Canada judge. In 1998, Estey concluded that "Bungling by police, politicians and strikers caused the violent clash," and recommended a major reorganization of protest policing at the Legislative buildings (Attorney General 2006: 5). Despite the blowback from this event, Toronto police continued to use pepper spray against protesters. In August 1996, Toronto police sprayed a crowd of fifty low-income residents spontaneously protesting the arrest of a community member outside a community center in the downtown Toronto neighborhood. Due to widespread criticism of the OPP actions at the Queen's Park Legislative Buildings, in 1997, the Toronto Police Service and the Ontario Provincial Police did a joint re-evaluation of public order policing in both Toronto and Ontario (ibid).

Therefore, by the time of the APEC Summit incident, the TPS were already engaged in re-evaluating and reorganizing their approach to crowd control. They were actively distancing themselves from the strategies used in the 1995 and 1996 incidents at the Ontario Legislature. However, they did not remove the weapon from their repertoire, but continued to endorse the weapon as useful against aggressive crowds. One of the key strategists in this evaluation was Sergeant Inspector Wesley Ryan, the unit commander of Toronto's Public Safety Unit, also on the Use of Force Committee. By 1998, a "Use of Force Report" recommended that "all front line police officers, whether in uniform or plainclothes, receive training in the use of oleoresin capsicum spray" (TPSB 1998). The rationale provided argued, "Public safety, officer safety, and Service liability concerns would be more thoroughly addressed if all front line police officers are trained in the use of belt-carried O.C. ... Some devices such as 'crowd control' sized O.C. aerosols can be very effective when used outdoors" (ibid.).

Nonetheless the controversy around pepper spray may have led decision-makers to be wary about ordering its use. The TPS did not use the spray as a crowd control tool from 1996 to 2004. In 2000, Toronto police did brandish OC containers against anti-poverty protesters. The aforementioned Wes Ryan, unit commander of the Public Safety Unit at the time, testified afterwards that the *Provincial Use of Force Guidelines* argue that OC spray can be used when police officers are faced with either active resistance or assaultive behavior (Cross Examination of Ryan,

OCAP June 15 trial). At the 2000 event, Ryan directed officers to display large spray canisters in order to show protesters that the police could potentially use this weapon. Although Toronto police did not use pepper spray at that event, they did deploy it three times in 2004, at an Ontario Coalition Against Poverty protest of the Liberal Party, to disrupt a sit-in by the immigrant justice group No One Is Illegal, and during the arrest of an anti-racist activist after confrontations between anti-racist activists and neo-Nazis. This last incident resulted in the sprayed activist filing a lawsuit against both the Police Services Board and the individual officer involved. The most recent use of pepper spray as a crowd control tool by Toronto police was in 2012, against anti-austerity protesters attempting to enter City Hall.

The 1997 experiments with pepper spray as a crowd-control tool in California and British Columbia provided police decision makers in the US and Canada with a raft of negative feedback from judges, public inquiries, civil liberties and human rights groups, the media, politicians and the general public. Nonetheless, newly established police forces adopted the tool, while other forces continued to employ pepper spray, including increasing its use against protesters. How do we explain the endurance of this practice?

Certification and Identification

The successful diffusion of an innovation requires that potential adopters know about the innovation, perceive its benefits, and its compatibility with existing identities and mandates. The implementation process involves experimentation and evaluation of feedback from those experiments. Diffusion theorists suggest that, at any point during this implementation process, negative feedback may lead to rejection. If experiments are seen to go well, an innovation is more likely to be gradually incorporated into existing routines and become part of ongoing practice (Rogers 2003: 170). This pattern has been observed in a wide range of innovations, and amongst a diverse set of populations. However, amongst police agencies, negative feedback doesn't always appear to affect the incorporation of an innovation. Why didn't public outrage, lawsuits, and government inquiries stop the diffusion of pepper spray to police forces? To answer this question, we need to look more closely at the mechanisms of certification and identification within the process of diffusion. The process of diffusion is neither automatic nor mechanical. Potential adopters are also active players. Sarah Soule shows how diffusion of an activist tactic is culturally constructed—by the media and by activists. When an innovation is compatible with existing understandings of the actor's own mandate and identity, it is more likely to travel (Soule 1999). But this process of interpretation is not simply about the innovation. It is also about the identities of past and potential users and the networks that link them.

The diffusion of innovations among policing networks has been paid limited attention (Buttle 2003, Lawless 1987, McCarthy and McPhail 1998, Manning 2008, Oliver 2000, Spelman et al. 1992 are some exceptions). Much of the work done thus far suggests that diffusion is often slow amongst police departments, especially if an innovation challenges the organizational structure, culture, or professional identity of the police. However, if an innovation does not have such characteristics, and is certified by opinion leaders in the field of policing, the structure of police networks, a shared culture of policing, and a strong professional identity can facilitate identification and boost the diffusion of an innovation.

Police agencies are tied to one another in different ways, and interact with one another for different reasons. Even in the decentralized context of US policing (1997), Alexander Weiss found that 40 percent of law enforcement planners contacted another agency at least once a month (Weiss 1997). A more recent study built on these findings and established that agencies were more likely to contact agencies that were geographically close to them, that were larger, that they perceived as being of a similar type as their own agency, and that were seen as experts in the relevant area (Roberts and Roberts 2006). They interacted when investigations or cases crossed jurisdictions, but also in order to make strategic and planning decisions. A shared occupational police culture facilitates the integration of police networks. As Della Porta and Reiter show, police culture has a tendency towards machismo and suspicion of outsiders (Reiner 2000). This strong culture facilitates solidarity amongst police officers and agencies, and shared understandings amongst police about the work, the profession, and the economic and political context. Despite local, regional and national variations, police also share a strong identity—facilitating both identification and certification.

Identification

It is widely understood that receivers are more likely to experiment with innovations when they identify with the past users of that innovation (Deffuant, Huet and Amblard 2005, McAdam and Rucht 1993: 60, Strang and Meyer 1993: 488). That is, adopters must see themselves as similar to earlier users of that innovation. They see themselves as sharing an identity, at least in part. As I noted earlier, Doug McAdam and Dieter Rucht specify three conditions that facilitate identification: a common institutional locus, adherents from the same strata, and a common language (1993: 71). Police organizations in the US and Canada, especially Anglophone Canada, would meet all of these conditions, to varying degrees.

Sean Chabot emphasizes the way these conditions are enacted, stating, "Identification is most likely when organizations see themselves as compatible, and share common meanings, a mutual subcultural language, and are alike in personal and social characteristics" (Chabot and Duyvendak 2002: 699). While these conditions offer a starting-point, they suggest that identities are fixed and identification is simply either present or absent. However, when one looks at the complexities that surround the incorporation of an innovation, it quickly becomes clear that the process of identification is a dynamic one, whose importance differs for different identities.

Charles Tilly shows how the process of defining a collective identity takes place through interaction and storytelling. Identities are constructed through activating we/they boundaries and de-activating previous boundaries. "We" tell stories about "us" and about "them." "We" begin to interact in different ways with "us" than with "them": "At least some actors on each side of the boundary reify it [an identity] by naming that boundary, attempting to control it, attaching distinctive practices to it, and otherwise creating a shared representation" (Tilly 2003). The process of identification is tied to more general processes of identity by making "us" see ourselves and articulate ourselves as being similar to a particular "them," whose ideas and practices we are much more likely to consider. Clearly, identification amongst police is facilitated by a shared professional identity, professional institutions, language, culture, and role. Anglo-American police see their job as rooted in the investigation of crime and in the response to calls for service (Reiner 1985). They are locked into the public mind as the essential sources of "crime control" (Manning 2008: 52). This role, their relationship to the state, and the occupational culture of the police reinforces the boundary between them and the rest of the population.

But this identity is not fixed and unchanging. Tilly's flexible understanding of identity, portrays identification as a process that is fluid and reversible. Because boundaries around identities may shift, or be thicker or thinner, or more or less malleable, identification may differ in its ease or significance. The identity boundary between police and outsiders is a relatively thick one, but may become particularly thick during crises of police legitimacy. Given the durability and thickness of identity boundaries between police and non-police, public criticism of the police may facilitate identification amongst police, and facilitating the diffusion of innovations, including controversial ones like pepper spray.

Certification

Identification is leveraged by the opinion of respected experts within the networks of potential adopters. When decision makers in a police agency are considering the adoption of a controversial new weapon, they will be interested in the opinions of other agencies, particularly agencies that they know, respect, and see as similar to themselves. The incorporation of an innovation by a police force is particularly likely when it is visibly certified by a high-status opinion leader, respected by the potential adopter, and whose context is seen as similar to the adopter's context. Such experts are more likely to be from large forces, from large cities, or with professional organizations who have developed their profile as successful in a particular field. Such opinion leaders, especially when they are nearby and perceived to be similar, have particular influence on others, but the influence is rarely bi-directional (Roberts and Roberts 2007). The status of such opinion leaders also reinforces the "thin blue line" of police identity.

When local police agencies in Canada and the US considered the adoption of pepper spray, they turned to researchers, and members of federal bodies, professional policing organizations, and high-profile police forces like the RCMP and the FBI who certified the weapon as an appropriate and effective tool, and later as an appropriate and effective crowd-control tool. This certification by experts increased the symbolic capital associated with the innovation, and reduced the risk associated with adoption—especially around controversial innovations. In a field that is increasingly transcending national borders, the certification by internationally recognized experts is having a particularly significant influence. The importance of certification by such leaders is visible in the *Use of Force Report* from the Toronto Police Service in 1998. When that document considered an increase in the use of pepper spray, it cited the ongoing and widespread use by US agencies, and FBI certification of its effectiveness. It also referred to (US) National Institute for Justice evaluations of the health impacts of OC spray use. It has also been noted by UK analyst John Buttle

(2003), that British law enforcement experts welcomed the use of pepper and other 'incapacitant' sprays, partly because they already had a track record in the US. He notes that Sir John Smith, then deputy commissioner of the Metropolitan Police, justified the adoption of an incapacitant spray without trial by suggesting its celebrated use in the US is applicable to policing in Britain (Statewatch 1994, in Buttle 2003: 107).

The Thin Blue Line

On October 17, 2013, RCMP officers in New Brunswick used pepper spray and beanbag projectiles against indigenous members of the Elsipogtog First Nation protesting shale gas exploration on a proposed fracking site on their territory. Flanked by snipers, the police arrived at dawn, attempting to remove a road blockade. When people attempted to stop them, the police used less-lethal weapons and an hour later, six police cars were in flames, 40 people were arrested and the police were justifying their strategy on the basis of weapons found in the camp. The police spraying protesters was not the front-page story it had been 16 years earlier in Vancouver, but it remains a controversial issue, and the reason for lawsuits, public inquiries, and part of a larger discussion about the use of less-lethal weapons and militarized protest policing strategies. Such ongoing controversy and debate about policing has further reinforced the "thin blue line." If anything, the "thin blue line" has become both stronger and more international, as police forces become increasingly integrated across borders, reinforcing their shared professional identity. While local variations in adoption continue, the ongoing diffusion and incorporation of less-lethal weapons as crowd control tools are likely to continue.

6

Experts, Agencies, the Private Security Sector, and Integration

On October 10, 2011, Occupy/99% protesters in Oakland, California gathered to protest increasing economic inequality and ordinary people's voicelessness in society, and also to create new models of relating that would be more just and sustainable. They were following the lead of Occupy Wall Street protesters, who had occupied Zuccotti Square in downtown Manhattan the previous month. Two weeks later, at 4:30 a.m. on October 25, 2011, 500 officers, pulled from the Oakland Police Department and 16 other police agencies, cleared the encampment at Frank H. Ogawa Plaza using tear gas and less-lethal projectiles including beanbag rounds, rubber bullets and flash-bang munitions (Flock 2011). Later that day, when protesters attempted to retake the square, Scott Olsen, an Iraq war veteran, suffered a skull fracture allegedly caused by a beanbag round. Police arrested 79 people, charging most of them with unlawful assembly and illegal lodging.

Oakland Mayor Jean Quan's decision to allow the police intervention at Frank H. Ogawa Plaza resulted in the resignation of her unpaid legal adviser, Dan Siegel, and Deputy Mayor Sharon Cornu. Dan Siegel announced via Facebook: "No longer Mayor Quan's legal adviser. Resigned at 2 am. Support Occupy Oakland, not the 1% and its government facilitators." Under fire, Mayor Quan explained that she had participated in a conference call with mayors from across the US, to discuss how to "deal with" the non-violent occupations taking place in US cities. Police chiefs from across the country took part in a similar telephone call. In the days following these calls, at least five other evictions of Occupy camps across the United States, Canada, and elsewhere took place.

The following week, author Naomi Wolf explored Mayor Quan's revelation about coordinated policing, arguing that, indeed, the near-simultaneous evictions of the Occupy movement in the US were informed and directed by the US Federal Government's Department of Homeland Security. Wolf argued that the elites were trying to crush the burgeoning Occupy movements that threatened their financial interests (Wolf 2011). This article was widely circulated through social media, recommended on Facebook 235,000 times, tweeted nearly 7,000 times, received close to 1,000 comments on the *Guardian* website where it was originally published, and viewed, over three days, by approximately a million people (Seaton 2011). The article resonated with a widespread perception on the left that police forces are both increasingly militarized and increasingly directed by political authorities.

This belief, however, oversimplifies the nature of collaboration that occurred. Instead of a top-down government conspiracy, there was a more complex interaction amongst police and civilian leadership. A phone conference among US mayors took place, and the Department of Homeland Security and the FBI gave advice to local law enforcement. The police NGO, the Police Executive Research Forum, had also convened two telephone calls amongst police executives, to discuss how to respond to Occupy (Holland 2011). The conversations taking place among police officers and agencies, in addition to the increased use of less-lethal weapons against protesters by police forces, are part of a changed and more integrated field of professional policing, one that is increasingly influenced by the business of security and defense industry corporations. These sectors and professional policing organizations have become more powerful within the field of policing since the mid-1990s, diffusing a professionalized, privatized approach to public order that values research, best practices, measurable results and police autonomy, altering the practices of protest policing.

As Pierre Bourdieu explains, social life can be understood by recognizing that there are fields of operation, organized around different kinds of practices, resources, and schemes of evaluation or legitimation (in Calhoun 2012: 303). The field of policing is structured by struggles amongst different police agencies, experts, and consultants for symbolic, political, and economic capital. The logics and practices that become dominant in a field gain influence and are more likely to be internalized by the players in that field. Both neoliberalism and globalization have altered the interplay and the value of particular logics within the field of contemporary policing by changing the boundaries of the field itself. The globalization of political and economic life has meant that previously distinct national police fields are increasingly integrated, increasing the competition for, and value of, internationally recognized "best practices." Often that research is done in partnership with military researchers— who may be more familiar with the international arena than their police equivalents. This is not simply a story of integration; the national police fields that have particularly high levels of political, economic, and symbolic capital are likely to be more influential in the integrated field. Simultaneously, neoliberal restructuring values privatization and deregulation, leveraging the influence of corporations and private security representatives over that of national governments.

In this changed field of policing, police understand and justify their strategy in ways that will be understood and appreciated not only by local political authorities and the public, but by opinion leaders in the field of protest policing. This is particularly the case with protest policing where globalizing movements and global economic and political instability present similar challenges to police in many jurisdictions. When existing protest policing strategies result in controversy, or new conditions or movements become apparent, police strategists are more frequently looking beyond their own traditional boundaries for tools and technologies that will help them succeed.

As police scholar Mathieu Deflem (2002) points out, since the 1960s, increased professionalization of policing has facilitated international collaboration, which has, in turn, accelerated since the 1990s. After the Seattle protests of 1999, key professional policing actors diagnosed a crisis in protest policing strategies. During the same period, international policing organizations grew, facilitating a shared professional identity, the sharing of information about tools and techniques, as well as information about the populations under control, and providing opportunities to promote and discuss "best practices." In general, Deflem argues that professionalization and international cooperation amongst police forces depends on increased autonomy from local and national political control. Although police agencies continue to prioritize bilateral or unilateral engagement within the international arena, transnational collaboration and coordination is rapidly increasing. When such interactions occur, within such initiatives, within professional organizations, agreements and in conferences, the value of research, cost effectiveness and measurable results are celebrated.

The transformation of a field also involves its "economies of worth" (Bolstanski and Thévenot 2006). These economies are the principles by which actors within an arena justify their actions as legitimate. The principles will reflect a particular vision of human nature. As the field of professional policing becomes globalized and privatized, the police are more and more justifying their practices (and the changes to these practices) in ways that reflect a vision of human nature within which competition and individual choice underline human behavior, and progress, based on the development of research based expertise and technical solutions are the appropriate responses. Such justifications are valued within the field of policing. This is particularly visible if we examine the operation of, and practices of, professional policing organizations that are influential on protest policing in Canada and the United States.

Professional public police organizations first emerged in an effort to formalize and legitimize the institution of public policing. Over the past fifty years, in response to criticisms of corruption, politicization, and ineffectiveness in fulfilling the mandate of crime control, public police have emphasized their professionalized identity. This has included an emphasis on training and standardization, and increasing autonomy from political dynamics and political authorities. After the 1960s, professionalization of policing intensified, with an escalated emphasis on research and technology as means of making policing more effective and professional. In the 1990s, international policing organizations began to grow, while national organizations became more integrated, corresponding with a more generalized globalization of a wide range of professions and institutions. As national subfields converged, uncertainty about the best forms, practices, and strategies of policing increased. In this reconfigured and globalizing field of policing, relationships outside of the local and national political context, and outside of public sector policing, became increasingly valued, as efforts to identify "best practices" in a globalized, neoliberal era simultaneously accelerated. Although national and regional policing traditions persist to this day, contemporary police organizations across the globe have clearly become analogous. As DiMaggio and Powell note, organizational forms within a field conform, as organizations attempt to limit risk (1983). The more it allows internal interaction, the more likely that an organizational field will display a tendency towards homogenization or "isomorphism."

As I discussed in the last chapter, the integration of national policing organizations and the growth of international policing bodies also facilitated the diffusion of particular innovations. In any system, diffusion is more likely when there is a perception of crisis, some shared identification between past and potential users of an idea, certification by respected opinion leaders, and an opportunity for potential users to deliberate about that idea in a relatively reflexive, diverse, egalitarian environment. With respect to policing, and protest policing in particular, all of these conditions are currently present, diffusing less-lethal weapons, barricading strategies and riot control units to police forces, who use them against protesters.

As national fields become integrated, dominant actors become influential over a wider set of players. As Craig Calhoun (2012) explains, the practices actors use reflect the cultural resources they have access to, strategic investments, positioning within social networks, and an embodied sense of how to act. Within increasingly integrated policing networks and institutions, trends such as community policing, intelligence-led policing, the use of Compstat, and "broken windows" models have each been promoted by opinion leaders (NYPD, RCMP, LAPD, MPDC). Such integration has also facilitated the diffusion of militarized units and less-lethal weapons to new users (Sheptycki 2000). Once incorporated, these tools begin to be used in crowd-control contexts. Their diffusion and acceptance is tied to the way struggles for legitimacy and authority have increasingly valued protest policing strategies and technologies certified by key actors in an increasingly professionalized, globalized field. I'll describe the activities and growing influence of three of these non-governmental and membership organizations, their affiliated conferences, research institutions, and publications—and then illustrate how the private sector funds and influences them.

Professional Policing Organizations

The International Association of Chiefs of Police (IACP)
Another key organization that has grown rapidly in recent years is the International Association of Chiefs of Police (IACP). This US-based organization "is the world's oldest (1893) and largest non-profit membership organization of police executives, with over 20,000 members in over 100 different countries. The IACP's leadership consists of the operating chief executives of international, federal, state, and local agencies of all sizes." Its mission is to:

Advance professional police services; promote enhanced administrative, technical, and operational police practices; foster cooperation and the exchange of information and experience among police leaders and police organizations of recognized professional and technical standing throughout the world. (IACP 2012d)

To these ends, it produces a magazine and website, publishes training materials, and holds annual conferences, including membership conferences featuring workshops on best practices, a massive trade fair, an international conference, specialized conferences, including one focused on Information Management: Training Conference and Technology Exposition, and an annual National Policy Summit in the United States. These conferences have grown in size and significance along with the organization. In 1958, the main conference was attended by 1,000 chiefs from 20 nations; by the time the 1987 conference was held, 8,000 chiefs attended with hundreds of thousands of other police representatives; in 2008, 15,000 police chiefs attended.[1] Each of these events includes speeches from high-ranking political leaders, award presentations for police officers, and agencies, initiatives, and products recognized as excellent by the association.

In the 1990s, in addition to an international headquarters with professional staff, the IACP added seven World Regional Offices, each chaired by a senior police executive. These offices promote the programs, services, and activities of the IACP in the geographical area served. In an era of increased professionalization, easier travel, and communication, it is no surprise that police organizations became more connected trans-nationally. These regions also host conferences, for the police chiefs in Europe, Asia, and Latin America. This international push was accelerated after 2002, when the IACP president established a clear internationalization plan (IACP 2012b). The IACP is currently one of the main professional organizations spreading ideas and practices amongst police forces.

The Canadian Association of Chiefs of Police (CACP)
Affiliated with the IACP, the Canadian Association of Chiefs of Police was founded in 1905. With the motto of "leading progressive change in policing," the organization describes its mandate as:

… the support and promotion of efficient law enforcement and to the protection and security of the people of Canada. Much of the work in pursuit of these goals is done through the activities and special projects of a number of committees and through active liaison with various levels of government and departmental ministries having legislative and executive responsibility in law and policing. (CACP n.d.)

The current membership of the CACP represents over 90 percent of the Canadian policing community (CACP 2013). The organization publishes five publications, holds annual conferences, and organizes committees on topics including Use of Force, Emergency Management, Professional Standards, and the Private Sector Liaison Committee. These committees are key conduits linking law enforcement agencies, government, and the private sector. For example, the Emergency Management Committee identified its initiatives for 2012–13 as including: organizing regional forums on emergency management trends, and a national conference on major event planning, as well as promoting and influencing research and development of best practices for major event planning and crowd management, promoting inter-operability, and the effective use of technology to first responders. Such activities influence the field and practices of protest policing.

The Police Executive Research Forum (PERF)
The Police Executive Research Forum is a US-based organization with some membership of Canadian police executives: "Founded in 1976 as a non-profit organization, the Police Executive Research Forum (PERF) is a police research organization or think-tank and a provider of management services, technical assistance, and executive-level education to support law enforcement agencies" (PERF 2012). Like the IACP, the organization is headquartered in Washington, DC and funded by US government grants, contracts, and partnerships with private foundations and other organizations. Unlike the IACP, which welcomes as members only those who hold police executive positions, PERF members also include "executives below the rank of chief; researchers and scholars; and others interested and involved in the criminal justice field." Like the IACP, PERF holds annual conferences, town hall meetings and thematic conferences, recent ones including one on "body worn cameras." The organization engages in collaborative research projects that include studies on the liability and effectiveness issues associated with conducted energy devices like Tasers, and one, sponsored by Lockheed Martin, on the technology needs of police agencies (PERF 2013). Although a US-based organization,

PERF is increasingly engaging internationally. In 2013, the organization facilitated discussions between Israel's police commissioner and his Palestinian and Jordanian counterparts. The organization explained its role as part of a joint effort to strengthen the rule of law in the region. But it wasn't simply brokering new relationships, it was bringing US police expertise into the region—police chiefs including Ed Davis from the Boston Police Department, Ray Kelly from the NYPD, and Charles Ramsey from the Philadelphia Police Department participated in the meetings, which covered topics including countering terrorism and managing large demonstrations (Cochran 2013).

The organization also issues reports that compile the "best practices" for police decision makers. These include a number relevant to understanding changing protest policing strategies including titles such as "Managing Major Events: Best Practices from the Field" (June 2011), "Police Management of Mass Demonstrations: Identifying Issues and Successful Approaches" (2006), and "Civil Rights Investigations of Local Police: Lessons Learned" (July 2013), in their *Critical Issues in Policing Series* and *Chief Concerns* series. The contents of such publications clearly endorse the importance of strategic incapacitation strategies. As I note at the beginning of this chapter, PERF drew a great deal of attention during the Occupy movement—being presented as a tool of the US government, who directed police chiefs to evict Occupy encampments. Both federal and private funds are crucial resources of PERF, but the influence of the funders is filtered by a logic that emphasizes police autonomy, research, and measurable evidence. It does not need to be directly controlled by political authorities in order to influence the timing and form of police strategy. As a think tank that is a key forum for the networking of and deliberation of US police leaders, which has gained political, economic, and social capital in the field of professional policing, PERF has significant influence.

Along with police unions, private sector actors, and others, each of the organizations described here contribute to international networks and help to circulate and diffuse ideas of "best practices" within the global policing field. They do this through organizing conferences or conventions, producing publications, consulting with government, and training other officers and agencies. These activities are funded by membership fees, but, significantly, also by security and defense corporations. How have these influential players in the field of professional policing influenced the way police forces responded to the Occupy movement? I analyze this below.

Policing Occupy

As I described earlier, Occupy protests took place simultaneously in cities across the US and Canada, thereby pushing police forces to turn to their professional organizations to inform their response. For example, conference calls amongst PERF members took place, as well as post hoc discussions at the 2012 Canadian Association of Chiefs of Police conference, and workshops at the International Association of Chiefs of Police Conference and Law Enforcement Education and Technology Exposition in San Diego in the fall of 2012. Typically, police executives from around the world gather at such conferences to learn about and discuss the latest trends in policing. In 2012 in San Diego, the Occupy movement was the subject of two educational workshops. The content of these sessions serve to illustrate a sampling of the criteria police consider when making decisions about police strategy in relation to protesters.

The first workshop was entitled "The Occupy Movement—How Municipal Governments, Law Enforcement, and the Private Sector Responded While Balancing Civil Rights, Budgets, and Media Coverage." The speakers on the panel included police and civilian authorities from Philadelphia, a city where the policing of the Occupy movement was seen as successful. The second workshop, "The Occupy Movement: What is the Police Chief's Role?" was described in the program as follows:

> The Occupy Movements across the county have been handled in a variety of ways. This workshop will talk about what worked and what did not, and will explore best practices. The focus will be on the preparation and communications done before and during the protests to ensure the rights of all are protected. The speakers for this workshop are Cathy Lanier, the Chief of the Washington DC police department, Ed Davis III, the Boston Police Commissioner and Susan Riseling, the Chief of Police at the University of Wisconsin, Madison. (IACP 2012b)

Such discussions, as part of IACP conventions, are certified as legitimate spaces for police authorities to evaluate new ideas and can facilitate diffusion of innovations and strategies. Importantly, the participants in these spaces are not only police executives. Indeed, many workshops are also attended by representatives of private sector corporations, eager to network and promote their products.

The most explicit opportunity for private sector promotion is of course the massive Education and Technology Exposition held at IACP conventions. In fact, IACP conference promotional material explicitly explains that sponsors of the conference are afforded additional access to "law enforcement decision-makers." A $50,000 sponsorship entitles a company to organize a "Super Session" workshop, held as part of the educational offering at the conference, as well as participate in VIP functions and receptions. Such access can facilitate the legitimacy and capital of a particular product or company. Therefore, companies provide a great deal of resources, in exchange for the opportunity to promote their products and services. While a similar system operates at CACP conferences, corporations are not able to organize "educational events," but they are offered "opportunities to present" their product in special sessions before and after plenary sessions, for a price. In 2012, the IACP exposition brought together 800 companies, whose products and services included: Communication/IT, Vehicles/Accessories, Weapons and Tactical/Protective Equipment, Administration and Training, Forensic/ Investigation, and Personal Equipment (includes uniforms, badges, footwear, etc.). Often awards are sponsored by one corporation, and given to another corporation, both of whom are simultaneously sponsoring the conference. These companies hosted receptions, luncheons, awards, and speakers, and were integrated into spaces where strategic policing questions, such as how to respond to the Occupy movement, were being considered.

In addition to conferences, professional publications also provided marketing opportunities for those who were interested in promoting their products as solutions to the challenges that the Occupy protests presented. The July 2012 issue of the IACP's *Police Chief Magazine* featured an article by Dale Peet, Senior Industry Consultant, SAS Institute, Cary, North Carolina; and Commander (Retired), Michigan Intelligence Operations Center on Fighting Crime Using Geospatial Analytics. Peet promoted the utility of mapping software for responding to Occupy protests, arguing that real-time visualization, predictive analysis, and geospatial analysis could help officials "to prioritize their resources to reduce the types of crimes associated with large protests." Other products, including body-worn video cameras, have also been promoted as a tool useful in responding to Occupy protesters (Neagle 2012).

The spaces offered by professional police organizations are also spaces colonized by defense and security industries. At the 2012 IACP conference in San Diego, the following companies promoted their less-lethal weapons: Aegis Industries, Alternative Ballistics LP, AMTEC Less Lethal, Armstar, Combined Systems Inc., Datrend Systems Inc., Kimber Mfg., Peacekeeper International, Pepperball Technologies Inc., Rescue Solutions International, Safariland, Security Devices International, TASER International, and Trident Police Products LLC. While direct influence of private security and defense corporations on policing decisions to adopt and use is impossible to determine conclusively, it is not farfetched to suggest that the collaboration between public police and private industry may be influencing policing strategies. A 2005 study showed that hundreds of US police officers were on the payrolls of companies the supplied equipment to police forces—for the most part as trainers—and the IACP recently accepted a $300,000 donation to its affiliated philanthropic foundation from TASER International (Johnson 2012). When police decision makers seek answers to the challenges they face, they turn to professional policing organizations and networks, which are themselves increasingly influenced by powerful commercial promoters of a particular product or service, such as less-lethal weapons.

These commercial promoters have accelerated the use of new technologies by police forces. According to a market report, the non-lethal weapons market will grow from $880.5 million in 2013 to $1,146.2 million by 2018 (Markets and Markets 2013).

According to the report, high levels of growth are expected, with austerity driving competition: "crowd dispersal non-lethal weapons segment is expected to have the highest demand in this market." The report predicts increased public-private partnerships, and "economic crisis and protest," along with "political dissent and unrest" as drivers of the market. Indeed, manufacturers like TASER International are proactive in their attempts to sell their technologies. Manufacturers become further integrated into the world of policing by helping police to test, train, regulate, and maintain the tools they sell, facilitating their adoption and use.

Examining the diffusion and incorporation of TASER International's conducted energy weapons offers a way to understand the way private industry is working to influence protest policing strategy. I introduced Tasers in Chapter 2, but we will now explore how Tasers have begun to become part of crowd control repertoire. Police officers in Canada and the US have used Tasers 32 times against protesters since 2000.[2] This usage includes incidents where police Tasered protesters who allegedly were resisting arrest; Tasers were also used to disperse protesters, and to force blockaders to unlock themselves. This use seems to be spreading. US police Tasered Occupy protesters three times between 2011 and 2013. On November 28, 2011, Washington State troopers Tasered Occupy Olympia protesters while removing them from a state building. On January 1, 2012, US Park Police Tasered an Occupy protester in Washington, DC. On May 21, 2013, a Department of Homeland security federal officer Tasered an Occupy Atlanta protester protesting at the Department of Justice building in Washington, DC. This is not to say that Tasers aren't being used in Canada. Before RCMP officers used Tasers to kill Robert Drzykanski at the Vancouver Airport in 2007, Canadian police were relatively heavy users of Tasers against protesters. Between 2001 and 2007, police Tasered protesters twelve times; seven of these incidents took place in Canada, with the RCMP being the user of the weapon in the majority of cases.

TASER International has seen dramatic growth and adoption of its weapons in both Canada and the US. Launched in 1993, the company was hampered by a non-competition clause affecting sales to law enforcement and military. But in 1998, the clause was dropped and TASER began to market its products to law enforcement agencies. According to the company's Annual Report in 2003:

> Our change in focus from the consumer market to the law enforcement market resulted from a market analysis that suggested the most effective method of penetrating the consumer and private security markets was through the de facto endorsement of the law enforcement community. In December 1999, we introduced the ADVANCED TASER for sale in the law enforcement market. (TASER International 2003)

In 2011, the Annual Report explained:

> … the decision to purchase TASER ECDs is normally made by a group of people, including the agency head, the agency's training staff and agency weapons experts. Depending on the size and cost of the device deployment and local procurement rules and customs, the decision may involve political decision-makers such as city council members or the federal government. The decision-making process can take as little as a few weeks or as long as several years. (TASER International 2011)

TASER International's marketing strategy with respect to law enforcement has been multipronged, with a "hands on" approach taken with respect to potential decision makers, to build trust in the company and its products. To do so, they have integrated themselves into professional law enforcement and military networks. TASER International sponsors sessions at professional conferences, put ads in professional publications, have established the TASER Foundation for Families of Fallen Officers, and provide personalized CD/DVD packages geared toward law enforcement leaders in the community. They also offer an Annual TASER Conference and run a certified master instructor school. They have organized more than 2,600 training classes around the world. The company has taken full advantage of the emerging online marketplace to promote its product, becoming a client of "PoliceOne," a website that describes its mission as

> ... provid[ing] officers with information and resources that make them better able to protect their communities and stay safer on the streets. We provide a secure, trusted and reliable online environment for the exchange of information between officers and departments from across the United States and from around the world. With more than 1.5 million unique visitors per month and more than 450,000 registered members, PoliceOne is becoming the leading destination for Law Enforcement professionals. (PoliceOne 2013)

TASER uses PoliceOne in order to

> ... build the business case for TASER use at departments nationwide ... [and] educate the market on the return of investment of adopting TASERs by disseminating case studies outlining the reduction of officer injuries and decreased liability for departments using TASERs. (ibid.)

The marketing strategy has worked. By the end of 2001, a thousand law enforcement agencies had bought Tasers (TASER International 2003: 6). After the 9/11 attacks, TASER seized a new opportunity, working with United Airlines and a Washington lobbying firm to "assist with safety studies and to initiate legislative changes which would allow the ADVANCED TASER to be deployed on board commercial aircraft." In 2002, the Homeland Security Act was passed, allowing airlines to deploy the TASER "weapon system." The following year, the company received federal funding to further develop less-lethal weapons, a move that, in the words of the company, "validated our position as a leader in less-lethal technologies" (ibid.: 6). By the end of 2002, more than 2,000 law enforcement agencies were using TASERs' M26 system and, by 2004, more than 6,000.

Then, in 2007, the corporation faced a publicity crisis. Between 1999 and April 2005, more than a hundred deaths in the United States and Canada were blamed on Tasers, incidents in which Tasers were used to apprehend or control the subject. TASER countered the accusation that the weapon could kill with aggressive litigation, arguing that, in none of these cases, was the Taser the cause of death. The company was forced to engage in an intensive marketing and public relations campaign, providing talking points and legal support to law enforcement agencies in relation to the more than a hundred deaths. The strategy for countering the criticism worked. Not only had TASER had sold its products to more than 16,000 law enforcement agencies by 2012, they had developed and sold additional technologies that employed video recording to document any use of a Taser, in order to counter criticisms of abuse. Through a strategic marketing campaign, the company made their products a "best practice" in professional policing, spreading the message that Tasers were safe and effective policing tools, life-saving devices that were better than any alternative. This strategy normalized the adoption of Tasers, and supported their use in an increasingly broad set of contexts, including crowd control and protest situations.

The marketing of TASER International products to law enforcement decision makers illustrates how less-lethal weapons became part of the public order toolkit, and why they were used against non-violent Occupy protesters. Private corporations are increasingly powerful players in the field of policing. Corporate participation at professional conferences and within policing organizations facilitates the diffusion of militarized technologies, certifying particular "best practices" as legitimate, cost-effective, effective, and linking them to a shared professional identity. In a time when the field of policing is rapidly integrating, and great value is given to globalized, high-tech solutions; corporations and their involvement in professionalized policing spaces have the potential to rapidly influence protest policing internationally.

Conclusion

When Oakland police used projectiles and tear gas against Occupy protesters, they, like the New York police using pepper spray, or the DC police using Tasers, were not making their tactical choices in isolation, nor solely in response to protesters in their city. Instead, they were making decisions within a field which had evaluated and certified the use of less-lethal weapons against protesters as appropriate and effective. This evaluation is partly a result of transformations of a field of policing that is increasingly integrated across geographic, political, and cultural boundaries, and one that has blurred the boundaries between public and private, and military and civilian security. In this field, struggles for legitimacy are increasingly influenced by private sector actors and international professional organizations, and are less sensitive to local political authorities or to an increasingly marginalized general public. Paradoxically, this neoliberal reorganization is partly a result of longstanding efforts to professionalize policing organizations and make them less driven by local political authorities, and partly a more general move away from democratic governance towards market logic. Such a transformed field is more vulnerable to perceptions of shared crisis and more easily influenced by private sector marketing of "solutions" that display technical, individualized, and militarized virtues. These solutions spread through the shared identity of professional law enforcement. Through the integration of professional policing networks and the involvement of corporations in these networks, this restructured field has contributed to police use of less-lethal technologies, barricading systems, and intelligence-gathering strategies against protesters framed as threats. In this way, the neoliberal globalization of the field of policing helps to explain why police are Tasering Occupy protesters.

7

Protest as Threat

We do not want to hold citizens who wish to go to downtown Montreal hostage. The Charter [of rights and freedoms] protects the right to freedom of expression, but there is no right to protest.

Sergeant Jean-Bruno Latour, SPVM spokesperson,
La Presse, March 22, 2012

Public dissent based upon difference of opinion is intrinsic in any democratic system. The core of the problem, however, is the evolution of these philosophical differences into the advocating of criminal activity and the creation of significant public security threats.

Integrated Security Joint Intelligence Group (JIG), "An Investigative
Baseline for the Primary Intelligence Investigative Team," 2010

In April 2013, I attended a meeting hosted by the Canadian Association of Chiefs of Police (CACP) and the Canadian Interoperability Technology Interest Group, entitled "Operation Planning and Management of Public Safety Events." Two hundred law enforcement decision makers from across Canada met in the ballroom of the Royal York Hotel in downtown Toronto, to try to develop a national standard for planning and managing major events, including protests, sports celebrations, drunken student street parties, public celebrations, and parades. The crowd was clean-cut, comprised of mostly white men over 50, dressed in business casual wear. Jane Wilcox, of the Toronto Police Service, launched the session, explaining that "one of the most important challenges facing police executives is the need to prepare their departments for major events—everything from large scale political protest marches and sporting events to natural disasters and acts of terrorism." She explained that the meeting, organized by the CACP Emergency Management committee, was driven by the need "to develop best practices that would assist in developing a national standard," to help Canadian police agencies coordinate and collaborate.

Much of the audience sat with arms crossed, attentive but skeptical. Following Wilcox was a high-energy facilitator named Chris who bounded across the stage, and after assuring the crowd that he was "ex-military," enthused about "tangible take homes" and the need for active engagement with the process. He then thanked the sponsors of the session: Harris, Rogers Communications, Intergraph Software, and the American Military University. According to the program, the first session of the two-day event was: designed to give the delegates the equivalent of a "Commanders Intent" briefing. CACP leaders and other Canadian chiefs of police would provide "a snapshot, high-level overview of various operational planning events and the planning models used to manage them over the past few years in Canada." They would outline their hopes that delegates would work together in order to develop the beginnings of a new National Strategy and Action Plans designed to identify best practices, tools, and processes for the planning and management of planned events of all sizes in Canada (CITIG 2013).

In this opening session, Superintendent Andy Hobbs of the Vancouver Police Department, Chief Charles Bordeleau of the Ottawa Police Service, and Jane Wilcox of the Toronto Police Service spoke about their experiences, describing their strategy for managing major events including Vancouver hockey riots, Occupy protests, Idle No More protests, Tamil protests in Toronto, "G-series events," the Olympics, fireworks displays, and presidential visits. They spoke about coordinating among multiple units and preparing after action reports, all speakers emphasizing the importance of risk assessments, threat assessments, and the use of intelligence to direct their approach.

Clearly, intelligence-led policing, with its emphasis on threat and risk assessments, has become central to the way police view an array of policing tasks, including protest policing. This chapter will show that this logic, the logic of risk and threat assessments, which underpins a policing strategy of strategic incapacitation, has a tendency to lead to militarized police action, pre-emptive policing and the arrest of large numbers of protesters. We've seen how the field of policing in Canada and the US has changed over the past twenty years, including a transformation in police management of protest and protesters. While police leaders are now more likely to make formal, explicit declarations about civil liberties and the importance of human rights in a democratic society, an increasingly integrated and privatized field of policing pre-empts and limits those same civil liberties and human rights. This transformation is a result of the way that the logics of public policing are blending with the logics of military control and intelligence. While police decision makers turn to professional policing organizations, private security and management theorists, there is increasing talk of "best practices" and cost effectiveness. Greater overlap with military researchers and state security officials means that police increasingly evaluate protest activity through the lens of "threat assessment," grouping it into a larger category that includes terrorism, war, and violent crime.

Of course, at its best, protest activity *does* threaten the status quo. But most protest is routinely unsurprising, that is, marching and rallying to demand policy change or participation in existing political regimes. Most of the time, protest activity cannot threaten the power and processes of the state or other authorities. Instead, it reproduces the existing order, assuring us that the system is democratic and effective, and that those social movements which are particularly worthy, united, numerous, and committed will have their concerns addressed. And yet, despite this ritualization of dissent, protest activity is increasingly managed as a "threat" by police and civil authorities, who criminalize protesters and justify a militarized response to protest. Since the terrorist attacks of 9/11, "Homeland Security" has become a central justification for a wide array of social practices, encouraging a dissolution and fusion of civil and military agencies and roles, national defense and domestic anti-crime work. In this reconfigured context, supported by new initiatives, funding, and institutions, the logic of risk and threat assessments provide police and political authorities with an unquestionable justification for practices, priorities, and policies. Security concerns trump the legal system, including civil liberties and human rights.

As Hornqvist notes, "Refugees, terrorism, anti-government demonstrations, organized crime, poverty, drugs and Islamic fundamentalism do not really have a great deal to do with one another. It would be difficult to identify what they had in common—if it was not for the concrete policy response" (2004: 10). This policy response categorizes all these activities as threats, despite the centrality of protest to the history and identity of the liberal, democratic nation-state.

The Western European state model, with its relatively broad suffrage and mechanisms for judicial and political accountability, emerged through struggle, in order to placate restive populations who threatened the power of authorities. At the beginning of the nineteenth century, these struggles created the form of the Western European social movement, as it addressed demands for inclusion and resources (Tilly 1995). The routinization of social movements led gradually to a routinization of protest policing (McCarthy and McPhail 1998). Social movement protest activity in Western Europe, as well as in Canada and the US in particular, is often highly managed by police, using permits, negotiation, established routes for marching, regulations for sound equipment, assigned locations, and signage. Protesters and protest are manageable, unthreatening and, some would argue, neutered.

Of course, sometimes, protest does disrupt the status quo. Instead of appealing to authorities as the arbiters of justice, transgressive, direct action protest puts pressure on decision makers by disrupting day-to-day economic and political routines and depleting authorities' resources.

Escalated Force to Intelligence-led Policing

Until the 1980s, police in Canada and the US responded to law-breaking during protest using an "escalated force" approach. When protesters broke the law, the police attempted to stop them through an escalating use of force (della Porta and Reiter 1998, McCarthy and McPhail 1997, McPhail, Schweingruber, and McCarthy 1998). Jennifer Earl and her collaborators (2003) analyzed newspaper coverage on protests in New York State between 1968 and 1973, and confirmed that larger and more militant (more threatening) demonstrations correlated with more repressive police action. The level and militancy of protest was less in Canada than in the US during the 1960s, but labor conflicts, the movements against nuclear weapons, against US involvement in Vietnam, and the student anti-war movement involved numerous sit-ins, street protests, and strikes, some of which involved police action. In both countries, although there is a long history of intelligence gathering on left-wing, ethnic and indigenous movements, this intelligence was distinct from the protest police strategy, which remained relatively unsophisticated.

Since then, police have attempted to use information to evaluate, anticipate, and preempt protest activity in a systematic manner. In Canada, as police experts observed the confrontations that US policing faced in the late 1960s and early 1970s, they began to consider crowd-control policies, and an expanded use of intelligence operations. (De Lint and Hall 2009: 100). As I've discussed, from the 1970s through the late 1990s, police in both countries favored liaising and negotiating with protest organizers, an approach that also corresponded with the gathering and use of intelligence. The emphasis on the centrality of intelligence to policing decisions didn't become explicit until the articulation of "intelligence-led policing" in the 1990s. As I discussed in Chapter 3, Ratcliffe defines this as:

> ... a business model and managerial philosophy where data analysis and crime intelligence are pivotal to an objective, decision-making framework that facilitates crime and problem reduction, disruption and prevention through strategic management and effective enforcement strategies that target prolific and serious offenders. (Ratcliffe 2008: 89)

Instead of traditional reactive policing, intelligence-led policing seeks to be proactive, preventative, scientific, and analytical. Such an approach uses intelligence to identify, prioritize, and intervene with protesters (and others), in order to minimize risk (Cope 2004: 190).

The approach first became popular in the UK, when police audits in 1993 and 1997 argued for the use of surveillance and intelligence, to intervene more strategically against repeat offenders involved in property crimes. In 2000, the Association of Chief Police Officers (ACPO) in the UK developed a National Intelligence Model (NIM). John Abbott, director general of the National Criminal Intelligence Service, introduced the model as follows:

> The National Intelligence Model (NIM) brings all the best practices in intelligence-led policing together, offering a blueprint for those who wish to develop better their ability to answer critical questions about strategy and tactics. It offers, for the first time, the realisable goal of *integrated intelligence* in which all forces might play a part in a system bigger than themselves. I believe it will become a major contributor to the continuing *professionalisation* of law-enforcement intelligence and have a major impact on the way we do our *business*. (NCIS, 2000, emphasis added)

The emphasis on integrating law enforcement and intelligence processes and networks, along with the highlighting of professionalization and a business orientation, signaled a new way of approaching police practices. Intelligence-led policing responded to a number of pressures police were facing in the context of neoliberal restructuring—pressures to justify cost-effectiveness, systematize procedures, and display "best practices" of law enforcement and intelligence gathering in a more businesslike organization (De Lint and Hall 2009: 201).

The NIM model describes four types of intelligence products for different types of operations:

- Strategic assessments—that provide decision-makers with a picture of the situation including the nature and extent of the problems, trends and threats, allowing them to create business plans with priorities and resource commitments.
- Tactical assessments—that inform day to day operations planning.
- Target profiles—that are person or organization specific to support or initiate a policing operation.
- Problem profiles—that identify established and emerging issues and present potential preventative options to assist decision-making. (NCIS 2000: 77)

Using these products, various social activities—political protest, public celebration, organized gang activity, extreme weather and terrorist attacks–are evaluated in standardized ways, thereby facilitating collaboration within and between agencies categorized as "emergency management," "major event planners," "first responders," and "homeland security." Broad categories are created, capable of generating reports, determining that threats can go up and down, and risk can be easily coded. These intelligence products also allow for the measurement of programs' cost effectiveness, and for forms to be filled in (Ericson and Haggarty 1997). More importantly however, such products also tend to direct attention away from the nature of the activity itself, its meaning, and its context.

In Canada, federal law enforcement leaders displayed an initial reluctance to embrace intelligence-led policing. This is tied to the way that, in 1984, the Royal Commission of Inquiry into Certain Activities of the RCMP found that members of that force had searched hundreds of homes and offices illegally, they had destroyed property, including a barn where militants were planning to meet, had planted evidence and attempted to disrupt social movements and radical political parties including the Parti Québécois, communist, peace, black nationalist and socialist organizations. This commission, and the public outrage surrounding it, led to the formal removal of intelligence-gathering functions from the RCMP, and the formation of the Canadian Security and Intelligence Service (CSIS) (De Lint and Hall 2009: 205). However, this division between policing and intelligence activities didn't endure for long. Gradually, with the rise of community policing, the emphasis on relationship building with businesspeople, social services, educational institutions and community leaders became a means for police to gather intelligence.

In the United States, the relative decentralization of policing and the historical centralization of intelligence gathering at the federal level meant that the two fields were more distinct than in Canada, where historical patterns limited the reception of intelligence-led policing. There was also a widespread suspicion of government intelligence gathering. From the mid-1970s until at least the mid-1980s, there was strong public criticism of the use of intelligence against domestic actors. This was rooted in revelations about the Federal Bureau of Intelligence's counter-intelligence program, COINTELPRO. This program was intended to "expose, disrupt, misdirect, discredit, or otherwise neutralize" black nationalist, socialist, communist, student, left, and far-right racist movements. When this program was revealed to the public, there was a significant outcry and the program was dismantled in 1971. The 1975 Senate Select Committee to Study Government Operations with Respect to Intelligence Activities, also known as the Church Committee, recommended significant changes to intelligence gathering.

By the late 1980s, there was a gradual return to systematic gathering of intelligence in both Canada and the US, using the language of prevention and relationship building favored by community and intelligence-led policing. As Ericson and Haggerty explain, the traditional police focus on deviance, control, and order is displaced in favor of a focus on risk, surveillance and security (1997: 18). In the context of this "risk society," threat and risk assessments began to be used, to develop police strategies for various policing initiatives. In the US, these involved operations within the War on Drugs, or anti-gang units, where militarized units were being introduced. In the early 1990s, the Los Angeles Police Department established a Threat Management Unit, to deal with cases of stalking and harassment. Shortly thereafter, the LAPD initiated a risk and threat assessment conference. Federal agencies began to build intelligence infrastructure that corresponded to the international standards of professional policing and international agreements. In 1998, the US Secret Service formed the National Threat Assessment Center (NTAC). In this context, the use of threat assessments by law enforcement officials was introduced to various federal concerns about infrastructure collapse, violent crime, drug trafficking, and terrorism. However, this period was relatively quiet for grassroots protest movements and threat assessments were rarely applied to social movements. Disruptive protesters were more likely to be labeled as gang members than terrorists. However, in the late 1980s, legislation against organized crime, and motorcycle gangs, the RICO Act (Racketeer Influenced and Corrupt Organization), began to frame political activists as involved in "organized crime." While only 300 suits against all groups were filed between 1970 and 1980, in 1986, 614 civil RICO suits were filed, and in 1988, 957 were filed; with the numbers continuing to climb (Silversmith 1994). This expanded use was supported by judicial interpretations that allowed campaigns that had more than one protest action that broke a law against a commercial enterprise to be defined as "racketeering." In this way, black nationalists, indigenous activists, environmentalists and animal rights activists were charged. Similar categorizations that lumped political organizations with gangs were seen in Canada. During the 1990s, RCMP files listed arrestees "gang affiliations," which included Anti-Racist Action, Earth First, Mohawk Warriors and OCAP. Such logics emphasized the formal affiliations of political opponents as justification for their criminalization, outside of any context, distinguishing such actors from the social movements who police tried to manage using communication and liaison models during this same period.

By the end of the 1990s, things had changed. In the post-Cold War context, and with the spread of digital communication, a new generation of activists were building networks to oppose the institutions and agreements pushing neoliberal globalization. The network structure and anarchist practices of some elements of these movements were not immediately understood by police decision makers, who underestimated their capacity and willingness to push beyond routine marches and rallies. Their mobilizations surprised authorities, and led the police at both the APEC summit in Vancouver in 1997 and the WTO summit in 1999 in Seattle to turn to militarized solutions in locally unprecedented ways.

After these events, police strategists in Canada further embraced the intelligence-led strategy. The preparations for APEC had involved unprecedented intelligence gathering and threat assessment activities, including the use of surveillance, spies, informants and open interviews with local activists (Pugliese and Bronskill 2001, in De Lint and Hall 2009: 252). However, the results were seen as too limited in predicting actual protester behavior. The failure of the Seattle strategy was also partly blamed on poor intelligence, and police experts responded to their own failures by describing these movements as threatening, and pushing for greater spatial control and broader use of less-lethal weapons (Fernandez 2008). The Department of Justice also funded a new series of public order trainings. By August 2000, at the Republican and Democratic National Convention protests, there was a much greater reliance on infiltration, surveillance, threat assessments, and the associated use of preventative detention of activists as a strategy for reducing the potential disruption of protest. As Warwyk (2004) argues, a new approach to public order was emerging: After Seattle, the police had to revise their readiness and rely ever more on intelligence to avoid a repeat of what was portrayed as a disaster. Part of the new approach meant that the police were under pressure to interpret the available intelligence correctly, and prepare appropriately for street protest. In this more intense environment, police forces have become networked and are studying protest by sending officers to act as observers. In Canada, what was done by a singular police force can no longer be done, as the size and complexity mounts. We are now seeing multi-police force participation with joint command entities as the normal approach for large events.

Post September 11, 2001–United States
The changes discussed above were just being established by the time of September 11, 2001.

Nine days after the attacks on New York and Washington, US President George W. Bush formally launched the War on Terror. Security, intelligence, and law enforcement leadership in the US, Canada and internationally entered an intensive period of reflection and reorganization. New institutions were formed, new funding for law enforcement initiatives released, and new collaborations took place under the new auspices of "Homeland Security." Notably, intelligence-led policing became the dominant framework in the US, the UK, and Canada (McGarrell, Freilich, and Chermak 2007). The US Federal Government launched an Office of Homeland Security, which became the Department of Homeland Security (DHS) in 2002. This new institution combined 22 different federal departments and agencies into a unified, integrated Cabinet agency, responsible for a number of new initiatives including an expanded role for the Federal Law Enforcement Training Center (FLETC). The new DHS also established a federal Homeland Security Grant Program for local and state law enforcement agencies, to help them purchase surveillance equipment, weapons, and provide advanced training for law enforcement personnel with the goal of "enhancing the country's ability to prepare for, prevent, respond to and recover from potential attacks and other hazards." The budget for these grants is enormous, with $1.5 billion allocated to assist states, urban areas, tribal and territorial governments, non-profit agencies, and the private sector in 2013, with $38 billion allocated since 2002 (DHS 2013b).

The new and enormous Homeland Security infrastructure was developed quickly. By 2013, it employed 240,000 people to carry out its missions (Murphy 2013). It rewarded local and state police forces for engaging in threat assessments, and integrating their information with federal systems. The NYPD reorganized its Intelligence Division and, to upgrade its intelligence gathering and analysis capability as well as creating a Counter-terrorism Bureau, charged the division with designing and implementing counterterrorism projects, training police officers to respond to terrorist attacks, and evaluating threats to the city's infrastructure. Combined, these two units have a budget of more than $100 million and employ approximately a thousand officers (Patel and Sullivan 2012).

In 2002, at a gathering funded by the US government and organized by the International Association of Chiefs of Police, over 120 criminal intelligence experts from across the US called for a National Intelligence Plan, with a core recommendation to "promote intelligence-led policing through a common understanding of criminal intelligence and its usefulness." To allay concerns about the building of a federal policing infrastructure, the experts argued for a critical counterbalance of civil rights (IACP 2002: v), insisting too that capacity, analysis, technology, and training issues needed to be addressed.

By 2003, the emphasis on intelligence-led policing was mainstream and institutionalized. The Department of Justice's Bureau of Justice Assistance published the IACP's *Intelligence-Led Policing: The New Intelligence Architecture* as part of its "New Realities: Law Enforcement in the Post 9/11 Era" series. The report argued that because effective intelligence operations may apply "equally well to terrorist threats and crimes in the community, homeland security and local crime prevention are not mutually exclusive." One outcome of intelligence-led policing is that distinctions between different types of policing are reorganized.

That same year, FBI Director Robert Mueller ordered the creation of Field Intelligence Groups (FIGs) in all 56 field offices. These offices were intended to combine the FBI's intelligence and investigative capabilities. The FIGs, in turn, had a mandate to work closely with the FBI-led Joint Terrorism Task Forces (JTTFs), various field office squads, and other agency components to support local and state law enforcement agencies (Spiller 2006). The DHS, along with the US Department of Justice's Office of Justice Programs, also established "fusion centers," terrorism prevention and response centers designed to promote information sharing at the federal level, between agencies such as the CIA, the FBI, the Department of Justice, the US Military, state and local government, and private sector partners. Fusion centers may also be affiliated with an Emergency Operations Center that responds in the event of a disaster, and, in addition, are often established for major summit or political conventions, if a risk and threat analysis merits it. As of August 2013, the Department of Homeland Security recognized at least 78 fusion centers.

The risk or threat analysis which can prompt the establishment of a fusion center is sometimes done by the Homeland Infrastructure Threat and Risk Analysis Center (HITRAC), which is a

> ... joint program of IP and the Office of Intelligence and Analysis, that provides risk, threat, and consequence analyses to give the Department of Homeland Security and its security partners an understanding of threats, infrastructure vulnerabilities, and potential consequences of attacks or natural disasters. They use the National Infrastructure Protection Plan to oversee the risk assessments. (DHS 2013a)

This plan identifies goals, objectives, assets, systems and networks; assesses risks, consequences, vulnerabilities, and threats; and prioritizes and implements programs. Each step of the plan has a feedback loop.

At the same time as this new integrated security infrastructure emerged, the USA PATRIOT Act broadened the definition of terrorism to include social movement activity. Section 802 of the Act defines the federal crime of "domestic terrorism" as "acts dangerous to human life" that violate the criminal laws, if their goal "appear[s] to be intended ... to influence the policy of a government by intimidation or coercion" (Boghosian and the NLG 2007: 12). When combined with the FBI definition of terrorism that includes "violence against property," the Act equated some protest activity with terrorism. Indeed, after 9/11, environmental and animal rights activists were identified by the FBI as the top domestic terrorism threat.

Post September 11, 2001—Canada
Canadian security infrastructure was also deeply altered by the attacks of 9/11 and ensuing US initiatives. The US government pushed for greater

border control and heightened integration of security, threat assessment, and intelligence infrastructure between the two countries. In Canada, national security initiatives and law enforcement became more integrated. As Superintendent Wayne Pilgrim, head of the National Security Investigations Branch, responsible for monitoring and coordinating the RCMP's post-9/11 initiative, states:

> "Prior to September 11, the national security program within the RCMP was, for the most part, isolated from mainstream law enforcement ... After September 11, many of the tangible and intangible barriers were taken down. This has facilitated partnership-building internally and externally. (Brian 2002)

The partners external to the RCMP included CSIS, the Department of Foreign Affairs and International Trade, Canada Revenue Agency, the Department of Justice, Transport Canada, Citizenship Immigration Canada, the Department of National Defence, and the Privy Council Office, among others. After eight years of funding cuts, the RCMP received increased resources in the federal budget of December, 2001, to deal with "threats to national security." The funded initiatives encompassed 17 distinct programs, including Integrated National Security Enforcement Teams (INSETs), comprised of representatives from the RCMP and partner agencies at municipal, provincial and federal levels of law enforcement (ibid.). According to Pilgrim, "At the heart of INSETs is the philosophy that they are intelligence-led and integrated ... We want to expand this concept to national security investigation areas across the country, so no matter where you are, the integration philosophy is being applied" (ibid.). Other organizations also received increased funding in 2001, including the Canadian Security Intelligence Service (CSIS), the Communication Security Establishment (CSE), and military intelligence.

In 2003, the government launched a new ministry called Public Safety Canada, a Canadian equivalent to the US Department of Homeland Security, to ensure coordination across all federal departments and agencies responsible for national security. The ministry's website notes that the "government approach to Canada's safety is highly organized and prepared to confront threats to national security. Public Safety coordinates an integrated approach to emergency management, law enforcement, corrections, crime prevention and border security" (Public Safety Canada 2013). The Canadian government developed a National Security Policy

(NSP) in the following year. Three of the main initiatives of the NSP were the formation of an Integrated Threat Assessment Centre within CSIS, the development of a new Emergency Management Framework, and Critical Infrastructure Strategy.[1]

All three of these innovations made intelligence evaluations central to national security. For example, at the Integrated Threat Assessment Centre, CSIS produces threat assessments concerning the scope and immediacy of a variety of threats posed by individuals and groups in Canada and abroad. Similar in some ways to the US PATRIOT Act, Canada's Bill C-36 was passed by Parliament in December 2001, amid concerns provisions allowing for "secret" trials, pre-emptive detention, expansive security and surveillance powers, and compatibility with the Charter of Rights and Freedoms. While some of these measures expired in 2007, they were reintroduced in the Combatting Terrorism Act (2012). Clearly, after the attacks of September 11, 2001, new institutions, resources, and collaborations transformed the field of policing in Canada and the US, including the subfield of protest policing. As a result, police adopted new ways of defining, analyzing, and evaluating protesters and protest.

Logics and Justifications

The logic of threat and risk assessments has become a dominant "logic of practice" that justifies policing decisions. The logics of such assessments are part of a larger social trend described by Ulrich Beck, Anthony Giddens, and others as the "risk society." They note that society is increasingly organized around evaluations of future harm. Beck defines it as "a systematic way of dealing with hazards and insecurities induced and introduced by modernisation itself" (Beck 1992: 21). As Eckberg (2007) argues, the traditional concept of risk is understood as the sum of the probability of an adverse event and the magnitude of the consequences. This concept has blossomed into a whole industry, complete with professionals, conferences, and competing models. In general, risk assessments define the components of risk in precise, usually quantitative, terms. In technical risk assessments, what is at stake is specified, calculated by multiplying the probabilities by the magnitude of the effects (Kolluru and Brooks 1995, in Renn 1998: 51). It all sounds quite convincing; the logic is seductive and tends to spread to new contexts. However, the value it gives to "what is at stake" and the existing infrastructure tend to automatically value the status quo and frames challengers to the current order as suspicious.

Luc Boltanski and Laurent Thévenot illustrate how such political justifications and evaluations of worth are coordinated. What is the principle of order that has allowed the police to develop and value "threat assessment" as the justification for militarized and pre-emptive protest policing? The logic of threat assessment is a response to the uncertainty of contemporary protest policing, as well as the uncertainty of how to maintain support from economic and political powerholders, and the general public. As Boltanski and Thévenot argue, "persons and groups confront uncertainty by making use of objects to establish orders and, conversely, they consolidate objects by attaching them to the order constructed" (Boltanski and Thévenot 2006: 17). The object in this case is, of course, the protest, and the order is that of threat assessment. This relationship answers the questions police face, including "Why did you pepper spray those protesters?", or "Why is that security fence necessary?" with a consistent response: "they posed a threat."

Both the questions and the answer to those questions imply a particular vision of the world and its values. In the justifications offered by threat assessments and risk calculations, a world is implied in which the worthy status quo is besieged by the forces of chaos and darkness. Information about these forces needs to be collected, analyzed, and acted upon, suggesting that threats and responses can be quantitatively or qualitatively measured, and responded to in an appropriate manner, with relatively predictable results. However, how this happens is contested.

"I wish we had a real science of threat assessment," a senior police decision maker sighed at the CACP conference with which I introduced this chapter. Indeed, despite the widespread adoption of risk and threat assessments by law enforcement, there is little agreement about how threat should be measured, what threat is and how to analyze it. Instead, what exists is a sequence of information gathering and coding procedures. According to a document issued in 2005 by the US Bureau of Justice Assistance, risk assessment and management follow sequential tasks:

1. Critical infrastructure and key asset inventory,
2. Criticality assessment,
3. Threat assessment,
4. Vulnerability assessment,
5. Risk calculation, and
6. Countermeasure identification. (Bureau of Justice Assistance 2005)

The first two tasks carried out by an assessing team are to identify the assets that might be targeted and to prioritize them. In the approach followed by Canadian authorities, targets are more important if identified as "Critical Infrastructure," a term defined as "processes, systems, facilities, technologies, networks, assets and services essential to the health, safety, security or economic well-being of Canadians and the effective functioning of government" (Public Safety Canada 2009: 2). If critical infrastructure is believed to be involved, and the particular infrastructure is seen as significant, resources will be directed towards eliminating that risk. Risk from protest activities is then made more significant when it targets institutions identified as "critical infrastructure." While risk assessments focus their attention on the target, threat assessments highlight the forces against that target. One US-based security contractor explained the distinction between risk and threat assessments, arguing that risk assessments are defined as probability of action multiplied by harm, whereas threat assessments are defined as capability to act multiplied by intent (Pilgrim 2010). Capability is assessed by looking at past performance, trends, the resources a particular actor has, and the ability to create opportunities for action. Intent is also established by past performance, public rhetoric, and initiative, in terms of creating opportunities (ibid).

Since the attacks of September 11, 2001, the threat and risk assessment logic has been widely promoted by the US government as a central element of counter-terrorism systems:

> Foremost among the demands that confront police in the post-September 11 environment is the ability to effectively and efficiently collect, assess, disseminate and act on intelligence information regarding threats posed by transnational and domestic terrorists... The need for technological interoperability, standardization and operational networking within and among all agencies has been amplified. These demands, coupled with the requirement that local jurisdictions conduct threat, vulnerability, and needs assessments to qualify for federal homeland security funding through the State Homeland Security Assessment and Strategy Program present clear challenges to law enforcement executives. (Bureau of Justice Assistance 2005)

In 2002, the RAND Corporation surveyed law enforcement agencies about their response to these demands. The survey examined law enforcement agencies in terms of their prior experience with and perceptions of terrorism, the formation of specialized counter-terrorism and intelligence units, coordination of counter-terrorism and intelligence activities, their information-sharing practices, their terrorism threat assessment activities, and the counter-terrorism intelligence support needs that they identified (Riley et al. 2005: xi–xii).[2] The year before 9/11, only 30 percent of local agencies had conducted threat assessments, but 60 percent had done so the year after 9/11. A correlation existed with the size of law enforcement agencies, in that the larger the local agency, the more likely it was to have done a threat assessment (ibid.: 22). Overall, it is clear that, by 2002, the US Department of Homeland Security initiatives to counter terrorism had increased the use of threat assessments as a law enforcement tool, especially at the state level.

How do threat and risk assessments evaluate protest activity? Public Safety Canada distinguishes "malicious" from "non-malicious" threats. Civil unrest (or protest) is categorized as a non-malicious, unintentional social threat, but listed as adaptive/malicious criminal threats are "extremist acts." The All Hazards Risk Assessment Framework classifies malicious threats as matters of national security (Public Safety Canada 2013). This is significant because national security intelligence discourse has adopted the category of "extremism" as a catch-all for a wide range of political groups and forms of direct action" (Dafnos 2014). While the framing of activists as gang members in the 1980s and 1990s led to a criminalization of protest, and a justification of surveillance, this reframing has different implications. The blurring of categories between criminality, terrorism, and protest facilitates collaboration amongst police, intelligence, military and other first responders, but it also increases the likelihood of a militarized response to protest, by taking the actors and actions being evaluated out of context. Given the logic of threat assessments as described here, protest, when it targets critical infrastructure, is much more likely to be evaluated as "extremism," and/or lead evaluators to overestimate both the capability and intent of protesters.

This designation of extremism is a result of the difficulty evaluating the capability and intent of protesters and partly as a result of the convergence between military, intelligence and law enforcement fields. When one reads threat assessment literature, it is clear that behind the neutral language, there is an ideal type—a Unibomber individual or al-Qaeda-like organization—with plans to attack a valued government or corporate target. However, increasingly, the movements that these threat assessments examine are significantly more fluid, geographically diffuse and unbounded. For example, if I wanted to evaluate the threat of upcoming protests against say, a G8 summit, for which loose networks of protesters from across a region were mobilizing, where would I start? A G8 summit, with plenty of world leaders and trade negotiators, would definitely be considered an important target for authorities to protect, whether labeled as a "National Special Security Event" in the US, or "critical infrastructure" in Canada. After setting up my fusion center to coordinate the collection and analysis of intelligence, I would try to evaluate the capability and intent of those organizing against that event. To do this evaluation, I would initiate two tasks: the first, an analysis of past performance, and the second, an analysis of ongoing organizing. Both tasks are more complicated than they seem. If one is analyzing past performance of a unified actor, one examines police documents, media coverage, interviews, organizational documents, etc. However, because summit protests are organized by networks of individuals and small groups, as well as large formal organizations from various towns, cities, and countries, the question of whose past performance I need to evaluate becomes relevant. If I follow the model given in threat assessments from the 1997 APEC protests in Vancouver and the 2004 RNC protests in New York, I would start by looking at the formal organizations active in the city and region, which can be analyzed relatively straightforwardly, in terms of current size, campaigns, and resources. Once I considered these, I must look elsewhere. If I followed the approach used for threat assessments around the APEC summit, I would examine the political opponents of each delegation to the summit, and then evaluate whether these opponents have any representatives who might attempt to target the event. If I followed the approach taken around the time of the RNC protests in New York City, or the G20 protests in Toronto or London, I would evaluate the history of locally active groups, and would then adopt a broader lens and consider the movement as a whole—in the case of protests against the G8, the global justice movement. In my evaluation of the past performance of the global justice movement and the threat it poses, I'd give the most attention to the most disruptive events—the window smashing, wall breaking, disruption of conferences, and, most of all, the past performance of the "black bloc". Despite the fact that this emphasis on disruption removes these events from any context or dynamics, and collapses many different events in different cities, and at different points in time, it can be used to create warnings like this one from the pre-RNC 2004 intelligence report:

"weapons used in the past have ranged from basic props to sling shots and Molotov cocktails." Such statements can be used as "intelligence" that such weapons may be used in the future. If I combine such decontextualized histories with an analysis of activist rhetoric, it will be easy to justify mass arrests, infiltration, and less-lethal weapons.

Moving from an analysis of historical action to contemporary capacity and intent, I would observe protesters both online and in person. Online surveillance is relatively straightforward—police are widely known to monitor chatrooms, Facebook groups, Twitter feeds and email lists. These media could be analyzed for patterns of interaction, as well as the content of communications—allowing me to offer a portrayal of organizing activity. However, given that many activists are aware of this surveillance and reluctant to organize protests, especially disruptive protests online—"live" surveillance and undercover infiltration would be useful. The logic of threat assessment and its bracketing of political analysis or ethical action make infiltration appear to be a reasonable strategy to gather information. There are many recent examples of police infiltrating organizations and social movement communities to assess "threat." One of the most dramatic cases is, of course, that of British police officer Mark Kennedy, who, as a member of the National Public Order Intelligence Unit (NPOIU), infiltrated the environmental direct action movement in the UK and Europe between 2003 and 2009.

The mandate of the NPOIU (formed in 1999) is "to provide the police service with the ability to develop a national threat assessment and profile for domestic extremism" (Creedon 2013). To do his assessment, Kennedy became deeply involved in the activist community, helping to plan protests, doing direct action and sleeping with numerous activist women before being revealed as a police officer. Two other British police infiltrators went as far as to have children with activist women without revealing their identities. Although some police leaders condemned the relationships as unprofessional, others including Bernard Hogan-Howe, the commissioner of the Metropolitan Police, saw them as inevitable (Lewis and Evans 2013). Such activity is not limited to the UK, in the months leading up to the G20 protests in Toronto, at least two Ontario Provincial Police officers infiltrated organizing bodies, Brenda Doherty posing as "Brenda Carey," a woman fleeing an abusive relationship, and Bindo Showan as "Khalid Mohamed," a building manager (Bennett 2013). Over the course of a year, both became active participants in the activist community, attending cottage weekends, parties, informal dinners and meetings. Brenda even moved into a collective house in Guelph, Ontario. Mohamed was accused of being an infiltrator in Guelph, but simply shifted his activity to Kitchener/Waterloo, subsequently becoming active in Toronto. Both disappeared as the mobilization began, reappearing in court to provide quotes from casual conversations and late-night jokes as evidence for charges of conspiracy to commit mischief. If I patterned my strategy on the approach of these officers, I too would build trusting relationships with activists in order to gain intelligence on "intent and capacity" of these activists to impact a particular event or target. Working with the assumption that I'm infiltrating because the activists are already engaged in criminal activity, the deeper I could penetrate activist networks, the more likely I'd be to discover the most secret information. Although as an infiltrator I would be engaged in face-to-face, emotional relationships with real people, I would need to either bracket the effects of my deception on the activist "targets" as irrelevant, or consider its trauma as informal punishment for engaging in protest activity. Combining an analysis of "past activity" based on worst-case scenarios, and current engagement based on informal conversations, the threat assessment framework flattens political and social activity into a "threat," something to be easily measured, and removed from its meaningful context.

Using evidence from the policing of the 2004 Republican National Convention protests in New York City, we can illustrate how the intelligence- and threat assessment-led strategy of law enforcement authorities constructed protest as a threat.

Construction of a Threat—RNC 2004

The Republican National Convention (RNC) in New York City in 2004 created a unique security context. The biggest city in the US, New York had been the site of the 9/11 attacks three years earlier. This was the first RNC since those attacks. A clear sense existed that this event was a potential terrorist target, if the patterns of the 9/11 attackers, of striking politically and economically important centers of power in the US, were to be followed by others. In attendance were 2,509 delegates, 2,344 alternates, 15,000 members of the media, 15,000 donors, governors, Congressional delegations and staff, and an additional 15,000 family members, friends, and other visitors. Events were held at Madison Square Gardens located at the center of the downtown core, the Javits Center, and 43 different hotels.

By June 2003, the RNC was designated a National Special Security Event (NSSE), which meant that the US Secret Service (USSS) acted as the lead federal agency responsible for coordinating all federal involvement. However, the NYPD was the lead local agency responsible for security (NYPD 2004). A massive security infrastructure was developed, named "Operation Overlord II," in apparent reference to a secret plan during World War II for the Allied invasion of Normandy, codenamed "Overlord."

When all was said and done, police and organizers declared the event security a success. Although there were dozens of protest events, only a few managed to disrupt the convention, and then only briefly. However, during the days of the convention, police arrested 1,806 people, the largest number of arrests in RNC history. Approximately 1,400 of these were arrested for non-criminal conduct such as "Parading Without a Permit" and "Disorderly Conduct." Arrestees were typically held for 24–48 hours in holding areas, for offenses that would otherwise result in only a few hours of detention. Afterwards, dozens of false arrest lawsuits were launched, by hundreds of people (Moynihan 2012). In 2012, Judge Richard Sullivan declared the NYPD mass arrests eight years earlier unconstitutional. NYCLU Executive Director Donna Lieberman commented, "This ruling is a victory for the right to protest—a core democratic principle. It places an important check on the abusive policing tactics used to suppress protests during the 2004 RNC." How does a situation where so many people were pre-emptively monitored (as described below), arrested, and abused become seen as a "successful operation"? The avoidance of disruption of the target is clearly valued over the disruption of arrestees' lives, usual political processes, and the ordinary routines of bystanders. This evaluation is justified through the logic of threat assessment frameworks, which categorize protest as a threat, and manage it through the lens of counter-terrorist operations.

The NYPD strategy for the RNC was dependent on intelligence-gathering operations developed in the post-9/11 era. By 2003, the NYPD had significantly expanded its capacity to collect and analyze intelligence, infrastructure which was central to the RNC policing strategy. According to documents released by the NYPD throughout the course of litigating federal lawsuits, as well as additional documents reviewed by the *New York Times*, teams of undercover NYPD officers traveled around the country, to Canada and Europe, for the purposes of infiltrating activist networks and meetings, gathering information for the daily intelligence reports they filed with the Intelligence Division (Dwyer 2007). David Cohen, the

NYPD's Deputy Commissioner for Intelligence, and an ex-senior official with the CIA, was central to coordinating this aspect of the operation (ibid.). A *New York Times* article reported that, in an affidavit dated September 12, 2002, Mr. Cohen contended that surveillance of domestic political activities was essential to fighting terrorism: "Given the range of activities that may be engaged in by the members of a sleeper cell in the long period of preparation for an act of terror, the entire resources of the N.Y.P.D. must be available to conduct investigations into political activity and intelligence-related issues" (ibid.).

These investigations were organized within a logic of threat assessment. The NYPD's Executive summary of their activities around the 2004 Republican National Convention begins with a "Situation and Threat Assessment" (NYPD 2004). The assessment explains that, although there are no specific threats against the RNC, political conventions and elections are potential terrorist targets, going on to say:

> The use of hazardous materials, including chemical and biological weapons, poses a significant threat as well. Additionally, it is anticipated that New York City will see a volume of protest activity not seen in decades. Organizers from *United for Peace and Justice* predict that 250,000 people will participate in their march and rally scheduled for August 29th. While the vast majority of the participants will be peaceful, the sheer size of the event will place a tremendous strain on the department's resources and severely impact vehicular and pedestrian flow in midtown. Open source information indicates that there will be some individuals and groups, who advocate the use of violence in opposition to the government, seeking to engage in criminal conduct that could significantly endanger public safety. (ibid.)

This description of the threats lumps together an odd assortment of activities. The use of chemical and biological weapons would obviously be a serious concern. It is odd, however, the way that it is introduced, without any evidence that there is in fact, a threat of such weapons present. The real topic of the assessments is protest activity, but its inclusion seems to need further specification—the size of the event and its implications for NYPD resources and traffic flow. The section concludes with this reference to the possibility of violence "in opposition to the government," but relies on "open source information," as its source of information, which seems to imply a Google search. Given that this summary is presented in the

"Executive Summary" for the operation, it seems hardly enough to justify a massive security operation. In response to this situation and threat assessment, the department stated its mission as being to ensure the safety of the citizens of, and visitors to, New York, providing for the security of the RNC, minimizing the inconvenience to commuters, residents, and merchants, and facilitating the rights of others to peacefully protest against the convention. The distinction between locals, visitors, and protesting "others" illustrates the way such protesters are being understood.

In addition to undercover field operations in over a dozen cities, files on groups or individuals were sometimes triggered by a simple web search for evidence of plans or ideas connected to the 2004 RNC. If an organization appeared to be making plans to organize or attend protests, a file was created (Dwyer 2007). Files were created on their political causes, the criminal records, if any, of the people involved and any plans for civil disobedience or disruptive tactics. If a senior police officer could argue that illegal activity was suspected, further investigation and monitoring could ensue.

In the months before the Convention, field and web reports were compiled into RNC Intelligence Situation Reports. These reports included different and inconsistent types of information, which shifted as the date of the convention loomed (NYPD 2004). They included sections on "Major Upcoming Events at the RNC," "Incidents or Demonstration Activities," and a distinct section on "Threats," including bomb threats, threats against protectees, losses, and thefts, etc. For example, on August 26, 2004, the RNC Situation Intelligence Report, categorized as "Suspicious Activity," two men were stopped while taking photographs of empty parking lots and streets in the vicinity of the RNC. They were stopped and had their identities checked. There was a "Middle Eastern man" loitering in a hotel bathroom, and two women were seen videotaping Madison Square Gardens from their vehicle. The report indicates that the man in the hotel was identified and released, and the Joint Terrorism Task Force is looking to find the two videographers. Intelligence operations deem such activity suspicious, and requiring intervention. But the reports also include notes like this one from April 14, 2004. Its headline reads "Local Anti-RNC Activist Group posts 'First Aid' Manuals on Internet Website." It continues:

- The information contained within the manuals prepares the reader to treat activists exposed to tear gas/pepper spray, in addition to

- activists injured by physical confrontation with disorder control personnel.
- The above indicates that participants of direct action protest(s) may be willing to physically resist and confront disorder control personnel.

Such an interpretation interprets protest activities in a way that highlights the most potentially confrontational elements.

The Intelligence Reports also include a section, "RNC Related Internet Discussions." For example, on August 4, 2004, the report noted that activists had posted a call for a direct action referred to as "Chaos on Broadway" on boards across Canada and the US, and that there had been online discussion around the "activist's belief" that the "recent increased level of security in relation to terrorism was announced prior to the RNC so that New York City can raise its alert status to Red, enabling martial law," and thereby disallowing ALL permitted protest activity. Along with such notes, there are extended synopses and evaluations of protester activity at previous convention and summit events seen to be relevant—in particular, the protests in 2000 against the Republican National Convention and Democratic National Convention in Philadelphia and Los Angeles, and the 2001 protests against the Free Trade Area of the Americas in Quebec City. The synopses and evaluations described the past event, its size, the number of arrests, and the charges (but not details on whether those charges ever became convictions). For example, the report noted that the charges laid at the DNC in 2000 in Los Angeles included Assault with a Deadly Weapon on a Peace Officer, Possession of Explosives, Carrying a Concealed Weapon and Possession of Dangerous Fireworks—all charges that suggest these protests were spaces where violent criminals ran amok. In some cases, the reports include details of the lawsuits that emerged as a result of police tactics. There were also reports of prior protests in the UK, and repeated and detailed descriptions of the use of "black bloc" tactics. When combined, these Intelligence Reports portray anti-RNC protesters as wily, organized, violent, powerful, somehow similar to terrorists.

Conclusion

These reports paint a vivid picture of a looming attack by threatening protesters. The way protesters and protest are evaluated is a result of a changed field of protest policing, one where military operations, intelligence infrastructure, policing, and emergency management intersect. In this field, the logic that allows integration of these different arenas is one that defines the critical infrastructure of the status quo as the target that must be defended, which, in turn, makes those that challenge that status quo suspect and threatening.

Clearly, this logic is evident in security operations for a wide range of events including the 2010 G8 and G20 summits. The story of the infiltrators "Brenda" and "Khalid" is a product of a Joint Intelligence Group (JIG), which was formed in 2009 in order to allow RCMP, OPP, local police, and other security services to coordinate their intelligence work. The investigative arm of JIG was called the Primary Intelligence Investigative Team (PIIT). The PIIT had a "mandate to detect, deter, prevent, investigate and/or disrupt threats to the 2010 G8." It used a "wide array of investigative techniques," which included open source information analysis, a review of police reports and more covert techniques such as the recruitment of confidential informants and undercover operations (Groves and Dubinsky 2011). In addition to known infiltrators, the police monitored large numbers of activists, color coding them according to perceived risk level as red (suspect), orange (person of interest) and yellow (associate) (ibid.). The police designated some protesters from anti-capitalist, First Nations, and environmental movements "criminal extremists." Nonetheless, despite this massive intelligence operation, chaos ensued. But the basic logic of the model was not challenged. What did the after-action reports suggest for the future? That there needs to be more intelligence gathering, analysis and sharing in order to disrupt threats.

Sometimes, there is a perception that protesters are targeted because of their political beliefs, effective organizing, and coalition work. This might be part of the story but it also needs to be understood in conjunction with the dominant logic of intelligence-led policing. According to this logic, effective organizing and coalition building is threatening to the status quo because it adds a level of uncertainty and unpredictability to protest. Therefore, when law enforcement works to evaluate a new, amorphous network, with unknown numbers, capacity, and intent, they tend to stop trying to understand protesters' motivations or actions, and instead plan for, and work to pre-empt their worst-case scenario. Given the characteristics of recent waves of protest, this will ensure repeated collisions between movements and law enforcement.

8

Urine-filled Supersoakers

One of the first social rules babies learn is that urine and feces are not toys. Our parents teach us that playing with our poo and pee can make us sick, and that those who do so are not acting "normally." We learn this lesson well, and early. Police repeatedly suggest that protesters violate this taboo. Since anti-WTO protests took place in Seattle in 1999, at police media conferences held prior to major protest events, authorities have repeatedly revealed they possess intelligence suggesting protesters plan to throw or squirt urine at the police. As early as 2000, before BIO2000, a biotech conference held in Boston, Boston Police Sgt. Detective Margot Hill told the *Boston Globe* that Seattle police department officers had briefed Boston police on the tactics of anti-globalization protesters, based on police experience at the WTO a few months prior. In their presentation to the Boston police, the Seattle officers displayed chunks of concrete, BB guns, wrist rockets, and large-capacity squirt guns loaded with bleach and urine. They explained that the anti-WTO protesters in Seattle had also drenched the streets with olive oil and ball bearings, to counter officers on horseback, and lined up peaceful protesters in front of their rowdier cohorts (Martinez 2000). This might sound like the global justice movement had escalated their militancy. Except that there is no evidence that protesters used or did any of these things in Seattle, except the evidence that the police themselves provided. Indeed, when a *New York Times* journalist reported the story of protesters shooting Seattle police with urine-filled squirt guns, citing information from a Detroit police source, the journalist had to retract the story after Seattle authorities confirmed no such thing had happened (Graeber 2004).

Since the 1999 protests, police have repeatedly told the same story in the lead-up to more than 20 protests in Canada, the UK, Australia, and most recently, the US. They claim to know that protesters are planning to squirt or throw urine, feces, and/or bleach at the police. In a quarter of the cases, police in the US and Canada have been more specific, claiming to have evidence that protesters are planning to fill large "Supersoaker" squirt guns with urine. In half of the cases, police have argued that protesters were planning to throw bottles of urine at the police. In a quarter of the cases, police claim to have confiscated bottles of urine from protesters, intended to be thrown at the police.[1] After each protest, police stories of urine and feces continue to circulate, despite the lack of visual evidence or criminal charges (Gostzola 2012). How should we understand the somewhat obsessive police retelling of this story?

In the previous chapter, I suggested that threat assessment logics promoted by well-resourced counter-terrorism initiatives categorize protesters as a threat, and justify increased budgets and a militarized response. The retelling of the urine story would complement such a strategy. But while this explanation is important, the restructuring of the field and its effect on logics of practice, and the distribution of resources are not the only factors at play. While this framework can explain the way police might tell such a story in an instrumental fashion to justify their resources and legitimacy, we must turn to the question of internalized beliefs and interpretive processes, or what Bourdieu calls "habitus," to explain why some police officers seem to believe the story, and why some officers continue to repeat it, despite the lack of evidence. Cultural and emotional dynamics are operating, influencing the construction of police knowledge about protesters. This chapter uses police testimony at court trials, in newspaper articles, in autobiographies, and in police publications to explore the power, meaning, and implications of the repeatedly told story that protesters shoot or throw urine at police. Mapping the telling of this story provides an opportunity to unpack how police knowledge of protesters contributes to the police use of riot control units, barricades, and attempts to control and limit protesters.

The urine story first surfaced in March 2000. It spread rapidly. In 2000 alone, in addition to the aforementioned Boston incident, in April, police in New York City described anti-police brutality protesters throwing bottles of urine at police; the same month, Washington, DC police suggested anti-World Bank and IMF protesters would use the tactic, and in June, Toronto police repeated the story about anti-poverty activists. In July, Philadelphia (RNC) and Los Angeles (DNC) police reported that anti-convention protesters were planning to use urine against police (Berbio et al. 2000, Jackman 2000, Parascandola 2000, Sullivan 2004).

While the story was used at all these events during the first half of 2000, the first written version didn't appear until October 2000, in an issue of *Police Chief Magazine*. The authors—Norman Beasley, an Arizona police officer who later became known for his promotion of fusion centers and threat assessments, Thomas Graham, veteran commanding officer of NYPD's Disorder Control Unit, and Carl Holmberg, who retired from his position as US Park Police Special Forces Commander in 2000—were leading authorities in either intelligence-led policing, or the policing of protest. They argued that protesters had changed:

> While the nature of today's protests has grown more violent and incendiary, seeming to strike without warning, today's protesters are also different from those of past years. They are often more affluent, mobile and educated than their 1960's counterparts, are more sophisticated, and highly organized, have greater resources, and receive more media exposure. Today's protesters are well financed and conduct training camps nationwide to teach activists how to "shut down" systems … Today's protesters also use more drastic tactics to accomplish their goals. They use various locking devices (sleeping dragons, tripods and bicycle lock necklaces) and caltrops to block vehicle and pedestrian traffic. They roll Dumpsters and 55-gallon water drums filled with cement or water into police lines, wield "wrist rockets" to shoot marbles or ball bearings and squirt guns filled with urine or bleach, and use paintball guns to "mark" plainsclothes officers. And they know that an angry, fluid crowd is more difficult to contain than a large, cohesive one. (Beasley, Graham, and Holmberg 2000)

Due partly to the legitimacy of the authors, and partly to the legitimacy of publication, this protester portrait spread and was repeated. From the article in *Police Chief Magazine* to federally funded preparations for the Free Trade Area of the Americas (FTAA) summit in 2003 in Miami, the FBI and Department of Justice appear to play central roles in perpetuating the spreading of this story to the larger law enforcement field, to the media, political leaders and to the public.

In 2004, in apparent response to ongoing questions from the media, activists and civil liberties organizations about the FBI's plans in relation to the mobilizations against the Republican and Democratic National Conventions, the FBI explained on their website:

> We are concerned about large-volume water guns (Super-Soakers) filled with ammonia, bleach or urine; projectiles such as rocks and bottles; incendiary devices such as Molotov cocktails and pyrotechnics; and

even improvised explosive devices such as pipe bombs. For example, at the November 2003 protests at the Free Trade of America conference in Miami, police were attacked with marbles and bolts launched from sling shots and wrist rockets, with rocks, with sticks embedded with razor blades and nails, and with bleach and urine. (FBI 2004)

Despite such warnings, there was no independent record of such attacks on police in Miami, nor was anyone ever charged. However, before the Miami protests, the story had been repeated by a private security consultant, presumably hoping to drum up business (Graeber 2007). The flyer listed possible potential tactics to be used by the soon-to-arrive "anarchists." Citing "police intelligence" as the source, this list included the following protester tactics:

- Wrist rockets—larger hunter-type sling shots that they use to shoot steel ball bearings or large bolts. A very dangerous and deadly weapon.
- Molotov cocktails—many were thrown in Seattle and Quebec and caused extensive damage.
- Crow bars—to smash windows, cars, etc. They also pry up curbs, then break the cement into pieces that they can throw at police officers. This was done extensively in Seattle.
- Squirt guns—filled with acid or urine.

When the protesters in Miami did not use these tactics, the police subsequently claimed effective policing had forestalled their use.

Effects of Stories about Urine

When a police spokesperson says, "the protesters are planning to throw urine at police," or some related story, there are implications. Whether or not the spokesperson believes the story, the telling dehumanizes protesters, and the idea that the protesters are somehow less than human can spread through the media to law enforcement, civilian authorities and the public, triggering a whole cascade of reactions before the protest event, including restrictions on protest, and increased police spending, and afterwards, justifying charges against and the use of militarized tactics against protesters. Examples of these effects include:

- Citing protesters' use of urine attacks on police at the 2000 Los Angeles Democratic National Convention, a Boston judge ruled in 2004, that the establishment of a protest zone to police the 2004 DNC was a "reasonable" way to contain demonstrators.
- Citing the same incident in Los Angeles (never confirmed by any source), Denver City Council passed a bylaw prohibiting the carrying of urine or feces for the purposes of throwing on people in anticipation of the 2008 DNC.
- In 2004, the NYPD cited past use of "urine or bleach in supersoakers" to justify mass arrests in the lead-up to the RNC (NYPD 2004).
- Ramsey County Attorney Susan Gaertner, who lead the prosecution of protesters arrested at anti-RNC protests in St. Paul, Minnesota in 2008, justified criminal charges of "conspiracy to riot, with the purpose of furthering terrorism" against activists declaring that activists were not charged with committing civil disobedience. Instead, she argued, "They are charged with planning to do things like break windows, trash squad cars, throw feces and urine at police officers" (Snyders 2008).
- In 2001, police in Long Beach, California defended their use of rubber bullets and beanbag projectiles against protesters, arguing that protesters had thrown bottles, some of which were filled with feces and urine.
- In 2003, at the Miami anti-FTAA protests, Lt. Bill Schwartz, spokesperson for the Miami Police Department argued that the police were pelted with rocks, feces in plastic bags and bottles of urine in his justification of police baton charges on protesters (Goldberg 2003).
- In 2013, Texas Department of Safety justified the searches of pro-choice activists by claiming that jars of urine and feces had been found in their bags (Schladen 2013).

The way the story of protesters' urine attacks justifies militarized responses can be better understood by looking closely at a single event. I'll explore the use of and effects of this story on the policing of an anti-poverty protest in Toronto in June 2000.

Case Study: June 15th, 2000—Anti-Poverty March, Toronto Ontario
By June 2000, the urine story had gained powerful momentum, and surfaced during police preparations against anti-poverty protesters in

Toronto. In some ways, this is surprising, because unlike the protests against the Organization of American States summit in Windsor, Ontario ten days earlier, anti-poverty organizers were planning a protest which would be largely a local affair. The thousand-strong march left from a downtown park and arrived at the Parliament buildings at Queen's Park with the demand of addressing the Provincial Parliament to argue against the Provincial cuts to social assistance, and social housing. In the context of the energetic days of the global justice movement, the protesters' rhetoric and tone was militant. The group had marched on the Federal Parliament buildings in Ottawa in February and November 1999, overturning barricades and being pepper sprayed by police. Gaining momentum, the June protest intended to bring the focus on the Provincial government.

The police were similarly determined. Like the protesters, less than six months after the Seattle protests, the Toronto police were incorporating new ideas about tactics, and the global justice movement from US, UK, and Canadian sources into their policing strategy for the anti-poverty protest. By examining police testimony recorded in transcripts from the trials of three OCAP leaders charged with counseling participation in and participating in a riot we can see the way that intelligence in general, and the urine story in particular became central to police preparations for the protest, and justifications of their actions. When asked by lawyer Peter Rosenthal during cross-examination about preparations police had made for the protest, Superintendent Adrian Maher explained:

> Well I would think with the prior Intelligence on this, the fact that we knew it was going to be a violent demonstration, not just the projectiles but the crowd itself—the bandannas going over the mouths—mattresses used to charge the barricades, that's a clear indication that there is going to be some violence.[2]

The intelligence that Maher refers to seems to be grounded in the information given by Toronto Police Service Intelligence Officer Steve Irwin, who noted in his testimony that the activists had said, "we will not be stopped."

Police testified that, months before the protest, they had been warned that protesters might use Supersoakers filled with urine. How had this idea been introduced to the Toronto police? Intelligence Officer Steve Irwin testified that police officers had watched videos of past protests and had learned that protesters had thrown or squirted urine on police in past protests (Cross Examination).

During the cross-examination of Steve Irwin, the source of the urine story is asked for, but not provided. Irwin notes that Staff Sergeant Gillispie "has researched this circumstance." Nonetheless, when briefing officers on the morning of the demonstration, Irwin underlines the information as being learned from Seattle, Washington, and Windsor. The detail clearly made an impact, as all of the dozen or so officers' notebooks provided as documents for court included the notation, "urine in supersoakers." Or simply, "urine." The Toronto Police Service Tactical Unit Head, Sergeant Wes Ryan, testified, "Intelligence gave us a briefing first thing in the morning and they advised us to expect things like bleach and urine, and squirt guns or super soakers, to expect projectiles." When asked how they had come to have this intelligence, Ryan only notes that it was a standard intelligence briefing.

Despite the vagueness of its source, such information influenced the police preparations for the day by leading police to consult with outside authorities about potential charges that might be laid. Lawyer Peter Rosenthal asks Irwin about the meaning of a section in the deployment plan for the 51 and 52 Divisions of the Toronto Police which reads: "On this date we will arrest persons observed to have water pistols in their possession for the offence of assault on the reasonable grounds that they are filled with some noxious substance; where the pistol is found to contain only water the person will be released, no charges" (January 17, 2002: 2). Irwin explains that such a phrase would suggest that "obviously someone has spoken to Crown Counsel and asked, 'what about this?'"

In addition to legal preparations, the story also stimulated a strong emotional response in officers. This may have influenced police interpretations of protester actions. During cross-examination at the preliminary hearing for the trial of three organizers of the June 15, 2000 anti-poverty protest in Toronto, Sergeant Brian Smith, a member of the Public Safety Unit, described his experiences at the protest:

That day we were assigned in front of the Legislature. When we originally started out there were two squads there. I was with one of the squads. I did not have my shield and it was just the twelve of us there. What eventually became the rioters attacked. As time went on we were able to disperse the crowd. I received numerous assaults. I was covered head to toe in paint, urine, faeces. My whole gun belt was destroyed. Parts inside my gun had to be replaced. I even had some ... I had a smell of gasoline on my uniform too.

The officer then goes on to describe an assault during which he was hit on the right side. "I did not see it coming and I was just flattened out on my left side," describing how he felt hands on him, and saw the face of someone grabbing him, who he identifies as one of the defendants. The lawyer then asks the officer, "Did you at all retaliate?" The officer replies, "No, the only thing in my mind is to get free. I mean it's ... one of the worst things that can happen is for an officer to be dragged into a crowd because the crowd only has one intent and that's to kill the officer" (*R. v. Clarke* 2002: 60) Clearly, this officer is telling a story about being terrified by the protesters. He obviously has a strong, emotionally charged interpretation of what occurred. His belief that protesters would kill him is not simply based on the story of urine in Supersoakers. The fear is likely rooted in his prior knowledge of protesters, combined with intelligence briefings about urine in Supersoakers and his personal observations of an unusually militant crowd, all of which led Sergeant Smith to manufacture the story of being "covered" in the urine he was warned about prior to the protest. The warning he received in intelligence briefings, about violent anti-poverty protesters, has set the stage for confrontation, fear, and even distortion of the truth.

Storytelling

The urine story continues to circulate among police authorities and, increasingly, the public. It was used in reference to anti-G20 protesters in Toronto (2010), student protesters in London, England (2010), and recently, pro-choice protesters in Texas (2013) (Cunningham 2010, Davenport, Moore-Bridger, and Parsons 2010, Luthra 2013). It is most frequently told with respect to protesters attending US protests, especially mobilizations against political conventions and G-series events, but the story is also told about anti-poverty, pro-choice, anti-police brutality and anti-capitalist protests. Strategic reasons alone can't explain the repetition of the urine story by police. Instead, in order to understand the popularity of this story, the relationship between the field of policing, and the internalized police knowledge of protesters must be examined.

Earlier chapters in the book drew upon the framework of della Porta and her collaborators in showing how changes in the configuration of political power and organizational features of police forces, combined with their interactions with protesters, influence protest policing.[3] But as della Porta and Reiter (1998) note, all of these influences are filtered through police knowledge, defined as "the police's perception of external reality," which includes their perception of their own role, the movement, the protest event and the protesters themselves. In order to use this conception of police knowledge to explain why the story of protesters attacking the police with urine and feces resonates and is retold, we can use Bourdieu's understanding of habitus, as "the socially constituted principle of perception and appreciation' that gives actors a feel for the rules of the game (De Bartolo 2008, Wacquant 1992: 21). Learned through both formal training and informal socialization, such a "principle of perception and appreciation" influences understandings of right and wrong, valuable and worthless, legitimate and illegitimate protest and protesters. As a participant joins a social group, they will adapt their behavior and attitudes in order to assist in their social survival (Bourdieu 1977). Recognizing that such principles, or habituses tend to be shared by those in similar positions within a field, we can begin to understand how the police story that protesters are planning to attack them with urine resonates with their understanding of protesters, who appear to be unpredictable and hostile.

Police Habitus

Police incorporate knowledge of protesters into their habitus through their civilian socialization, through their participation in police subculture and through the on-the-job accumulation of training, formal intelligence briefings and past interactions with particular movement organizations or activists. Before becoming police officers, individuals will have developed conceptions of protesters through basic socialization, the media, and possibly through interactions with protesters they know. Research suggests that police recruits at their time of enlistment are more conservative than other members of the public (Cook 1977, Potter 1977). Early studies found that there was a "police personality" that tended to be attracted to the police—one that is authoritarian and conservative—but this idea has been challenged in recent years and replaced with a more complex framework (Balch 1972). Despite increasing racial and gender diversity in the police, recent studies suggest that police officers have more conservative and authoritarian attitudes than the general public (Mignon and Holmes 1999), and would be unlikely to have had positive interactions with politically motivated protesters.

As police cadets, individuals gradually become socialized into their professional identity and the culture of the police. In Chapter 4, I show how an identity is constructed through boundaries, interactions, and stories. Police training builds and reinforces a shared professional identity by activating the boundary between police and civilians, increasing the interactions within the boundary, and limiting the interactions across that boundary. Training builds and reinforces police identity through story-telling about who police are and aren't, and about those who the police interact with on a regular basis, including protesters. Interestingly, research on police academy training tends to reduce authoritarianism, but not racist, attitudes. Once recruits begin their field training, their authoritarianism and aggressiveness again increases (Rosenbaum, Schuck, and Cordner 2011, Wortley and Homel 1995).

Specialized public order or crowd control training will explicitly tell stories about protesters, and how to relate to them as well as past protest. Training documents for a workshop offered to Waterloo Regional Police officers participating as part of the Integrated Security Unit at the 2010 G20 protests included extensive reference to the OCAP protest of June 15, 2000 discussed in this chapter. The instructors explained that John Clarke had incited the riot, but wasn't convicted due to bad note taking and poor communication by police. They explain that the failures at this past event underline the importance of clear communication and record keeping at the upcoming one. The trainers also teach the officers the difference between protesters and anarchists, explaining that "protesters are there to be heard and to express themselves, and anarchists may have similar goals (or not) but choose distinctly different methods. Not all protesters are anarchists. An anarchist is someone who believes that governments should be abolished, and are willing to use a lawless action to attain their goal" (Waterloo Regional Police Service 2010, original emphasis). Even though protesters in this context are presented as relatively benign, compared with the incomprehensible anarchists, they are not presented as rational, political actors. This is even more the case during the realistic enactments of protests that police trainers utilize to prepare public order units. During such events, which are often widely promoted to friendly media, police act as protesters, chanting nonsensically as they perform sit-ins, attempt to push through police lines, and throw projectiles. Such trainings also recreate the division between "well-meaning and passive protesters" and "violent, criminal anarchists."

Police Culture

Police subcultures also influence police knowledge of protesters and protest (Wahlstrom 2007: 392). Rob Reiner (1992, 2000) describes police culture as being action oriented, pessimistic, conservative, suspicious, cynical, macho, and pragmatic. Ruess-Ianni and Ianni (1983) describe the ethos of police culture as including bravery, autonomy, secrecy, isolation, and solidarity. Law enforcement observers note that police culture makes it difficult for officers to admit weakness or obtain assistance dealing with their own mental and emotional health (Malmin 2012). Although the characteristics vary by force and rank, overall, police culture contributes to a general suspicion about both protesters, and their activities. The conservative and macho aspects of the subculture also reduce the likelihood that a police officer will break the "thin blue line" of police solidarity, facilitating police brutality and abuse. Indeed, Winnipeg Police Service Inspector Robert G. Hall cited a study by the National Institute of Ethics done in 1999 and 2000 that found that 79 percent of US police recruits acknowledged the existence of a "Code of Silence" and it didn't bother 52 percent of them (Hall 2002). While interaction with protesters can reduce the hostility between protesters and police, longstanding cultural norms can contradict this process (Wahlstrom 2007).

Police Learning

Most explicitly, officers gain information about particular protesters and social movement organizations from formal intelligence briefings, interactions with the protesters themselves, and direct command, depending on their rank. Officers will respond to this information differently and emphasize different elements differently in different contexts. I'll talk more about this later. Police knowledge about protesters changes over time but, like any regularized interaction, tends to follow particular scripts, sometimes being particularly reliant on stereotyped understandings of "good" (predictable, cooperative, with clear, resolvable goals) and "bad" (unpredictable, ideological, uncooperative, professional, with radical goals) protesters (della Porta and Reiter 1998: 25–6, Noakes, Klocke and Gillham 2005: 208). "Good" protesters are often portrayed by police as routine collectivities, apolitical much like festival goers or sports fans, but as ones who are tied to "democracy" and "freedom." "Bad" protesters are also presented as apolitical, but also criminal and threatening. Police appear particularly likely to characterize protesters as "bad" when there is a great deal of uncertainty about and/or limited information on, the protesters (Wahlstrom 2007: 397). Such uncertainty is particularly likely when a protest attracts unknown actors from beyond the local context, when those protesters don't negotiate with police, when multiple police agencies must work together, when regular budgets are supplemented, and when there is a significant amount of media and political attention on the event. In such situations, police legitimacy is under scrutiny and agencies justifying militarized action will be particularly likely to characterize protesters as "bad" or "troublemakers."

Conclusion

Police perceptions of and stories about protesters can be complicated. Like any set of stories, they vary and often contradict one another. And like many stories, they tend to fit into particular genres–stories of heroes and villains; stories of overcoming obstacles and of restoring order; stories of well-meaning people, and of manipulated fools. Some of the punchlines in these stories activate boundaries that justify the existence of political institutions, of democracy, constitutions, and human rights, while others justify extreme action and heroism. However, the story about protesters shooting or throwing urine at police goes beyond a simple stereotype of bad protesters—it holds a particular emotional intensity. Such a story is not one simply of threat, but is also rooted in widespread and deep taboos about those who touch human waste. This potency goes beyond the police, to the general public, who would easily recognize the taboo about touching human waste, and indeed even throwing it at people. This triggers emotional reactions. Of course the interactions between police and protesters are often emotionally laden (Jasper 2011). Arrests, police beatings, and the use of less-lethals can provoke feelings of shock, fear, and anger. Police too, respond emotionally to protest contexts. Research shows that police may feel irritation, contempt, and anger with protesters

(Wahlstrom 2007). A story of urine attacks can transform distrust into disgust and horror.

The story dehumanizes and depoliticizes the protesters, although it doesn't decriminalize their action, presenting the urine attacks as clearly pre-meditated and intentional. Consider also the stories of activist training about excrement throwing, or protester plans for squirting urine found in the memoir of retired cop Richard Greelis, who writes about his time as an undercover police officer at the 2008 Republican National Convention. Greelis describes how National Lawyers Guild and other radical legal activists and videographers monitor protests, how they film police actions and turn off their video cameras while "protesters surreptitiously pelted officers with rocks, garbage, excrement and urine squirted from Supersoakers" (Greelis 2009: 381). He also reports that an activist house was found that contained "buckets" of urine—something that was later downscaled to one bucket of urine, that could be explained by the lack of an operational toilet in the house (Jardin 2008). Greelis tells us too that during the RNC in St. Paul/Minneapolis, an intelligence team arrested a young man with a "backpack laden with bottled urine" (Greelis 2009: 407).

When police tell this story, does it always mean that they believe protesters plan to throw urine on them? Probably not. But they often act as if they do. Once a story like this becomes certified by police spokespeople, repeated in the media and by city councilors, used to justify laws, restrictions on normal life, and lay charges and justify actions, it becomes intensely real. So much so that some police officers will describe being soaked with urine even though nothing of the kind has happened to them.

Given the centrality of intelligence-led policing in developing protest police strategy, and the desire to evaluate threat, stories that trigger hostile emotional reactions to protesters are likely to trigger police militarization and pre-emptive control. As I've noted, intelligence-led policing attempts to identify threats in order to direct available policing resources appropriately. In the high-pressure situation of a summit protest, with the strain to perform, long lead time, complex chain of command, and high budget, there is a lot of room for a story like "protesters with urine" to trigger a cascade of reactions.

At each stage of police preparation for a protest—gathering, interpreting, and sharing intelligence; the public presentation of intelligence as a justification of strategy; and the interpretation of protester behavior and rhetoric—a story, for example, about how protesters plan to squirt urine on police, becomes further certified, gains legitimacy, and triggers the likelihood of militarized policing. The confluence of the two trends—intelligence-led policing and militarized policing—when combined with police stereotypes of protesters, and limited interactions with protesters, creates a recipe for trouble. As policing networks are increasingly globalized, and ongoing uncertainty about how best to manage protests continues, this recipe, despite the fact that its veracity is repeatedly undermined, continues to spread to new cities and contexts.

9
Crisis and Control

In the best-selling "Hunger Games" series, the corporate/government entity known as the "Capitol" forces randomly selected young people to fight each other to the death for popular entertainment. The Games are widely watched and are intended to distract the population from the deprivations in their own lives, and from the system as a whole. The contemporary equivalent might be the cop shows, watching police arrest poor people, people of color, and immigrants. Or, for the anti-capitalist crowd, the streams of "riot porn" on YouTube: footage of battles between the police and protesters, showing us that dissent is unwise but that it's possible, indeed heroic, to challenge the police.

Whether the goal is an end to the tar sands, tuition increases, or immigrant detention, we must return to the streets to challenge the legitimacy of the leaders and systems that are destroying our communities and earth's balance. But like a nightmare of digital animation, the number of police multiply, gaining more weapons, building higher fences, aiming more cameras. As their police lines build, filling those streets, especially with marginalized or vulnerable communities, seems more and more dangerous. The police are militarizing the field of protest policing, and pre-empting our mobilizations.

The preceding pages try to explain why this nightmare has become our reality. To do so, I wanted to push beyond explanations that fix the police as a consistent demon, and beyond explanations that determine their behavior solely as a result of capitalism, or of state power, or of micro-level interactions. As I discussed in Chapter 1, it is important to see the police both as a tool of economic elites and political powerholders, to maintain their power and as a force with relative autonomy which struggles to maintain its own position. To link the macro to the micro, I argued that elements of neoliberal globalization have both transformed the field of policing, and increased the influence of professional policing organizations, the security and defense industries, military actors and private security consultants in that field and has led police to interpret protest activity as threatening.

To review the argument from previous chapters, it would read as follows:

- Global integration and neoliberal restructuring increase the volatility and effects of economic fluctuations, and decrease the capacity of most states to manage those fluctuations, leading to ongoing political and economic crises.
- Global integration and neoliberal restructuring have rapidly increased diffusion and brokerage amongst both police actors and those challenging the system, leading to waves of protest, with corresponding overreactions by police, corresponding threats to the legitimacy of police, and increasingly polarized interactions between police and protesters.
- Such processes reinforce the "thin blue line" of police identity, increasing the likelihood of greater integration and isomorphism amongst police practices.
- The effect of global integration and neoliberal restructuring on these threats has increased the influence of already dominant police agencies, defense industry actors and professional policing networks in global policing networks who offer "best practices" to police agencies working to maintain their power and legitimacy within the context of these crises.
- These challenges also increase the likelihood that police agencies rely on stereotyped understandings of protesters, further facilitating militarized strategies. For the reasons given earlier, these conditions are becoming more frequent.

This argument rests on a number of assumptions. To begin with, I'm assuming that police institutions are in some ways very similar to other state institutions, but that they also play a unique role in defending the status quo. They are similar in the pressures that they face to other publicly funded state institutions in that they compete for various forms of capital, they face crises of legitimacy and mandate, and they are under pressure to privatize, justify spending, increase their use of new technologies, display their results, and integrate transnationally. In the face of challenges, they, like other institutions, rely on their existing knowledge of change and social order, and tend to react most strongly against critics when they believe their resources are under threat. At the same time, I recognize that policing institutions are in some ways very different to other state institutions, as their mandate and resources often continue to grow while other publicly funded operations are cut. They are also, of course, traditionally the sole purveyors of armed force legitimized by the state, operating domestically.

While there are broad shared characteristics amongst police agencies, particularly police agencies within a single nation-state, local and national political, economic and social contexts affect the autonomy and practices of police, and the dynamics in the national and local field can facilitate or limit both the manifestation and experience of local crises in protest policing, influencing the incorporation of new approaches, or the maintenance of existing ones. However, the pressures of globalizing policing fields or large-scale events that garner national or international attention have a similar influence on policing in different spaces. Mega-security events, such as the summit gatherings of international leaders, institutions and political conventions create defining moments for particular agencies and leaders, and reorganize the relations of the police, and their struggles for legitimacy, resources, and autonomy both locally and within broader networks, making both crisis, and militarization more likely. For two examples of international events that created the conditions for both militarization and crisis, we need only to look at the G20 summits in London and Toronto.

Throughout this text, I've located the militarization of protest policing within broader logics and practices that are tied to a globalizing and neoliberalizing field of policing. In this way, the logic of the strategic incapacitation model is a transparent mode of social control. This becomes clear to me if I imagine myself as a police commander whose job and legitimacy depended on effectively maintaining the status quo. I'd want to focus my attention on those protesters most likely or willing to disrupt. I'd try to prevent them from organizing and from acting, and I'd use the strategy that seemed to achieve this end most easily, while avoiding "on the job" and "off the job" trouble from the public or other authorities. I would try to convince the activists that they didn't need to disrupt, and encourage them to trust me. If they resisted my advances, I'd try to limit their influence, separate them and their nefarious deeds from others who might be inspired by their militant approach. Through physical separation, or sowing distrust between them and the others, I'd try to contain and isolate them. I'd work to maintain the appearance of order, through careful management. Regardless of its politics, I would evaluate protest and protesters in terms of the threat that it posed to the existing order. Some groups, of course, I would find difficult to evaluate, making them suspicious and demanding more serious intervention. Within this logic, protest needs to be managed, contained, and potentially eliminated.

One can see this logic in action within the court transcripts surrounding arrests from the early 2002 protests against the World Economic Forum. In these transcripts, Thomas Graham, then deputy chief of the NYPD, who arrested 16 animal rights activists from Stop Huntington Animal Cruelty (SHAC), explains his approach to a small march within the high-profile convergence protest, the first large demonstrations in New York City since the attacks of 9/11. SHAC had a reputation for using direct action tactics, including property destruction in their attempts to pressure Huntingdon Life Sciences, the largest animal-testing operation in Europe, to stop testing chemicals, cosmetics, and other products on the 70,000 animals in their facility. In New York, the SHAC activists didn't have a permit to march, and refused to negotiate with police, which, combined with their past history, caused Graham concern. During his examination, Graham was asked when the SHAC protest became unlawful; he explains that

> Had this group negotiated with us, my perception of lawlessness would have been after the window broke ... But because this group did not negotiate with us, as far as I'm concerned as of Madison Avenue, when I saw the conduct between Fifth and Madison Avenue, there was enough to take people into custody. It was illegal ... once they blocked the sidewalk going down 76th Street—they weren't blocking Fifth Avenue. But once they crossed the street en masse—because they were all stretched out all over the place.

This internationally renowned expert in public order is arguing that even before a window got smashed, he perceived the protesters as unlawful because the protesters hadn't negotiated with the police before walking down the sidewalk. The second time he understands them as unlawful is when they had crossed the street en masse. The justification of this evaluation was tied to the prior intelligence about SHAC, a group who Graham notes:

Manhattan North [precinct] has reported to me or had reported to me that they have had acts against residences prior to 2002, where they target executive's residences. There's a couple of 19th Precinct locations they target. They tend to be a little bit more willing to take a collar. They'll break a window. They'll throw paint. They'll throw blood. They don't even throw real paint. They throw water-based paint that you can wash away.

The logic described in this testimony illustrates the way that negotiated management has broken down, and intelligence-led policing, with its influence on strategic incapacitation clearly justifies mass arrest by 2002. Many other examples can be seen throughout the book, from the Metropolitan Police Department's kettling and arrest of 400 anti-capitalist and anti-war protesters in Washington, DC, due to intelligence reports that the protesters intended disruption, and because one protester had broken a window. Similarly, the SPVM used pepper spray projectiles on student protesters in Montreal who intended to march without a permit, and the Toronto Police Services' riot control units at the G20 summit kettled protesters in order to stop them from marching, similar to the mass arrest of Occupy Wall Street marchers in New York. In each case, police used their powers to control the actions of unarmed demonstrators, justified by a perception that those who challenge the status quo are threatening, because they refused to negotiate and operate within existing routines. As Graham notes in his discussion of the SHAC protest, "This group was not willing to negotiate at all. I don't know why they even allowed the march in the first place." Clearly, protesters could be stopped simply for marching down the sidewalk without a permit. Within the logic of strategic incapacitation, the maintenance of order trumps any right to protest.

This logic, and the attendant tactics and technologies, are diffusing through professional policing networks. Graham was one of the authors of the article written in *Police Chief Magazine* in 2000 that argued that the anti-globalization protesters were willing to use violent tactics, and a new model of policing was required. He retired as a deputy chief, the commanding officer of the Disorder Control Unit in 2009, and from the NYPD in 2010. He now operates his own consultancy firm. Similarly, after finishing his work with the NYPD, the LAPD and other major police agencies in the US, Chief William Bratton launched his own consultancy firm until he was reappointed as NYPD Police Commissioner. As a consultant he advised over a hundred police forces. His expertise is sought after, respected, and legitimated. Experts like Graham and Bratton are increasingly powerful in a field of law enforcement more internationally integrated than ever before (Roberts and Roberts 2007).

The widespread influence of such leaders within the field of policing illustrates the increasing diffusion of new tools and strategies, including Tasers, pre-emptive mass arrest and control barriers. This new repertoire of protest policing can best be understood within its changing economic and political context. As repeated crises erupt in different cities and nation-states, police organizations struggle for legitimacy with other players, and influence local and national policies and practices for protest policing. Understanding these policies and practices requires an examination of the interplay amongst these different actors, and the operation of diffusion processes on the police decision to arrest, or to ignore protesters.

Understanding the dynamics behind the militarization of protest policing may offer strategic insights to those struggling against the militarization of protest policing in their own particular location. Within an unequal, capitalist state system, police agencies are unlikely to avoid abuse and corruption. However, the form, nature, and extent of this abuse and corruption vary. Understanding that there is variation in the dynamics of and levels of police legitimacy in different cities, activists can analyze the current struggles amongst the police and different powerholders and put pressure on them accordingly. It is useful to look for the triggering incidents for tactical change in a particular force, and recognize the way the spread of innovative "best practices" promoted by professional policing organizations are offered as solutions. As I've discussed earlier, a similar sequence of processes can be identified behind the introduction of CEDs, pepper spray, LRADs and threat assessment models to police forces. If we pay attention to the ways that protest policing creates legitimacy problems for police agencies, we can begin to be more strategic in our attempts to challenge their militarization. The story I described in this book suggests that when police are critiqued for their past protest policing strategy, or are put into a position where they are uncertain about the most appropriate strategy to take in a future protest, they turn to the experts, and are particularly likely to incorporate practices promoted by private sector and military analysts. This doesn't mean we shouldn't challenge the police on their current practices. But it does suggest that when we do so, we must be strategic, and ensure that we call into question not simply a particular technology or practice, but link that challenge to the legitimacy of both the policing "experts" and their supporters, and the policing logics of controlling populations as a whole. To be clear, I'm not suggesting that we dismiss attempts to reform police behavior and policy. Even when such campaigns don't challenge the police as a whole, such demands for police accountability and against particular programs and technologies can provide tools that can increase oversight, and limit police abuse—at least temporarily or in certain contexts. The difference between a Taser and a de-escalation technique can mean the difference between death and life. A demand for better note taking by police as part of a lawsuit by those victimized by the police can redistribute wealth from city budgets, and build the capacity of those seeking a more just system.

Due to its widespread criminalization of protest, including protest by relatively privileged sections of the population, strategic incapacitation triggers movements that challenge the police. When police arrest, beat, gas, and imprison protesters, and infiltrate their groups, they reveal the brutality of a system that affects hundreds of thousands of people, especially people of color, poor people, every day. Some of these activists build organizations and successful campaigns against youth prisons, against police practices like the NYPD's "Stop and Frisk," and against immigration detention. Successful lawsuits, such as the class action lawsuit by Partnership for Civil Justice Fund in Washington, DC, put pressure on police agencies and their civilian supporters, costing them money for their abuses, while challenging existing practices, and establishing new ones in ways that will, at least temporarily, make them more accountable to, and reliant on, civilian oversight bodies. In contexts where the police face little organized resistance, protest policing strategies may become more and more vicious.

If the goal is to strengthen a social system that treats people with dignity, that ensures that people have what they need to flourish, that ensures that diverse relationships of care, responsibility, equity, and justice are valued, then we need to demilitarize our relationships. This process will be under way for generations to come, but as it stands, there is a great deal we don't yet know about the workings of the repressive arm of the system and how to most effectively challenge and contain it. By unpacking the dynamics that drive social, economic, and political inequalities and the forces that maintain them, we gain leverage and capacity for this work.

Notes

Chapter 1   Introduction

1. See also Todd Gordon, 2006. *Cops, Crime and Capitalism: The Law and Order Agenda in Canada*; Mark Neocleous, 1996. *Administering Civil Society: Towards a Theory of State Power.*

2. Although I build on research that uses interviews with police, and make direct use of police documents, along with my observations of and conversations with police at policing conferences and events, I did not do any formal interviews with police decision makers. Such interviews are understandably difficult to access for they are understood to be critical of police practice. Other activist/scholars like Alex Vitale (2005) have also tried to interview police, to no avail.

Chapter 2   Policing Waves of Protest

1. LexisNexis search of all North American media sources for the keywords "pepper spray," "protesters," and "protest" in a search of all available North American media sources.

2. LRAD Product Overview: <http://www.lradx.com/site/content/view/15/110/>.

3. For British debate around kettling published in *The Guardian*, see O'Connor (2009), Christian (2009), Lewis (2009).

4. This figure is obtained by analyzing a dataset of Occupy arrests developed by Occupy Research activists. Only arrests that have been confirmed are included: <http://occupyarrests.moonfruit.com/>.

Chapter 3   To Serve and Protect Who? Policing Trends and Best Practices

1. Following the approach of Charles Tilly and his collaborators on the Contention in Great Britain and Contention in France projects, I searched for the terms "protest," "protesters," "demonstrators," "demonstrated" and "rallied," using the Factiva newspaper search engine. I reviewed each "hit" for evidence of a protest over ten people in each city. With the goal of creating a profile of protest policing rather than contention in general, I restricted myself to the dominant English-language newspaper in each city. The four newspapers included in the sample were the *Toronto Star*, the *New York Times*, the *Montreal Gazette* and the *Washington Post*. It is clear that this small sample of events is only a fraction of the protest events occurring. Past research suggests that this method may only capture 5–10 percent of the total events (Wood 2004). While each newspaper will have its particular reporting style and politics, all of these newspapers are contemporary North American publications, using similar practices around newsworthiness. They are biased in relatively consistent ways that will still

allow us to pick up the ebbs and flows of protest, and particularly the dramatic incidents where protesters and police clash. However, the specifics of police practices are not always covered. Arrests or the use of less-lethal weapons are more consistently included in coverage. The use of barricades, surveillance or riot control units are not. Most of the time, standard media practice is to emphasize "both sides" of a conflict, downplaying the disproportionate use of force

Chapter 4   Local Legitimacy and Struggles for Control

1. NB: Montreal has a complex municipal structure, which came into being in 2006. In 2004, a city-wide referendum undid *some* of the consequences of the 2002 amalgamation: 15 localities voted to become nominally independent again, meaning that they ceased to be boroughs (*arrondissements*) of Montreal. As a result, the mayors of these 15 so-called "reconstituted municipalities" (*villes de banlieue reconsitutuéés*) do not sit on the city council (*conseil municipal*). Rather, they attend a *parallel* assembly—the agglomeration council—along with the "overall" mayor of Montreal and 15 borough mayors (of the overall mayor's choosing). In theory, the public security commission (CSP) answers to the agglomeration council. In practice, however, the CSP is beholden to the city council, since the agglomeration councils' 16 "city members" hold 87.3 percent of the voting rights, and because the executive committee, whose planning jurisdiction includes the SPVM, reports directly to the city council (see "Democratic Life" in the "City Hall" section of the Montreal website, accessed February 27, 2009 <http://ville.montreal.qc.ca/portal/page?_pageid= 133,301697&_dad=portal&_schema=PORTAL>).

2. Cases and/or allegations of professional misconduct by SPVM officers are usually adjudicated first by the force's internal affairs department (an adjunct to the office of the police chief), and then passed on to the committee.

3. Montreal experienced a 25 percent reduction in the crime rate between 2002 and 2012 Montreal 2012, *Operating Budget at a Glance.*

4. Author's notes, Operational Planning and Public Safety Events Workshop. February 19 and 20, 2013, Toronto.

5. Police Services Act, RSO 1990, c. P.15.

6. There has been a significant amount of controversy about the effectiveness of the SIU, attributed to a perceived pro-police orientation among investigators, but also from a lack of cooperation from the police.

7. Adequacy and Effectiveness of Police Services, O. Reg. 3/99.

8. The regulation also contains a section regarding Emergency Response Services that includes tactical units. This section includes requirements for procedures for tactical units and perimeter/containment functions (sections 21–4).

9. <http://www.toronto.ca/wes/techservices/oem/history2.htm>.

Chapter 5   Officers Under Attack—The Thin Blue Line, Pepper Spray, and Police Identity

1. Mace, or CS or CN sprays, were taken off the market because of a high number of injuries associated with them, and because of their inability to influence individuals affected by alcohol and/or drugs.

2. It is important to note that the use of pepper spray against protesters is difficult to evaluate. Although its use is often a relatively dramatic and newsworthy event, we have no sense of whether all incidents would be recorded in the media. I looked at an event catalogue of all protest events covered in the media sources included in the search engine Factiva's search of mass media between 1993 and 2008, results of a search of all North American media sources using the keywords "pepper spray," "protesters," and "protest." According to these results, OC spray was first used against protesters in the US and Canada in 1993, although as I noted earlier, the RCMP approved its use as a crowd-control tool a year earlier.

3. AP newswires; *San Francisco Chronicle*, April 29, 1997; July 14, 1998 AP newswires; *Kitchener-Waterloo Record*, June 5, 1997; July 5, 1997 *Washington Times*; September 28, 1997 *Austin American-Statesman*, March 12, 1997 and November 29, 1997; D22, B1 *Boston Herald*; January 20, 1998, *Boston Globe*.

4. The review of pepper spray in Berkeley took place due to a conflict that erupted between University of California Police Department and affirmative action supporters on April 28, 1997.

Chapter 6   Experts, Agencies, the Private Security Sector, and Integration

1. "Police Meet to Sharpen their Style," *Miami News*, October 26, 1958; "'Iron-clad case' helps Toronto nab police conference," *Financial Post*, June 28, 1986; "Police Chiefs Get Look at Cop Car of the Future," *NBC San Diego*, November 10, 2008.

2. Based on a Lexis-Nexis search of all media using the search terms "protesters," "TASER," "Tasered," "demonstrators," "protested," between 2000 and 2012.

Chapter 7   Protest as Threat

1. The Threat Assessment Centre was renamed in 2011 as the Integrated Terrorism Assessment Centre.

2. RAND researchers administered the survey to a stratified random sample of 209 local agencies and all 50 state-level agencies.

Chapter 8   Urine-filled Supersoakers

1. Data compiled from doing a search of all media using Lexis Nexis.

2. All quotes in this section, unless otherwise attributed, come from Ontario Court of Justice, *HRH vs. J. Clarke, G. Heroux, S. Pilipa*. Justice R. Khawly. Toronto, January 17, 2002: Preliminary Inquiry, and Cross Examinations of

Superintendent Aidan Maher, Detective Constable Stephen Irwin, Sgt. Wes Ryan, and Sgt. Brian Smith, by Peter Rosenthal.

3. Della Porta and colleagues also argue that police occupational culture and public opinion are significant influences.

References

ACLU (American Civil Liberties Union), 1999. "ACLU Urges CA Appeals Court to Declare Use of Pepper Spray Dangerous and Cruel." August 12, press release. Available at <https://www.aclu.org/racial-justice_prisoners-rights_drug-law-reform_immigrants-rights/aclu-urges-ca-appeals-court-declar>. [Accessed January 15, 2014]

Adkins, L.D., 2003. "Oleoresin Capsicum: An Analysis of the Implementation of Pepper Spray Into The Law." Unpublished dissertation, East Tennessee State University.

Amnesty International, 2012. "Amnesty International Urges Stricter Limits on Police Taser Use as U.S. Death Toll Reaches 500," February 15. Available at <http://bit.ly/1bcrB4f>. [Accessed January 15, 2014]

Anderson, L., J. Hirschmann, and V. Jones, 2005. "When Police Play Russian Roulette …": The Case for a Moratorium on Police Use of Pepper Spray, The Ella Baker Centre for Human Rights. Available at <http://www.nopepperspray.org/when_police_play_russian_roulette_ella_baker_center.pdf>. [Accessed January 16, 2014]

Anon. (likely Colonel Charles Rowan and Sir Richard Mayne), 1829. General Instructions. London Metropolitan Police Force <https://www.gov.uk/government/publications/policing-by-consent>. [Accessed January 15, 2014]

Armstrong, E.A., 2002. Forging Gay Identities: Organizing Sexuality in San Francisco, 1950–1994. Chicago, ILL: University of Chicago Press.

Associated Press, 2012. "Chicago police to deploy range of protest tactics," May 16. Available at <http://bit.ly/KfMaoP>. [Accessed September 28, 2013]

Attorney General of Ontario, 2006. OPP Public Order Units: A Comparison of 1995 to 2006, Government of Ontario. Available at <http://bit.ly/17yb1fS>. [Accessed September 1, 2013]

Bala, N., J.P. Hornick, M.L. McCall, and M.E. Clarke, 1994. State Responses to Youth Crime: A Consideration of Principles. Ottawa: Department of Justice Canada.

Balch, R.W., 1972. "Police Personality: Fact or Fiction." Journal of Criminal Law and Criminology, 63:1, article 10.

Barber, J., 2000. "Craig Bromell and his own spin on yesterday's facts." Globe and Mail, January 27.

Bayley, D.H., 1992. "Comparative Organization of the Police in English-Speaking Countries." Crime and Justice, 15, pp. 509–45.

——, 1998. "Policing in America: Assessment and Prospects." Ideas in Policing, Police Foundation [pdf] Available at <http://www.policefoundation.org/pdf/Bayley.pdf>. [Accessed September 1, 2013]

Bayly, M., 2006. "Faces of Resistance: Images and Stories of Progressive Activism at the Turn of the Millennium (1997–2006)." Available at <http://www.cptelecom.net/mbayly/facesofresistance7.htm>. [Accessed September 1, 2013]

Beahen, W., 2008. "Evolution of Use of Force by Police in the Canadian Context." In CACOLE Conference *Commission for Public Complaints Against the RCMP.* Regina, SK, 16–18 June.

Beasley, N., T. Graham, and C. Holmberg, 2000. "Justice Department's Civil Disorder Initiative Addresses Police Training Gap." *Police Chief Magazine,* LXVII(10), pp. 113–22.

Beck, U., 1992. *Risk Society, Towards a New Modernity.* London: Sage Publications.

Bennett, A., 2013. "Unmasked: Searching for lessons in Toronto's 2010 G20 debacle." *Maisonneuve,* Winter. Available at <http://maisonneuve.org/article/2013/03/6/unmasked/#sthash.21BXanOU.dpuf>. [Accessed March 6, 2013]

Berbeo, D., D. Greenberg, D. Huffaker, J. Kandel, and J. Smith, 2000. "Protest Clashes End Quickly L.A. Police Move Fast to Break Resistance." *Los Angeles Daily News,* August 17.

Boghosian, H., and the NLG (National Lawyers Guild), 2007. *Punishing Protest: Government Tactics That Suppress Free Speech* [pdf]. New York: National Lawyers Guild. Available at <http://www.nationallawyersguild.org/NLG_Punishing_Protest_2007.pdf>. [Accessed September 1, 2013]

Boltanski, L., and L. Thévenot, 2006. *On Justification: Economies of Worth,* translated by Catherine Porter. Princeton, NJ: Princeton University Press.

Bourdieu, P., 1977. *Outline of a Theory of Practice.* Cambridge: Cambridge University Press.

——, 1986. "The Forms of Capital." In J. Richardson, ed. *Handbook of Theory and Research for the Sociology of Education.* New York: Greenwood, pp. 241–58.

——, 1990. *The Logic of Practice.* Cambridge: Polity Press.

——, 1993. *The Field of Cultural Production: Essays on Art and Literature.* Cambridge: Polity Press.

——, and L. Wacquant, 1992. *Invitation to a Reflexive Sociology.* Cambridge: Polity Press.

Bourrie, M., 2003. "Police 'Excessive' at 2001 Quebec FTAA Protest – Report." *Common Dreams.* [online] Available at <http://www.commondreams.org/headlines03/1115-10.htm>. [Accessed September 1, 2013]

Brian, J., 2002. *High levels of collaboration continue one year post-9/11.* Available at <http://www.rcmp-grc.gc.ca/secur/fea-ved2-eng.htm>. [Accessed September 1, 2013]

Brodeur, J.P., 1983. "High Policing and Low Policing: Remarks about the Policing of Political Activities." *Social Problems,* 30 (5), pp. 507–20.

Brogden, M., 1987. "The Emergence of the Police – The Colonial Dimension." *British Journal of Criminology,* 27 (1): 4–14.

Buntin, J., 2012. "Cathy Lanier Changes Policing in D.C. and Maybe Nation." *Governing the States and Localities*, July 2012, Available at <http://bit.ly/MpqMoq>. Accessed [1 September 2013]

Bureau of Justice Assistance, 1994. *Understanding Community Policing: A Framework for Action* [pdf] Government of the United States of America. Available at <https://www.ncjrs.gov/pdffiles/commp.pdf>. [Accessed September 1, 2013]

——, 2000. *Operation Cooperation: Guidelines for Partnerships between Law Enforcement and Private Security Organizations* [pdf]. Government of the United States of America, Available at <http://www.ilj.org/publications/docs/Operation_Cooperation.pdf>. [Accessed September 1, 2013]

——, 2004. *Intelligence-Led Policing: The New Intelligence Architecture as part of its New Realities: Law Enforcement in the Post 9/11 Era* [pdf] Government of the United States of America, Available at <https://www.ncjrs.gov/pdffiles1/bja/210681.pdf>. [Accessed September 1, 2013]

——, 2005. *Assessing and Managing the Terrorism Threat* [pdf] Government of the United States of America, NCJ 210680. Available at <https://www.ncjrs.gov/pdffiles1/bja/210680.pdf> [Accessed September 29, 2013]

Buttle, J.W., 2003. "'What's good for them, is good for us': Outside influences on the adoption of incapacitant sprays by the British police." *International Journal of Police Science and Management*, 5 (2), pp. 98–111.

CACP (Canadian Association of Chiefs of Police), n.d. *Our History*. Available at <http://www.cacp.ca/index/aboutus>. [Accessed January 15, 2014]

——, 2013. *Our History*. Available at <http://www.cacp.ca/index/aboutus>. [Accessed January 15, 2014]

Calhoun, C., 2012. *The Roots of Radicalism: Tradition, the Public Sphere and Early Nineteenth Century Social Movements*. Chicago, IL: University of Chicago Press.

Canadian Security Intelligence Service, 2000. "Anti-Globalization—A Spreading Phenomenon." *Perspectives*. Available at <http://www.csis-scrs.gc.ca/eng/miscdocs/200008_e.html>[Accessed September 1, 2013]

Cauvin, H.E., 2007. "D.C. Settles Suit Over Protest Arrests." *Washington Post* [online], 1 March. Available at <http://wapo.st/cBInYm> [Accessed September 28, 2013]

CBC News, 2001. "RCMP slammed in APEC report." *CBC News*, August 7. Available at <http://bit.ly/19gYtZO>. [Accessed September 1, 2013]

CCRB (Civilian Complaint Review Board), 2000. *Report of the Pepper Spray Committee* [pdf] New York City Government, Available at <http://www.nyc.gov/html/ccrb/pdf/pepperreport.pdf>. [Accessed September 28, 2013]

——, 2012. *Annual Report*. Available at <http://www.nyc.gov/html/ccrb/downloads/pdf/ccrb_annual_2012.pdf>. [Accessed January 18, 2014]

Cetron, M.J., and O. Davies, 2008. "55 Trends Now Shaping the Future of Policing." *The Proteus Trends Series*, 1(1), pp. 1–200.

Chabot, S., and J.W. Duyvendak, 2002. "Globalization and transnational diffusion between social movements: Reconceptualizing the dissemination of the

Gandhian repertoire and the 'coming out' routine." *Theory and Society*, 31, pp. 697–740.

Chan, J., 2004. "Using Pierre Bourdieu's Framework for Understanding Police Culture." *Droit et Societe*, 56-57, pp. 327–47.

Cherkis, J., 2009. "Affadavit: Ramsey Ordered Pershing Park Arrests." *Washington City Paper*. [online] 18 November. Available at <http://bit.ly/18gEefa> [Accessed September 29, 2013]

——, 2011. "Occupy Wall Street Mass Arrest Resembles Infamous, Costly Police Tactic, Critics Say." *Huffington Post* [online], 4 October. Available at <http://huff.to/ou3fAb>. [Accessed September 1, 2013]

Christian, L., 2009. "G20: Questions need to be asked about 'kettling'." *Guardian* [online], April 2. Available at <http://bit.ly/KvpSzL>. [Accessed January 15, 2014]

Christoff, S., 2012. "Police violence on the rise in Montreal." *Rabble.ca* [online], March 23. Available at <http://rabble.ca/news/2012/03/police-violence-rise-montreal>. [Accessed September 29, 2013]

Chung, A., 2008. "Wearing their protest in public." *Toronto Star* [online] September 28. Available at <http://bit.ly/18dVUIl> [Accessed September 28, 2013]

Churchill, W., 1998. *Pacifism as Pathology: Reflections on the Role of Armed Struggle in North America*. Winnipeg: Arbeiter Ring.

CITIG, 2013. "Enhancing Operational Planning and Public Safety Event Management in Canada." February 19–20, 2013, Toronto. Available at <http://www.cacp.ca/index/eventscontent?contentId=1318>. [Accessed January 22, 2014]

City of Toronto, 2012. *Tax Supported Operating Budget*. Available at <http://bit.ly/190lnoC>. [Accessed September 28, 2013]

Cochran, A., 2013. "Middle East police heads meet in effort to strengthen law in region." *CBS This Morning*. 21 August. Available at <http://cbsn.ws/174nSqb>. [Accessed September 29, 2013]

Coleman, J., 1957. *Community Conflict*. New York: Free Press.

Collective Opposed to Police Brutality, 2003. "Opèration 15 Mars 2002," unpublished document.

Colman, A., and L.P. Gorman, 1982. "Conservatism, Dogmatism, and Authoritarianism in British Police Officers." *Sociology*, 16 (1), pp. 1–11. Available at <http://www.le.ac.uk/psychology/amc/consdogm.pdf>. [Accessed September 29, 2013]

Colquhoun, P., 1797. *Treatise on the Police of the Metropolis*. Google ebook [online] Available at <http://bit.ly/15Gnrip>. [Accessed September 30, 2013]

Commission for Public Complaints Against the RCMP, 2000. *APEC—Commission Interim Report*. Government of Canada, Available at <http://www.cpc-cpp.gc.ca/cnt/decision/ph-ap/apec/APECintR-eng.aspx>. [Accessed September 29, 2013]

——, 2012. *Public Interest Investigation into RCMP Member Conduct Related to the 2010 G8 and G20 Summits, Final Report*. May 2012. Available at <http://

www.cpc-cpp.gc.ca/cnt/decision/cic-pdp/2012/g8g20/g8g20Rep-eng.aspx>. [Accessed September 29, 2013]

Contenta, S. 1994. "The beating that forced police reform The image of Richard Barnabe's face made Montrealers fear abuse of power." *Toronto Star*, December 30, A19.

Cook, P.M. 1977. "Empirical survey of police attitudes." *Police Review*, 85, pp. 1042–78.

Cope, N., 2004. "Intelligence Led Policing or Policing Led Intelligence?" *British Journal of Criminology*, 44, pp. 188–203.

Corruption Prevention and Education Unit (Australia), 1997. *New York Police Department Preventing Crime and Corruption*. Available at <www.icac.nsw.gov.au>. [Accessed September 1, 2013]

Creedon, M. 2013. "Operation Herne: Report 1: Use of Covert Identities. Derbyshire Constabulatory." Available at <http://www.derbyshire.police.uk/Documents/About-Us/Herne/Operation-Herne---Report-1---Covert-Identities.pdf>. [Accessed January 19, 2014]

Crimethinc., 2013. *The Age of Conspiracy Charges*. Available at <http://www.crimethinc.com/texts/recentfeatures/conspiracy.php>. [Accessed September 1, 2013]

Cronin, P., and S. Reicher, 2006. "A study of the factors that influence how senior officers police crowd events: on SIDE outside the laboratory." *British Journal of Social Psychology*, 45 (1), pp. 175–96.

Cunningham, E., 2010. "McGuinty did dirty moral job at G20." *The Hamilton Spectator*, July 13.

Curtis, C., 2010. "Montreal Police Protest: More Than 2,500 Officers March Against Budget Cuts." *The Link* [online], October 26. Available at <http://thelinknewspaper.ca/article/543/>. [Accessed September 1, 2013]

Dafnos, T., 2014. "Negotiating Colonial Encounters: (Un)Mapping the Policing of Indigenous Peoples' Activism in Canada." Unpublished dissertation, Chapter 3. York University.

Davenport, J., B. Moore-Bridger and R. Parsons, 2010. "Emergency Brain Surgery for Student 'Hit on Head with Police Truncheon'." *Evening Standard* [online], December 10. Available at <http://www.standard.co.uk/news/emergency-brain-surgery-for-student-hit-on-head-with-police-truncheon-6545658.html>. [Accessed September 28, 2013]

Davison, N., 2007. *The Development of "Non-Lethal" Weapons During the 1990s*, Bradford Non-Lethal Weapons Research Project, University of Bradford. Available at <http://bit.ly/1cdPYjP>. [Accessed September 1, 2013]

DC City Council (Council of the District of Columbia), 2004. *Report on Investigation of the Metropolitan Police Department's Policy and Practice in Handling Demonstrations in the District of Columbia*. Draft Report. Committee on the Judiciary, Kathy Patterson, Chair, March 11. Available at <http://www.dcwatch.com/police/040311.htm>. [Accessed September 30, 2013]

DeBartolo, P.J., 2008. *NYPD Protest Policing: An Analysis of Discourse, Dissent, and Redefinition*. M.A. thesis, Central European University. Available at <http://bit.ly/146j6EA>. [Accessed September 1, 2013]

Deffuant, G., S. Huet, and F. Amblard, 2005. "An Individual-Based Model of Innovation Diffusion Mixing Social Value and Individual Benefit." *American Journal of Sociology*, 110 (4), pp. 1041–69.

Deflem, M. 2003. *Policing World Society: Historical Foundations of International Police Cooperation*. New York: Oxford University Press.

De Lint, W., 1998. "New Managerialism and Canadian Police Training Reform." *Social Legal Studies*, 7(2), pp. 261–85.

——, and A. Hall, 2009. *Intelligent Control: Developments in Public Order Policing in Canada*. Toronto: University of Toronto Press.

Della Porta, D., 1997. *Police Knowledge and Public Order: Some Reflections on the Italian Case*. EUI Working Papers. RSC No. 97/11, European University Institute, Italy. Available at <http://search.library.wisconsin.edu/catalog/ocm37733149>. [Accessed October 1, 2013]

——, and O. Fillieulle, 2004. "Policing Social Movements." In D.A. Snow, S.A. , and H. Kriesi, eds. *Blackwell's Companion on Social Movements*. Oxford: Blackwell.

——, and H. Reiter, 1998. *Policing Protest: The Control of Mass Demonstrations in Western Democracies*. Minneapolis: University of Minnesota Press.

——, and H. Reiter, 2006. "The Policing of Global Protest: The G8 at Genoa and its Aftermath." In D. Della Porta, A. Peterson, and H. Reiter, *The Policing of Transnational Protest*. Burlington, VT: Ashgate.

——, and S. Tarrow, 2012. "Interactive Diffusion: The Coevolution of Police and Protest Behavior With an Application to Transnational Contention." *Comparative Political Studies*, 45 (1), pp. 119–52.

——, A. Peterson, and H. Reiter, 2006. *The Policing of Transnational Protest*. Burlington, VT: Ashgate.

Democracy Now, 2009. "'I Made Major Mistakes'—Ex-Seattle Police Chief Admits Response to 1999 WTO Protests Was Too Heavy-Handed." *Democracy Now*, March 30. Available at <http://www.democracynow.org/2009/3/30/i_made_major_mistakes_ex_seattle>. [Accessed September 1, 2013]

Denson, E., 1998. "Pepper Spray, Pain and Justice," Civil Liberties Monitoring Project. Available at <http://www.civilliberties.org/win98spray.html>. [Accessed October 1, 2013]

Desai, S., and I. Taylor, 2007. *Two Crowd Control Case Studies*. Defence Rand Canada, Available at <http://cradpdf.drdc-rddc.gc.ca/PDFS/unc66/p528392.pdf>. [Accessed September 1, 2013]

DHS (Department of Homeland Security), 2013. *About the Infrastructure Analysis and Strategy Division*. Available at <http://www.dhs.gov/infrastructure-analysis-and-strategy>. [Accessed September 1, 2013]

——, 2013b. "DHS Announces Grant Allocation for Fiscal Year (FY) 2013 Preparedness Grants." Available at <http://www.dhs.gov/news/2013/08/23/

dhs-announces-grant-allocation-fiscal-year-fy-2013-preparedness-grants>. [Accessed September 28, 2013]

——, 2013. *Police Discretion with Young Offenders: 7.0 Support for community policing.* Government of Canada, Available at <http://www.justice.gc.ca/eng/rp-pr/cj-jp/yj-jj/discre/org/supp-appu.html>. [Accessed September 1, 2013]

DiMaggio, P.J., 1982. "The Structure of Organizational Fields: an analytical approach and policy implications." Paper presented at the *SUNY-Albany Conference on Organizational Theory and Public Policy.*

——, and W.W. Powell, 1991. "The Iron Cage Revisited: Institutional Isomorphism and Collective Rationality in Organizational Fields." *American Sociological Review*, 48 (2), pp. 147–60.

District of Columbia Police Union, 2012. "D.C. Police Union Files Suit to Stop Chief Lanier from Interfering in Negotiations for Police Compensation." [online] District of Columbia Police Union, May 7. Available at <http://bit.ly/1emuYMp>. [Accessed September 24, 2013]

Draaisma, M., 2007. "Is pepper spray an appropriate tool for police?" *CBC News*, July 16. Available at <http://www.cbc.ca/news/background/tasers/pepper-spray.html>. [Accessed September 1, 2013]

Dunn, C., A. Eisenberg, D. Lieberman, A. Silver, and A. Vitale, 2003. *Arresting Protest: A special report of the New York Civil Liberties Union on New York City's Protest Policies at the February 15, 2003 Antiwar Demonstration in New York City*, New York Civil Liberties Union. Available at <http://www.nyclu.org/files/nyclu_arresting_protest.pdf>. [Accessed September 1, 2013]

Dupuis-Deri, F., 2013. *À qui la rue? Répression policière et mouvements sociaux.* Montréal: Écosociété.

Dwyer, J., 2007. "City Police Spied Broadly Before G.O.P. Convention." *New York Times.* March 25. Available at <http://nyti.ms/13D8uzG>. [Accessed September 1, 2013]

Dye, S., 2009. "Policing in Local Law Enforcement: A Commitment to Getting Out-of-the-Car." *Police Chief Magazine.* Available at <http://bit.ly/17moBPV>. [Accessed September 1, 2013]

Earl, J., S.A. Soule, and J.D. McCarthy, 2003. "Protest under Fire? Explaining the Policing of Protest." *American Sociological Review*, 68 (4), pp. 581–606.

Eckberg, M., 2007. "The Parameters of the Risk Society." *Current Sociology*, 55 (3), pp. 343–66.

Eilstrup-Sangiovanni, M., 2009. "Varieties of Cooperation: Government Networks in International Security." In M. Kahler, ed. *Networked Politics and Governance: Agency, Power and Governance*, Ithaca, NY: Cornell University Press, pp. 194–227.

Ericson, R., and K. Haggerty, 1997. *Policing the Risk Society.* Oxford: Oxford University Press.

——, and K. Carrier, 1993. "Community Policing as Communications Policing." In D. Dolling and T. Feltes, eds., *Community Policing: Comparative Aspects of Community Oriented Police Work*, Holzkirchen: Felix-Verlag, pp. 31–52.

Faulkner, S.D., and L.P. Danaher, 1997. "Controlling Subjects: Realistic Training vs. Magic Bullets." *FBI Law Enforcement Bulletin*, 66(2), pp. 20–26. [Accessed September 28, 2013]

FBI (Federal Bureau of Investigation), 2004. *Responding to Your Concerns: FBI Interviews at Special Events.* Available at <http://www.fbi.gov/news/stories/2004/august/responding_081804>. [Accessed September 1, 2013]

Fernandez, L.A., 2008. *Policing dissent: social control and the anti-globalization movement.* Piscataway, NJ: Rutgers University Press.

Fields, M., and S. Castor, 2011. "Intelligence-Led Policing: The Future Is Now." *The Police Chief*, 78, pp. 72–5. Available at <http://bit.ly/1fgTidP>. [Accessed September 1, 2013]

Flock, E., 2011. "Occupy Oakland: Did police use flashbangs and rubber bullets on protesters?" *Washington Post*, October 26. Available at <http://wapo.st/tePuKS>. [Accessed September 28, 2013]

Forcese, D., 2002. "The Politics of Police Unions." In D. Forcese, ed. *Police: Selected Issues in Canadian Law Enforcement.* Ottawa: Golden Dog Press.

——, 2000. *Police: Current Issues in Canadian Law Enforcement.* Toronto: Dundurn Press.

Forst, B., and P.V. Manning, 1999. *Privatization of Policing: Two Views.* Washington, DC: Georgetown University Press.

Gabriel, D., 2012. *Towards the Creation of the US-Canada Police State. "Counterterrorism" and War on Drugs used to Justify Sweeping Reforms.* Available at <http://www.globalresearch.ca/index.php?context=vaandaid=29446>. [Accessed September 1, 2013]

Ganeva, T., and L. Gottesbeiner, 2012. "9 Terrifying Facts about America's Biggest Police Force." *Salon.com*, September 28. Available at <http://bit.ly/14Ahk40>. [Accessed September 1, 2013]

Gascon, G., and T. Foglesong, 2010. "Making Policing More Affordable: Managing Costs and Measuring Value in Policing." *National Institute of Justice.* Available at <http://www.nij.gov/pubs- sum/231096.htm>. [Accessed September 1, 2013]

Gates, B. 1986. "'Iron-clad case' helps Toronto nab police conference." *Financial Post*, June 28.

Gee, M., 2012. "Report critical of G20 tactics, Chief Blair defensive." *Globe and Mail*, May 16. Available at <http://www.theglobeandmail.com/news/toronto/report-critical-of-g20-tactics-chief-blair-defensive/article4216411/>. [Accessed September 28, 2013]

Gillham, P.F., and G. Marx, 2000. "Complexity and Irony in Policing and Protesting: The World Trade Organization in Seattle." *Social Justice*, 27(2), pp. 212–36

——, B. Edwards, and J.A. Noakes, 2013. "Strategic incapacitation and the policing of Occupy Wall Street protests in New York City." *Policing and Society*, 23(1), pp. 81–102.

Gives, K., and T. Heat. 2012. "City Council NYPD Budget Hearing Goes Beyond Dollars and Cents." *WNYC*, March 15. Available at <http://www.wnyc.org/story/192569-blog-kelly-takes-and-gives-heat>. [Accessed January 15, 2014]

Globe and Mail, 2012. Editorial: "Canada's police among the best paid in the world," March 20. Available at <http://bit.ly/17MBzu5>. [Accessed September 1, 2013]

Goldberg, M., 2003. "This is not America." *Salon.com* [online], December 16. Available at <http://www.salon.com/2003/12/17/miami_police/>. [Accessed October 1, 2013]

Goldstein, J., 2007. "Operation Overlord II: NYPD Planned RNC Arrests." *New York Sun*, January 31. Available at <http://bit.ly/1dWLRvY>. [Accessed September 1, 2013]

Good, T., 2008. "Repression at the Republican Convention: The Criminalization of Dissent." *Peacework*. Issue 389 – October.

Gordon, T., 2006. *Cops, Crime and Capitalism: The Law and Order Agenda in Canada.* Halifax: Fernwood.

Gosztola, K., 2012. "The Hysterical Fear of Urine and Feces Being Thrown at Police During G8 Protests." *The Dissenter*, February 14. Available at <http://bit.ly/19Ck136>. [Accessed September 1, 2013]

Graeber, D., 2004. "Lying in wait: on the eve of mass protests, police tell tales that turn out not to be true." *The Nation*, 278(15), April 19. Available at <http://www.thenation.com/article/lying-wait>. [Accessed September 28, 2013]

——, 2007. "On the Phenomenology of Giant Puppets, broken windows, imaginary jars of urine, and the cosmological role of the police in American culture." Available at <http://balkansnet.org/zcl/puppets.pdf>. [Accessed September 1, 2013]

Granovetter, M.S., 1973. "The Strength of Weak Ties." *American Journal of Sociology*, 78(6).

Greelis, R., 2009. *Cop Book*, Edina, MN: Beaver's Pond Press. [Accessed September 28, 2013]

Groves, T., 2011. "Living among us: Activists speak out on police infiltration." *Briarpatch Magazine*, June 20. Available at <http://briarpatchmagazine.com/articles/view/living-among-us>. [Accessed September 1, 2013]

——, and Z. Dubinsky, 2011. "G20 case reveals 'largest ever' police spy operation." *CBC News* online, November 22. Available at <http://www.cbc.ca/news/canada/g20-case-reveals-largest-ever-police-spy-operation-1.1054582>. [Accessed January 23, 2014]

Habernero, Detective, 2000. "A Short and Sordid History of Pepper Spray." *Earth First Journal*, December/January. Available at <http://www.nopepperspray.org/sordid.htm>. [Accessed September 1, 2013]

Hall, R.G., 2002. "A Brief Discussion of Police Culture and How It Affects Police Responses to Internal Investigations and Civilian Oversight." Canadian Association for Civilian Oversight of Law Enforcement (CACOLE). Conference

Paper. 2002 Conference. Available at <http://bit.ly/161mQvh>. [Accessed September 23, 2013]

Harman, A., 1995. "Toronto's Public Order Unit." *Law and Order*, September, pp. 97–100. Available at <http://bit.ly/15RKaa8>. [Accessed September 1, 2013]

Harvey, D., 2005. *A Brief History of Neoliberalism*. New York: Oxford University Press.

Hedström, P., R. Sandell, and C. Stern, 2000. "Mesolevel Networks and the Diffusion of Social Movements: The Case of the Swedish Social Democratic Party." *American Journal of Sociology*, 106 (1) (July), pp. 145–72.

Hennelly, B., 2012. "City Council and NYPD Budget Hearing Goes Beyond Dollars and Cents; Kelly Gives and Takes Heat." *WNYC*, March 15. Available at <http://wny.cc/1eaYJ2B>. [Accessed September 1, 2013]

Hirsch, E.L., 1990. "Sacrifice for the Cause: Group Processes, Recruitment and Commitment in a Student Social Movement." *American Sociological Review*, 2 (55), pp. 243–54.

Holden, G.A., 2009. *Lessons From 9/11: Organizational Change in the New York City and Arlington County, Va., Police Departments* [pdf] United States Department of Justice. Available at <https://www.ncjrs.gov/pdffiles1/nij/227346.pdf>. [Accessed September 1, 2013]

Holland, J., 2011. "Naomi Wolf's 'Shocking Truth' About the 'Occupy Crackdowns' Offers Anything but the Truth." *Alternet*, November 26. Available at <http://bit.ly/tiHLAS>. [Accessed September 1, 2013]

Hoogenboom, A.B., 1997. "Policing the Future: 13th European Policing Executive Conference." International Association of Chiefs of Police. Dordrecht, Netherlands: Martinus Nijhoff Publishers.

Hornqvist, M., 2004. "Risk Assessments and Public Order Disturbances: New European Guidelines for the Use of Force?" *Journal of Scandinavian Studies in Criminology and Crime Prevention*, 5(1), pp. 4–26.

IACP (International Association for Chiefs of Police), 1976. *Executive Summary: Major Recommendations for Management of Effective Police Discipline*. Gaitersburg, MD.

——, 2002. *Criminal Intelligence Sharing: A National Plan for Intelligence-Led Policing at the Local, State and Federal Levels* [pdf]. Available at <http://www.cops.usdoj.gov/Publications/criminalintelligencesharing_web.pdf>. [Accessed October 1, 2013]

——, 2010. *International Association of Chiefs of Police FY 2011–2016 Strategic Plan*. Available at <http://bit.ly/Aeuhqj>. [Accessed September 28, 2013]

——, 2012a. *Ad Hoc Committee on International Initiatives (AHCII)*. Available at <http://bit.ly/14v1iq2>. [Accessed January 22, 2014]

——, 2012b. "Law Enforcement Conference and Expo Program, San Diego, CA." Available at <http://bit.ly/14v1iq2>. [Accessed January 22, 2014]

——, 2012c. *Sponsor and Advertising Opportunities, IACP* [online]. Available at <http://bit.ly/14v1iq2>. [Accessed January 22, 2014]

——, 2012d. *Welcome to IACP 2012.* Available at < http://bit.ly/14v1iq2 >. [Accessed January 22, 2014]

Institute for Non-Lethal Defense Technologies, 2005. *Less-Lethal Operational Scenarios for Law Enforcement. Final Draft* [pdf] Penn State Applied Research Laboratory. Available at <https://www.ncjrs.gov/pdffiles1/nij/grants/232756. pdf>. [Accessed October 1, 2013]

Interpol, 2011. "Innovation will be focus of planned extension of INTERPOL's global reach to Singapore" [media release], September 14. Available at <http:// bit.ly/17SHV7l>. [Accessed September 1, 2013]

Jackman, C., 2000. "Bloody finale to talks." *Hobart Mercury*, April 19.

James, J.W., and S.D. Mastrofski, 2011. "Innovations in Policing: Meanings, Structures, and Processes." *Annual Review of Law and Social Science*, 7, pp. 309–34.

Jardin, X., 2008. "Report: Massive, warrantless raids on peace protesters in Minneapolis, ahead of RNC." *Boing Boing*, August 30. Available at <http://boingboing.net/2008/08/30/report-massive-warra.html>. [Accessed September 23, 2013]

Jasper, J.M., 2011. "Emotions and Social Movements: Twenty Years of Theory and Research." *Annual Review of Sociology*, 37:14.1–14.19.

Johnson, C.L., 2010. *Police Use of Intelligence Networks for Reducing Crime.* El Paso, TX: LFB Scholarly Publishing.

Johnson, K., 2012. "Police organization gets $300 K at group tied to stun-gun maker: Analyst says donation from TASER Foundation raises ethics concerns." *USA Today*, October 22. Available at <http://www.usatoday.com/story/news/ nation/2012/10/21/taser-police-chiefs/1627299//>. [Accessed September 1, 2013]

Jones, N., 2010. "A Brief History of Riot Control." *Time Magazine*, 6 August. Available at <http://ti.me/15NhXIh>. [Accessed September 1, 2013]

Jones, T., and T. Newburn, 2002. "The Transformation of Policing: Understanding Current Trends in Policing Systems." *British Journal of Criminology*, 42, pp. 129–46.

Kaminski, R.J., Edwards, S.M., and J.W. Johnson, 1999. "Assessing the incapacitative effects of pepper spray during resistive encounters with the police." *Policing: An International Journal of Police Strategies and Management*, 22, pp. 7–29.

Kane, L., 2013. "Toronto police board keeps chief's SIU investigations secret." *Toronto Star*, December 14.

Karagama, Y.G., J.R. Newton, and C.J.R. Newbegin, 2003. "Short-term and long-term physical effects of exposure to CS spray." *Journal of the Royal Society of Medicine*, 96 (4), pp. 172–4.

Katz, E., 1968. "Diffusion (Interpersonal Influence)." In David Shils, ed. *International Encyclopedia of the Social Sciences.* London: Macmillan and Free Press.

——, 1999. "Theorizing Diffusion: Tarde and Sorokin Revisited." In M. Durfee and P. Lopes, eds. *Annals of the American Academy of Political and Social Science*, Vol. 566, special issue on diffusion, pp. 144–55.

Kirton, J., J. Guebert, and S. Tanna, 2010. *G8 and G20 Summit Costs*. University of Toronto. Available at <http://bit.ly/avFSs4>. [Accessed September 1, 2013]

Kitschelt, H., 1986. "Political Opportunity Structures and Political Protest: Anti-Nuclear Movements in Four Democracies." *British Journal of Political Science*, 16, pp. 57–85.

Klein, N., 2007. *The Shock Doctrine: The Rise of Disaster Capitalism*. Toronto: Knopf Canada.

Klotz, R.W., 2000. "How Can the Cops Stop Seattle From Happening Here?; With a Change of Face," *Washington Post*, April 9. Available from <http://www.highbeam.com/doc/1P2-516142.html>. [Accessed September 28, 2013]

Kolodner, M., 2001. "Eyewitness in Quebec." *International Socialist Review*. 18, June–July. Available at <http://isreview.org/issues/18/eyewitness_quebec.shtml>. [Accessed 25 September 25, 2013]

Koopmans, R., 2005. "Repression and the Public Sphere: Discursive Opportunities for Repression." In C. Davenport, H. Johnston, and C. Mueller, eds. *Repression and Mobilization* [Social Movements, Protest, and Contention Series], vol. 21, Minneapolis: University of Minnesota Press, pp. 33–57.

Koper, C.S., 2004. "Hiring and Keeping Police Officers." *US Department of Justice, National Institution of Justice*. Available at <https://www.ncjrs.gov/pdffiles1/nij/202289.pdf>. [Accessed September 1, 2013]

Kraska, P., 2001. *Militarizing the American Criminal Justice System*. Richmond, VA: Northern University Press.

——, and V.E. Kappeler, 1997. "Militarizing American Police: The Rise and Normalization of Paramilitary Units." *Social Problems*, 44(1), pp. 1–18.

Kriesberg, L., 1973. *The Sociology of Social Conflicts*. Englewood Cliffs, NJ: Prentice Hall.

Law Enforcement Training Network, 2004. *Less-Lethal Force, Part 1: OC-Pepper Spray Updates LETN-163-0017*, Critical Information Network. Available at <http://www.twlk.com/law/tests/LETN1630017ct.pdf>. [Accessed September 1, 2013]

Lawless, M.W., 1987. "Institutionalization of a Management Science Innovation in Police Departments." *Management Science*, 33(2), pp. 244–52.

Lennard, N., 2012. "NYPD tactics at 2004 RNC ruled illegal." *Salon.com* [online], October 2. Available from <http://bit.ly/1dWYaIS>. [Accessed September 1, 2013]

Lewis, P., 2009. "A history of police kettling." *Guardian*, April 14. Available at <http://www.guardian.co.uk/uk/2011/apr/14/history-police-kettling>. [Accessed September 1, 2013]

——, and R. Evans. 2013. "Police chiefs confused over whether they have authorised their spies to sleep with activists." *Guardian Online*, October 18. Available at <http://www.theguardian.com/uk-news/undercover-with-paul-lewis-and-rob-evans/2013/oct/18/undercover-police-and-policing-espionage>. [Accessed January 8, 2014]

Li, G., 2008. *Private security and public policing.* Statistics Canada. Available at <http://bit.ly/14B2KY6>. [Accessed September 1, 2013]

Lingamneni, J.R., 1979. "Resistance to Change in Police Organizations: The Diffusion Paradigm." *Criminal Justice Review*, 4(2), pp. 17–26.

Linebaugh, P., 1991. *The London Hanged: Crime and Civil Society in the 18th Century.* London: Verso.

Losure, M., 2002. *Our Way or the Highway: Inside the Minnehaha Free State.* Minneapolis: University of Minnesota Press.

LRAD, 2013. "Company History." Available at <http://www.lradx.com>. [Accessed January 2, 2014]

Luthra, S., 2013. "Evidence of Excrement Remains Elusive." *Texas Tribune*, July 30, 2013.

Maas, B., 2008. "DNC Security Planners Prepare For The Worst." *CBS*, August 13. Available at <http://www.freerepublic.com/focus/f-news/2061912/posts>. [Accessed January 8, 2014]

Mahoney, J., and A. Hui, 2010. "G20-related mass arrests unique in Canadian history." *Globe and Mail*, June 29. Available at <http://bit.ly/1ebi4kc>. [Accessed September 1, 2013]

Malmin, M., 2012. "Changing Police Subculture." *FBI Law Enforcement Bulletin* April 2012. Available at <http://1.usa.gov/18wumyN>. [Accessed September 22, 2013]

Manning, P.K., 1995. "TQM and the Future of Policing." *Police Forum*, 5 (2). Available at <http://bit.ly/18DtN6k>. [Accessed September 29, 2013]

——, 1997. *Police Work: The Social Organization of Policing.* Prospect Heights, IL: Waveland Press.

——, 2008. *The Technology of Policing: Crime Mapping, Information Technology and the Rationality of Crime Control.* New York: New York University Press.

Marin, A., 2011. *G20 Summit: Caught in the Act,* Ombudsman of Ontario. Available at <http://bit.ly/m2zckU>. [Accessed September 1, 2013]

Markets and Markets, 2013. *Non-Lethal Weapons Market (2013–2018).* September 13. Available at <http://www.marketsandmarkets.com/Market-Reports/non-lethal-weapons-market-1236.html>. [Accessed September 29, 2013]

Martinez, J., 2000. "Police prep for protests over biotech conference at Hynes." *Boston Herald* [online], March 4. Available from <http://bit.ly/16Nwi18>. [Accessed September 28, 2013]

Mascoll, P., and J. Rankin, 1996. "OPP defends riot squad called 'animals' by pickets." *Toronto Star*, March 19, A1.

Mawby, R.I., 2008. "Models of policing." In T. Newburn, ed. *Handbook of Policing*, 2nd edn., Portland, OR: Willan Publishing, pp. 17–46.

McAdam, D., 1983. "Tactical innovation and the pace of insurgency." *American Sociological Review*, 48, pp. 735–54.

——, 1995. "'Initiator' and 'Spinoff' Movements: Diffusion Processes in Protest Cycles." In M. Traugott (ed.), *Repertoires and Cycles of Collective Action*. Durham, NC: Duke University Press.

——, and D. Rucht, 1993. "The Cross National Diffusion of Movement Ideas." *Annals of the American Academy of Political and Social Science*, 528(1), pp. 56–74.

McCarthy, J., and C. McPhail, 1998. "The Institutionalization of Protest in the United States." In D.S. Meyer and S. Tarrow, eds. *The Social Movement Society*, New York: Rowman and Littlefield, pp. 83–110.

——, C. McPhail, and J. Crist, 1999. "The Emergence and Diffusion of Public Order Management Systems: Protest Cycles and Police Response." In H. Kriesi, D. Della Porta, and D. Rucht, eds. *Globalization and Social Movements*, London: Macmillan. pp. 49–69.

McGarrell, E.F., J.D. Freilich, and S. Chermak, 2007. "Intelligence-led Policing as a Framework for Responding to Terrorism." *Journal of Contemporary Criminal Justice*, 23 (2), pp. 142–58.

McHenry, K., 2012. *History of FBI infiltrating Food Not Bombs to entrap volunteers as 'terrorists'*. Available at <http://bit.ly/146e9eX>. [Accessed September 28, 2013]

McLeod, R., 2002. *Parapolice. A Revolution in the Business of Law Enforcement*. Toronto: Boheme Press.

McPhail, C., D. Schweingruber, and J.D. McCarthy, 1998. "Policing Protest in the United States: 1960–1995." In D. Della Porta and H. Reiter, eds. *Policing of Protest: The Control of the Mass Demonstration in Western Democracies*, Minneapolis: University of Minnesota Press.

Menzies, K., 2004. "Policing as Force and Policing as Risk." In S.E. Nancoo, ed., *Contemporary Issues in Canadian Policing*, Mississauga: Canadian Educators Press.

Mignon, S.I., and W.M. Holmes, 1999. "Police Recruits' Attitudes toward the Death Penalty." *Criminal Justice Policy Review*, 10 (1), pp. 29–47.

Mihm, S., 2004. "The Quest For The Nonkiller App." *New York Times Magazine*, July 25. Available at <http://nyti.ms/1alXIzK>. [Accessed September 1, 2013]

Miller, W.R., 1977. *Cops and Bobbies: Police authority in New York and London*. Chicago, IL: University of Chicago Press.

Montreal (City of), 2012. *2012 Operating Budget at a Glance*, Available at <http://bit.ly/17d4ckf>. [Accessed September 28, 2013]

Moore, B., 1993. *Social Origins of Dictatorship and Democracy*. Boston, MA: Beacon Press.

Moore, T., 2012. "NYPD SUE! Surge in lawsuits vs. Police Department part of costly trend for the city." *Daily News*, December 26. Available at <http://nydn.us/1bRrWhk>. [Accessed September 28, 2013]

Morgan, J., 1987. *Conflict and Order: The Police and Labour Disputes in England and Wales, 1900-1939.* Oxford: Oxford University Press.

Moynihan, C., 2012. "City Seeks to Dismiss False-Arrest Suits Stemming From 2004 Republican Convention." *New York Times*, May 31. <Available at http://nyti.ms/1eyloDM>. [Accessed September 1, 2013]

MPDC, 2011/12. *Council of the District of Columbia, Committee on the Judiciary. 2011. Fiscal Year 2012, Committee Budget Report.* Available at <http://bit.ly/1aCFNqg>. [Accessed January 15, 2014]

Murphy, C., 2007. "'Securitizing' Canadian Policing: A New Policing Paradigm for the Post 9/11 Security State?" *The Canadian Journal of Sociology,* 32 (4), pp. 451–77.

——, and P. McKenna, 2007. *Rethinking Police Governance, Culture and Management* [pdf] Public Safety Canada. Available at <http://www.publicsafety.gc.ca/rcmpgrc/_fl/eng/rthnk-plc-eng.pdf>. [Accessed September 1, 2013]

Murphy, D., 2013. "Dept. of Homeland Security Wasting Billions." *Counterpunch,* April 19. Available at <http://www.counterpunch.org/2013/04/19/dept-of-homeland-security-wasting-billions>. [Accessed January 16, 2014]

Myers, D.J., 2000. "The Diffusion of Collective Violence: Infectiousness, Susceptibility, and Mass Media Networks." *American Journal of Sociology,* 106 (1) (July), pp. 173–208.

Narr, T., J. Toliver, J. Murphy, M. McFarland, and J. Ederheimer, 2006. *Police Management of Mass Demonstrations: Identifying Issues and Successful Approaches* [pdf] Police Executive Research Forum. Available at <http://policeforum.org/library/critical-issues-in-policing-series/MassDemonstrations.pdf>. [Accessed September 25, 2013]

NCIS (National Criminal Intelligence Service), 2000. *The National Intelligence Model.* Available at <http://bit.ly/15gCors>. [Accessed September 1, 2013]

Neagle, C., 2012. "Occupy protests send police shopping for wearable cop cams." *PoliceOne.com,* June 18. Available at http://bit.ly/LxaPl8>. [Accessed September 24, 2013]

Neocleous, M., 1996. *Administering Civil Society: Towards a Theory of State Power.* London: Palgrave Macmillan.

Noakes, J., and P.F. Gillham, 2006. "Aspects of the New Penology: the Police Response to Major Political Protests in the United States." In D. Della Porta, A. Peterson, and H. Reiter, eds., *The Policing of Transnational Protest,* Burlington, VT: Ashgate, pp. 97–115.

——, and P.F. Gillham. 2007. "Police and Protester Innovation Since Seattle." *Mobilization,* 12(4), pp. 335–40.

——, B. Klocke, and P.F. Gillham, 2005. "Whose Streets? Police and Protester Struggles over Space in Washington, DC, 29–30 September 2001." *Policing and Society,* 15 (3), pp. 235–54.

Nopepperspray.org, 2006. *No Pepper Spray on Nonviolent Protesters.* Available at <http://www.nopepperspray.org/>. [Accessed September 1, 2013]

Normandeau, A., and B. Leighton, 1990. *A Vision of the Future of Policing in Canada: Police-Challenge 2000*. Solicitor General's Office of Canada.

NYCLU (New York Civil Liberties Union), undated. *Civilian Complaint Review Board and Civilian Oversight of Policing*. Available at <http://bit.ly/17SQGQJ>. [Accessed September 1, 2013]

——, 2003. *Arresting Protest: A special report of the New York Civil Liberties Union on New York City's Protest Policies at the February 15, 2003 Antiwar Demonstration in New York City*. Written by C. Dunn, A. Eisenberg, D. Lieberman, A. Silver, and A. Vitale. Available at <http://bit.ly/KvpSzL>. [Accessed January 15, 2014]

NYPD (New York Police Department), 2004. *2004 Republican National Convention. NYPD Executive Summary*. Available at <http://www.nyclu.org/RNCdocs>. [Accessed January 2, 2014]

Occupy Wall Street, 2012. Occupy Arrests Dataset. *Occupy Research*. (email, personal communication, 2012).

O'Connor, J., 2009. "The Upside of Kettling." *Guardian* [online], April 2. Available at <http://bit.ly/1aZMx2t>. [Accessed September 1, 2013]

O'Hanley, S., 2005. "Montreal police reprimanded by UN: Pig roast, Hour Community." Available at <http://hour.ca/2005/11/10/pig-roast/>. [Accessed September 28, 2013]

Oliver, P., and D. Myers, 1998. "The Coevolution of Social Movements." *Mobilization: An International Journal*, 8 (1), pp.1–24.

Oliver, W.M., 2000. "The Third Generation of Community Policing: Moving Through Innovation, Diffusion, and Institutionalization." *Police Quarterly*, 3 (4), pp. 367–88.

Ontario Association of Police Service Boards, 2012. *The Rising Costs of Policing*. Available at <http://bit.ly/14COAaM>. [Accessed September 29, 2013]

Ontario Court of Justice, 2002. *HRH vs. J. Clarke, G. Heroux, S. Pilipa*. Justice R. Khawly. Toronto, January 17. Preliminary inquiry: Transcripts and disclosure documents.

OPC (Office of Police Complaints), 2012. *Government of the District of Columbia. Police Complaints Board Office of Police Complaints. Annual Report Fiscal Year 2012*. Available at <http://1.usa.gov/1idK6Nz>. [Accessed January 15, 2014]

OPP (Ontario Provincial Police), 2006. *OPP Public Order Units: A Comparison of 1995 to 2006*, Attorney General of Ontario. Available at <http://bit.ly/17yb1fS>. [Accessed September 1, 2013]

——, 2011. *Consolidated After Action Reports—Summits 2010*. Available at <http://www.opp.ca/ecms/files/265483322.4.pdf>. [Accessed September 28, 2013]

Organization for Economic Co-operation and Development, 2011. *An Overview of Growing Income Inequalities in OECD Countries: Main Findings*. Available at <http://www.oecd.org/dataoecd/40/12/49499779.pdf>. [Accessed September 1, 2013]

O'Toole, M., 2011. "Six plead guilty to G20 mischief charges; charges against 11 others dropped." *National Post*. November 22. Available at <http://news.

nationalpost.com/2011/11/22/six-plead-guilty-to-g20-mischief-charges/>. [Accessed September 29, 2013]

Panetta, A., and A. Blatchford, 2013. "'It would be preferable for him to withdraw from his current role,' Marois says after Montreal Mayor arrested." *National Post*, June 17.

Parascandola, R., 2000. "Video Leads to Two Arrests in Funeral Riot." *New York Post*, April 21.

Parenti, C., 2000. *Police and Prisons in the Age of Crisis*. New York: Verso.

Patel, F., and A. Sullivan, 2012. *A Proposal for a NYPD Inspector General* [pdf] Brennan Center for Justice at New York University School of Law. Available at <http://www.brennancenter.org/sites/default/files/legacy/Justice/NYPDInspectorGeneral-web.pdf>. [Accessed October 1, 2013]

Peel, T., and J. Richman, 2011. "As Port protest looms, Oakland Police face tough questions over use-of-force." *Costa Contra Times*, December 10. Available at <http://www.mercurynews.com/occupy/ci_19519989>. [Accessed September 1, 2013]

Peet, D., 2012. "Fighting Crime Using Geospatial Analytics." *Police Chief Magazine*, July. Available at <http://bit.ly/LoG63u>. [Accessed September 1, 2013]

PERF (Police Executive Research Forum), 2011a. *Managing Major Events: Best Practices from the Field*, Police Forum. Available at <http://www.policeforum.org/dotAsset/1491727.pdf>. [Accessed January 28, 2014]

——, 2011b. "Police Leaders at PERF/BJA Meeting Discuss CompStat: Best Practices and Future Outlook." *Subject To Debate*, 25 (2). Available at <http://www.policeforum.org/library/subject-to-debate/2011/Debate_Mar-Apr2011_web.pdf>. [Accessed September 1, 2013]

——, 2012. *About Police Executive Research Forum*. Available at <http://www.policeforum.org/about-us/>. [Accessed September 1, 2013]

——, 2013. "PERF Plays Role in Unprecedented Middle East Policing Project." Announcement Archives, August 27. Available at <http://www.policeforum.org/news/detail.dot?id=5169940>. [Accessed January 22, 2014]

Phillips, K., and J. Godfrey, 1999. "A dangerous weapon in dangerous hands; Will Oleoresin Capsaicin spray reduce fatal shootings by police?" *Alternative Law Journal*, 24 (2).

Pilant, L., 1993. "Less-Than-Lethal Weapons: New Solutions for Law Enforcement." *International Association of Chiefs of Police*, December. Available at <https://www.ncjrs.gov/pdffiles1/nij/grants/181653.pdf>. [Accessed September 1, 2013]

Pilgrims Group, 2010. *Threat and Risk: What's the Difference?* Available at <http://www.pilgrimsgroup.com/news.php?id=94>. [Accessed September 1, 2013]

Pilon-LaRose, H., 2013. "Intervention policière rapide à la manifestation du 22 March 2013." *La Presse*. Available at <http://bit.ly/XwjSHF>. [Accessed September 28, 2013]

Poisson, J., J. Yang, and B. Kennedy, 2011. "Exclusive: Toronto police swear off G20 kettling tactic." *Toronto Star* [online], June 22. Available at <http://www.thestar.

com/news/gta/2011/06/22/exclusive_toronto_police_swear_off_g20_kettling_
tactic.html>. [Accessed January 15, 2014]

PoliceOne, 2013. "PoliceOne Marketing Program Drives Rapid Adoption of the
TASER." Available at <http://ddq74coujkv1i.cloudfront.net/_misc/PDFs/Taser_
Case_Study.pdf>. [Accessed September 28, 2013]

Potter, L.J., 1977. "Police Officer Personality." Unpublished M.Ed. thesis, University
of Bradford.

Public Safety Canada, 2009. *National Strategy for Critical Infrastructure*. Available at
<http://www.publicsafety.gc.ca/cnt/rsrcs/pblctns/srtg-crtcl-nfrstrctr/srtg-crtcl-
nfrstrctr-eng.pdf>. [Accessed January 15, 2014]

——, 2013. *About Public Safety Canada*, Government of Canada. Available at
<http://www.publicsafety.gc.ca/cnt/bt/index-eng.aspx>. [Accessed September
1, 2013]

Pue, W., ed., 2000. *Pepper in Our Eyes: The APEC Affair*. Vancouver: UBC Press.

Pugliese, D., and J. Bronskill, 2001. "RCMP create 'Public Order Program' to
keep the public in check." *Ottawa Citizen*, August 18. Available at <http://www.
ottawacitizen.com/national/010818/653833.html>. [Accessed September 28,
2013]

Rafail, P., 2010. "Asymmetry in Protest Control? Comparing Protest Policing in
Montreal, Toronto, and Vancouver, 1998–2004." *Mobilization*, 15 (4).

——, S.A. Soule, and J.D. McCarthy, 2012. "Describing and Accounting for the
Trends in U.S. Protest Policing, 1960–1995." *Journal of Conflict Resolution*, 56
(4), pp. 733–62.

Rakobowchuk, P., 2011. "Montreal police use stun grenades to disperse students
following protest." *Prince George Citizen*, April 1.

Rapaport, D., 1999. *No Justice, No Peace: The 1996 OPSEU strike against the Harris
government in Ontario*. Montréal, QC and Kingston, ON: McGill-Queen's
University Press.

Rashbaum, W.K., 2004. "Police Create Panel on Abuse Claims at Convention." *New
York Times*, November 5. Available at <http://nyti.ms/17okwOj>. [Accessed
September 1, 2013]

Ratcliffe, J.H., 2008. *Intelligence-Led Policing*. Cullompton, UK: Willan Publishing.

Reiner, R., 2000. *The Politics of the Police*, 3rd edn. Oxford: Oxford University Press.

Renn, O., 1998. "The role of risk perception for risk management." *Reliability
Engineering & System Safety*, 59 (1) (January), pp. 49–62.

Richmond Police Department, 2008. *Crowd Management Team Operating Manual*.
Available at <http://bit.ly/15U2Ztb>. [Accessed September 1, 2013]

Riley, K.J., G.F. Treverton, J.M. Wilson, and L.M. Davis. 2005. *State and Local
Intelligence in the War on Terrorism*. Santa Monica, CA: RAND Corporation.

Robbins, C., 2012. "Law suits against the NYPD Rose 20% and Could Cost NYC $154
Million." *Gothamist*, October 3. Available at <http://gothamist.com/2012/10/03/
lawsuits_against_the_nypd_have_rise.php>. [Accessed September 27, 2013]

Roberts, A., and J.M. Roberts Jr., 2007. "The Structure of Informal Communication Between Police Agencies." *Policing: An International Journal of Police Strategies and Management*, 30 (1), pp. 93–107.

Rogers, E.M., 2003. *The Diffusion of Innovations*. New York: Free Press.

Rosenbaum, D.P., A. Schuck, and G. Cordner, 2011. *The National Police Research Platform: The Life Course of New Officers*. National Institute for Justice, Office of Justice Programs. Available at <http://www.nationalpoliceresearch.org/storage/Recruits%20Life%20Course.pdf>. [Accessed October 1, 2013]

Ross, B., 2013. "Cop who pepper sprayed Occupy Wall Street protestors to refuse questions from civilian board: Attorney." *New York Daily News*, August 28. Available at <http://nydn.us/1dRQrtN>. [Accessed September 1, 2013]

Royal Canadian Mounted Police, 2012. *INTERPOL Ottawa: Law Enforcement's Gateway to the World*. Available at <http://www.rcmp-grc.gc.ca/interpol/index-eng.htm>. [Accessed September 1, 2013]

Ruddick, J., 1998. *TM-08-98 OC Spray – a Review of its Possible Risks Including Carcinogenicity*, Canadian Police Research Centre, April. Available at <http://publications.gc.ca/collections/collection_2007/ps-sp/PS63-1-1998-8E.pdf>. [Accessed January 19, 2014]

Ruess-Ianni, E., and F.A.J. Ianni, 1983. "Street Cops and Management Cops—The Two Cultures of Policing." In M. Punch, ed. *Control in the Police Organization*, London: MIT Press, pp. 251–74.

Safir, H., 2011. "Protests and Security: Rights, Risks and Tools." *Vigilant Resources International*, November 15. Available at <http://bit.ly/1dsaS1M>. [Accessed September 1, 2013]

Schladen, M., 2013. "Texas DPS not talking about abortion protest." *El Paso Times.com*, August 5. Available at <http://www.elpasotimes.com/news/ci_23795309/protesters-reportedly-had-feces-and-urin-disrupt-vote>. [Accessed September 24, 2013]

Scholl, C., 2013. *Two Sides of a Barricade: (Dis)order and Summit Protest in Europe*. Albany, NY: SUNY Press.

Schuster, H., 2005. "Domestic terror: Who's most dangerous? Eco-terrorists are now." *CNN*, August 24. Available at <http://www.cnn.com/2005/US/08/24/schuster.column/>. [Accessed September 30, 2013]

Seaton, M. 2011. Naomi Wolf: reception, responses, critics. *Guardian* [online], November 28. Available at <http://www.theguardian.com/commentisfree/cifamerica/2011/nov/28/naomi-wolf-reception-responses-critics>. [Accessed January 21, 2014]

Seglins, D., 2008. "Toronto police. CBC News investigation: The report that led to the charges and the Crown's problems." *CBC.ca*, April 28. Available at <http://www.cbc.ca/news/background/torontopolice/>. [Accessed September 1, 2013]

Shaffer, G., D. Davis, and L. Powell, 1993. "Police break up Chicano rights march." *Orange County Register*, September 17, B1.

Sheptycki, J., 2000. *Issues in Transnational Policing*. New York: Routledge.

Silversmith, J.A., 1994. "Not So Suave: the Problem with RICO Laws." *Perspective*, January, online at *Third Amendment*. Available at <http://www.thirdamendment.com/rico.html>. [Accessed September 28, 2013]

Skogan, W.G., and S.M. Hartnett, 2005. "The diffusion of information technology in policing." *Police Practice and Research*, 6 (5), pp. 401–17.

Skolnick, J.H., 1966. *Justice without trial: law enforcement in democratic society*. New York: Wiley.

Smith, B.L., 1940. *Police Systems in the United States*. New York: Harper & Bros.

Smith, N., 1996. *New Urban Frontier: Gentrification and the Revanchist City*. New York: Routledge.

——, 2001. "Global Social Cleansing: Postliberal Revanchism and the Export of Zero Tolerance." *Social Justice*, 28 (3), pp. 68–74.

Snyders, M., 2008. "Eight RNC Protesters Accused of 'Furthering Terrorism' Thanks To Statute." *Common Dreams*, November 12. Available at <https://www.commondreams.org/headline/2008/11/12-0>. [Accessed 3 January 2014]

Solstice, 1999. "Police Evict Anti-road Occupation." *Slingshot*, Issue 64.

Sossin, L., 2004. *The Oversight of Executive Police Relations in Canada: The Constitution, the Courts, Administrative Processes and Democratic Governance*, Attorney General of Ontario. Available at <http://bit.ly/1dnncBA>. [Accessed September 1, 2013]

Soule, S.A., 1999. "The Diffusion of an Unsuccessful Innovation." *Annals of the American Academy of Political and Social Science*, 566, pp. 120–31.

SPCUM, 2001. *Bilan Annuel 2000*. Montreal: SPCUM.

Spelman, W. et al., 1992. *The diffusion of innovations and the creation of innovative police organizations*. Cambridge, MA: Taubman Center for State and Local Government, John F. Kennedy School of Government, Harvard University.

Spiller, S., 2006. "The FBI's Field Intelligence Groups and Police Joining Forces." *FBI Bulletin*, 75(5), pp. 1–6.

SPVM (Service de Police de la Ville de Montreal), 2008. *At the Heart of Montreal: New Service Coverage Framework* [pdf] Available at <http://www.spvm.qc.ca/upload/documentations/anglais_au_coeur_vie.pdf>. [Accessed September 30, 2013]

——, 2013. *Public Order Section – Operations*. Available at <http://bit.ly/17UGZBi>. [Accessed September 1, 2013]

Starr, A., L.A. Fernandez, and K. Scholl 2011. *Shutting Down the Streets: Political Violence and Social Control in the Global Era*. New York: NYU Press.

Statistics Canada, 2011. *Trends in police personnel and expenditures, Canada, 1962–2010*, Government of Canada, Available at <http://bit.ly/14JGrMD>. [Accessed September 1, 2013]

Steinmetz, G., 2008. "The Colonial State as a Social Field: Ethnographic Capital and Native Policy in the German Overseas Empire before 1914." *American Sociological Review*, 73 (4), pp. 589–612.

Stenning, P.C., 2000. "Powers and Accountability of Private Police." *European Journal on Criminal Policy and Research*, 8 (3), pp. 325–52.

Strang, D., and J.W. Meyer, 1993. "Institutional conditions for diffusion." *Theory and Society*, 22 (4), pp. 487–511.

——, and S.A. Soule, 1998. "Diffusion in Organizations and Social Movements: From Hybrid Corn to Poison Pills." *Annual Review of Sociology*, 24, pp. 265–90.

Sullivan, E., 2004. "'Unpredictable' protesters challenge agency; Federal Protective Service on guard against anarchists at conventions." *Federal Times*, August 2.

Sylvestre, M.E., 2010. "Disorder and Public Spaces in Montreal: Repression (and Resistance) through Law, Politics and Police Discretion." *Urban Geography*, 31 (6), pp. 803–24.

Tarrow, S., 2011. *Power in Movement: Social Movements and Contentious Politics.* New York: Cambridge University Press.

TASER International, 2003. *TASER International Annual Report.* Available at <http://investor.taser.com/annuals.cfm>. [Accessed September 1, 2013]

——, 2009. *TASER International Annual Report.* Available at <http://bit.ly/1dHNm1K>. [Accessed January 15, 2014]

——, 2011. *TASER International Annual Report.* Available at <https://materials.proxyvote.com/Approved/87651B/20120404/AR_126127/>. [Accessed January 5, 2014]

Thorne, S., and L. Schmidt, 2001. "Ottawa police stun, arrest demonstrators." *Hamilton Spectator*, November 17.

Tilly, C., 1992. *Coercion, Capital, and European States, AD 990–1992.* New York: Wiley.

——, 1995. *Popular Contention in Great Britain, 1758–1834.* Cambridge, MA: Harvard University Press.

——, 1997. *Roads from Past to Future.* Lanham, MD: Rowman and Littlefield.

——, 2003. "WUNC." In Jeffrey T. Schnapp and Matthew Tiews, eds. *Crowds.* Stanford, CA: Stanford University Press, pp. 289–306.

——, and L.J. Wood, 2012. *Social Movements 1768–2012.* Boulder, CO: Paradigm Publishers.

Toronto Police Services Board v. *Toronto Police Association*, 2004. Arbitration re: A Shift Change for the Community Oriented Response (C.O.R) Unit. Available at <http://bit.ly/14V5T55>. [Accessed September 29, 2013]

TPSB (Toronto Police Service Board), n.d. Board Mandate. Available at <http://www.tpsb.ca/V/Board_Mandate/>. [Accessed January 22, 2014]

——, 1998. *Use of Force Committee Final Report.* Available at <http://bit.ly/18NFlSp>. [Accessed September 1, 2013]

——, 2000. *Annual Report.* Available at <http://www.torontopolice.on.ca/publications/files/reports/2000annualreport.pdf>. [Accessed October 1, 2013]

——, 2011a. *Annual Statistical Report.* Available at <http://bit.ly/15hPd87>. [Accessed September 1, 2013]

——, 2011b. G20 Summit, Toronto Ontario, June 2010. "Toronto Police Service After-Action Review." Available at <http://www.torontopolice.on.ca/publications/files/reports/g20_after_action_review.pdf>. [Accessed September 29, 2013]

United Press International, 2012. *Security Industry: Growth forecast for non-lethal weapons.* Available at <http://bit.ly/15gEJ49>. [Accessed September 1, 2013]

Urbina, I., 2009. "Protesters Are Met by Tear Gas at G-20 Conference." *New York Times*, September 25. Available at <http://nyti.ms/1b2LM8Y>. [Accessed September 1, 2013]

US Bureau of Labor Statistics, 2012. *Occupational Employment and Wages, May 2012 33-3051 Police and Sheriff's Patrol Officers.* Available at <http://www.bls.gov/oes/current/oes333051.htm>. [Accessed January 21, 2013]

US DOJ (United States Department of Justice), 1993. *Law Enforcement Management and Administrative Statistics.* Washington, DC: Office of Justice Programs. Bureau of Justice Statistics.

——, 2007. *Local Police Departments 2007*, Bureau of Justice Statistics. Available at <http://www.bjs.gov/content/pub/pdf/lpd07.pdf>. [Accessed September 1, 2013]

——, 2013. *Community Policing Defined.* Available at <http://www.cops.usdoj.gov/default.asp?item=36>. [Accessed September 1, 2013]

Vallis, M., 2010. "Amputee alleges G20 police ripped off his prosthetic leg." *National Post*, July 6. Available at <http://bit.ly/cibX43>. [Accessed September 1, 2013]

Vitale, A.S., 2005. "From Negotiated Management to Command and Control: How the NYPD Polices Protests." *Policing and Society*, 15, pp. 283–304.

——, 2007. "The Command and Control and Miami Models at the 2004 Republican National Convention: New Forms of Policing Protests." *Mobilization*, 12 (4), pp. 403–15.

——, 2012. "Managing Defiance: The Policing of the Occupy Wall Street Movement." Unpublished paper, Politics and Protest Workshop, CUNY Graduate Center. Available at <http://politicsandprotest.ws.gc.cuny.edu/archives/spring-2013/>. [Accessed September 28, 2013]

Wacquant, L.J.D., 1992. "The Structure and Logic of Bourdieu's Sociology." In P. Bourdieu and L. Wacquant, eds. *An Invitation to Reflexive Sociology*. Chicago, IL: Chicago University Press.

——, 2001. "The Advent of the Penal State Is Not a Destiny." *Social Justice*, 28 (3), pp. 81–7.

——, 2009. *Punishing the Poor: The Neoliberal Government of Social Insecurity.* Durham, NC: Duke University Press.

Waddington, D.P., 2007. *Policing Public Disorder: Theory and Practice.* Cullompton: Willan Publishing.

Waddington, P.A.J., 1994. "Coercion and Accommodation: Policing Public Order after the Public Order Act." *The British Journal of Sociology*, 45 (3).

——, 2000. "Orthodoxy and Advocacy in Criminology." *Theoretical Criminology*, 4 (1), pp. 93–111.

——, 2003. "Policing Public Order and Political Contention." in T. Newburn, ed., *Handbook of Policing*. Cullompton: Willan Publishing, pp. 394–421.

Wahlstrom, M., 2007. "Forestalling Violence: Police Knowledge of Interaction with Political Activists." *Mobilization*, 12 (4), pp. 389–402.

Warwyk, W., 2004. *The Collection and Use of Intelligence in Policing Public Order Events*. Attorney General of Ontario. Available at <http://bit.ly/19Fz5wX>. [Accessed September 1, 2013]

Waterloo Regional Police Service, 2010. "G8/G20 Summit." Available at <http://www.sendspace.com/file/8dz3t9>. [Accessed October 1, 2013]

Weber, M., 1946. "Politics as a Vocation." In H.H. Garth and C. Wright Mills, eds., *Essays in Sociology*. New York: Macmillan, pp. 26–45.

Weisburd, D., and C. Lum, 2005. "The Diffusion of Computerized Crime Mapping in Policing: Linking Research and Practice." *Police Practice and Research*, 6 (5), pp. 419–34.

——, R. Greenspan, S. Mastrofski, and J.J. Willis, 2008. *Compstat and Organizational Change: A National Assessment*. National Institute of Justice. Available at <http://1.usa.gov/1dHNa20>. [Accessed January 15, 2014]

Weiss, A., 1997. "The communication of innovation in American policing." *Policing: An International Journal of Police Strategies and Management*, 20 (2), pp. 292–310.

White, M.D., and J. Ready, 2010. "'Don't Taze Me, Bro': Investigating the Use and Effectiveness of the Taser." In C. McCoy, ed. *Holding Police Accountable*. Washington, DC: Urban Institute Press, pp. 73–94.

Williams, K., 2007. *Our Enemies in Blue: Police and Power in America*. Cambridge, MA: South End Press.

——, 2011. "The Other Side of the COIN: Counterinsurgency and Community Policing." *Interface* 3 (1), pp. 81–117. Available at <http://bit.ly/15agdpB>. [Accessed September 1, 2013]

Willis J.J., T.R. Kochel, and S.D. Mastrofski, 2010. *Compstat and Community Policing: Taking Advantage of Compatibilities and Dealing with Conflicts*. Final report. Washington, DC: US Department of Justice, Office of Community-Oriented Policing Services.

Winfield, G., 2012. "Going Underground." *CBRNE World*, December. Available at <http://www.cbrneworld.com/_uploads/download_magazines/Going_under ground.pdf>. [Accessed September 28, 2013]

Wolf, N., 2011. "The shocking truth about the crackdown on Occupy." *Guardian* [online], November 25. Available at <http://www.theguardian.com/commentisfree/cifamerica/2011/nov/25/shocking-truth-about-crackdown-occupy>. [Accessed January 16, 2014]

Wood, L., 2004. "Breaking the Bank and Taking to the Streets." *Journal of World-Systems Research*, 10 (1), pp. 69–89.

——, 2012. *Direct Action, Deliberation and Diffusion: Collective Action After the WTO Protests in Seattle*. New York: Cambridge University Press.

Wortley, R.K., and R.J. Homel, 1995. "Police Prejudice as a Function of Training and Outgroup Contact: A Longitudinal Investigation." *Law and Human Behaviour*, 19 (3).

Young, B., 2007. "City to pay $1 million to settle lawsuit over WTO arrests." *Seattle Times*, April 3. Available at <http://bit.ly/1fgYfTO>. [Accessed September 1, 2013]

Zajko, M., and D. Beland, 2008. "Space and protest policing at international summits." *Environment and Planning : Society and Space*, 26, pp. 719–35.

Index